Survival Tactics

Survival Tactics

The Top 11 Behaviors of Successful Entrepreneurs

Ted Sun

Westport, Connecticut
London

Library of Congress Cataloging-in-Publication Data

Sun, Ted, 1972–
    Survival tactics : the top 11 behaviors of successful entrepreneurs / Ted Sun.
      p. cm.
    Includes bibliographical references and index.
    ISBN-13: 978-0-275-99470-9 (alk. paper)
  1. Entrepreneurship.   I. Title.
    HB615.S96   2007
    658.4′21—dc22   2007016354

British Library Cataloguing in Publication Data is available.

Library of Congress Catalog Card Number: 2007016354
ISBN-13: 978–0-275-99470–9
ISBN-10: 0–275-99470–8

First published in 2007

Praeger Publishers, 88 Post Road West, Westport, CT 06881
An imprint of Greenwood Publishing Group, Inc.
www.praeger.com

Printed in the United States of America

The paper used in this book complies with the
Permanent Paper Standard issued by the National
Information Standards Organization (Z39.48–1984).

10 9 8 7 6 5 4 3 2 1

To all those who work hard and desire a change in reality.
You have a better life—choose to see it.

Contents

PART V: YOUR SUCCESS

Tables and Figures

TABLES

FIGURES

Acknowledgments

Where do I even start? So many people have had a profound influence in getting this work to you. At the top of the list are those who've made the greatest impact from a personal growth perspective. My grandparents, Tsu Shi and Mary Chu, who have lived an incredible life. Through their survival tactics during World War II, they moved to America. I was born in China, but they wanted a better life for me and brought me to the United States. My parents, Steve and Florence Sun, who pushed me to grow and constantly pursue education, although I'm not sure if their intent was the pursuit of multiple doctorate degrees. To my mentor and good friend, Dr. Lloyd Williams, who has been an inspiration for me since the day we met. He's been a guiding force in my development with an incredible amount of unconditional love and support. His guidance through my first doctorate influenced a rare early completion of my dissertation. Dr. Williams's continued support and encouragement helped me complete this book as well as the start of a second doctorate, which heavily influenced this volume. Thanks to his guidance, this book is a multidisciplinary approach that draws from the best of business and psychology bodies of knowledge.

I'd also like to thank those who've had an active hand in the research as well as the writing of this book. To Helena Brus's magnificent attention to detail fine-tuned my writing. My dissertation committee were instrumental in guiding the research to be the best possible. They included Dr. Frank Toney, Dr. Paulette DeGard, and Dr. Michael Vandermark. Also, a thank you goes out to Robert M. Parker at Central Ohio Transit Authority, who helped with the statistical research in regression analysis.

The research would not have happened without the assistance of various partners who helped obtain research participants. These include a wide range of organizations to individual entrepreneurs who knew many others that met the requirements of being successful. These include Debbie Bowden, Center for Entrepreneurship at The Ohio State University; Craig Hohnburger with Action

International; Andy and Sarah Hippensteele at Ash Image; John Butterfield at the Worthington Chamber of Commerce; Alan Mooney with Mooney Financial Services; and Dr. Pam Popper with the Wellness Forum.

I would like to make a special note of thanks to Stan Wakefield, whose diligent work as an agent brought this work to the publishing world, and to Kristi Gerner, my extremely talented graphics illustrator and good friend. Finally, thanks to those who have played a major role in teaching me some incredible lessons about myself within the nontraditional intelligences such as emotional, somatic, and spiritual—Chandra Passero for your somatic awareness, Philip Yassenoff for your emotional confidence, Natalie Marrone for your depth and awareness of energy, and Alison K. Hazelbaker for your wisdom in connecting my wisdoms. I appreciate all of you in the roles you've played in my life.

In writing this, I feel like it's a quick review of my history over the past decade. So many people have had an influence in my journey to this point that I can't begin to acknowledge everyone. As I journey toward a new chapter of life, I look forward to the future blessing and the endless growth of acknowledgments I'll get to make in the next book.

PART I

YOU AND ENTREPRENEURSHIP

CHAPTER ONE

Are You An Entrepreneur?
Says Who?

According to the Small Business Administration, a small business is defined as one that employees fewer than 500 people.[1] Entrepreneurs are responsible for starting these small businesses. Furthermore, in the conversations of many organizational leaders, entrepreneurial attitudes are also highly encouraged.[2] In such a situation, you don't have to own a business at all, but have a innovative mind and behave as if you have ownership. So what exactly is an entrepreneur? Are you an entrepreneur if you're a business of one person? What about your family—isn't that an organization in itself where you may play the CEO role and your employer is your best client?

In more than 19 years of being an entrepreneur, I've encountered all types of entrepreneurs looking for the American dream. Some had just started their business and were looking to grow. Others had their business for a few years and were seeking stability. A few worked in corporate America with a business on the side, hoping to do it full-time someday. On the edge of what I call entrepreneurship are those typical employees who see themselves as the president of their own company, regardless of who they work for. Whether or not you consider yourself an entrepreneur, take a look at these challenges. Are these ones you face over and over again?

> I've been in this business for a few years now. When I started, I wanted to create a business that could give me the freedom to spend more time with my family. Today, I still have to spend 60–80 hours each week, making sure the business continues to survive. I'm forced to miss a lot of events with my family, and I don't like it. But this is what it means to own your own business. You have to work hard to get ahead.

> My company just decided to outsource my department to India. I can't believe that after all the time I put into that company, they're going to lay me off. Worse yet, I'm being asked to train my replacement in India. I just bought my dream house; how am I going to make the payments?

I can't seem to stop having people problems at work. Someone is always upset, and I have to deal with them. Just when life is getting to be fun with some new projects, someone always drags me back down. Does life have to have so many ups and downs?

The other day, one of the key staff members quit and went off to another company. Now I'm faced with more work than ever. In addition to all the new projects, I have to take some of the work from the departing staff member. There's never enough time to get things done. I already do the job of two people. When is it enough?

Money is always a problem. I never seem to make enough. Just when a new client signs a deal, there are more expenses to suck that money away. The cost of marketing seems to always go up, and my vendors are constantly reducing due dates on invoices. Am I ever going to have enough money to get what I want?

My health is never perfect. Just as I was getting over a pulled back muscle, my neck started to get sore. I've been to the doctor's office several times. He's giving me medication from muscle relaxers to antidepressants. I didn't even think I was depressed. Sometimes, I have trouble falling asleep. There always seems to be something wrong with me. Make it stop!

These are the types of problems that average Americans face every day while chasing the American dream. In the process of chasing a dream, the people got lost. If you face any of these challenges, you're an entrepreneur. At the core of entrepreneurship, independence is the root of America. According to the founding principles of America, there is an entrepreneur in each individual. Some manifest entrepreneurial spirit more than others. The good news is that you're not alone in this. Countless Americans struggle between starting their own businesses to gain the independence and continuing employment for perceived security. The balance of family and work is always on the mind of the entrepreneur.

How much balance do you have in your life?

The bad news is that there is no quick fix. These common issues require a deep level of understanding to address the root cause so that they can be permanently solved.

LEARNING YOUR ENTREPRENEURIAL ROOTS

To grasp the root cause of these problems, let's look at how the United States got started in entrepreneurship. Back in the days from the mid-1700s to the late 1800s, or what's called the federalist days, life was much simpler in certain respects. All Americans considered themselves entrepreneurs. The federalist era was a time of an agrarian society, and most entrepreneurs owned small shops that served the agricultural population or owned their own farms. This way of life dominated entrepreneurship, and every business was a small business.[3] The American dream was defined as working hard to become more successful than one's parents. It was a dream about breaking away from the boundaries into a world where the sky was the limit.[4] Does this sound familiar to you? What limits do you have in your mind about your reality? What limits do you place on your own success?

The pilgrims were among the first entrepreneurs in the history of the United States. To reach the New World, they made agreements with London backers for the money required for their trip. Once the debt was paid off, the pilgrims became completely independent, requiring no outside influence for its economic prosperity.[5] As the first entrepreneurs, the pilgrims saw entrepreneurial success as freedom and independence. Today, research has found that the same ideas still exist. Independence and control over one's life was one of top four intangible measures of success.[6]

Within the federalist era, another defining principle of an entrepreneur was one's character. Character was the ultimate judge of personal wealth.[4] Because the dependency on others was high, entrepreneurs functioned as part of small communities. Characteristics such as honesty, integrity, and self-reliance were highly valued. People lived simple lives to serve the community. In today's society, similar groups share this value. For example, the National Association of Women Business Owners (NAWBO) found that women entrepreneurs define success in their relationships with customers and employees as well as control over their lives. Another study further supported this fact in their findings—the intrinsic definition of success is recognition by the community and security in one's family.[7]

Building on these principles, entrepreneurs gave birth to the great American industrial power. Some of the most famous entrepreneurs in U.S. history are Henry Ford, Andrew Carnegie, and John D. Rockefeller. Each of them arrived at entrepreneurship in the early 1900s. Ford started with the creation of a mechanical plow. He eventually learned enough to create the first automobiles in 1896. It sold for $200. Today, Ford Motor Company is one of the largest automakers, selling cars all over the world. These entrepreneurs had one characteristic in common—the ability to dream and the drive to pursue that dream. The sense of purpose and belief lead these men to possess great self-confidence to take risks and the leadership required for success.[8] This characteristic was derived from the American dream that was deeply embedded in our cultures by the late 1800s and early 1900s.[4]

YOU ARE ONLY AS GOOD AS A MACHINE

The entrepreneurs of the early 1900s created the huge industrial machine. Large enterprises suddenly needed skilled workers to work in their assembly lines. As a result of this demand, the vocational movement in the early 1900s created a new educational system that produced employees.

In the federalist days, a formal educational system did not exist. Most people trained via apprenticeships. Students who attended universities such as Harvard were paid to attend. Many of the graduates still did not know how to read.

Imagine a Harvard graduate that didn't know how to read![4] The new system stripped away the experiential learning system of apprenticeships, in which every student was expected to think for themselves within a few years.

Large organizations needed skilled workers in their assembly lines. As organizations grew bigger due to automation, the value of traditional skills disintegrated. Radical innovations in education were created to meet the demand for skilled workers. This new system of education prepared people to be controlled and led by management. Taylor's scientific principles of management saw people as interchangeable parts of a machine, so the educational system trained people to act and think as robots while creating a huge dependency on management.[4] Many workers began to depart from the federalist view of community and moved toward minimum effort for the greatest rewards.[9] As organizations grew in size, they designed limited social systems with controlling structures that prohibited free movement.[3] Because the only knowledge we had at the time concerning governance of large bodies was the military, much organizational structures and theory were based on military models. For example, if your role is a programmer (or an accountant or a soldier), your ability to take on activities outside of your role is very limited. In many organizations, there's a cultural rule that says "worry about your own backyard" or "don't mess with someone else's sandbox." In this structure, you take the projects that are given to you or follow orders like the typical mission statement. You are now thinking as an individual; the principle of scarcity stood at the center of economic and business thought.[4] Community only comes after you are taken care of first. Individualism rules the way people think and reason.

Within this system, you need the approval of others. Sound like anyone you know? As children, your worth is judged by a teacher. As adults, your worth is judged by your manager or boss with performance evaluations and pay raises (if you're lucky). In this system, you are not capable of being creative. That is why each employee needs to work within a box of strict job responsibilities. The structures provide the best way for you to advance in society. The American dream went from the sky as a limit to the glass ceiling that nearly everyone has above their head today. How often have you felt yourself bumping into your glass ceiling? For some, the glass ceiling is about getting out of debt; for others, it's a mental trap that greatly limits your potential built with the fear of failure and/or success.

In the organizational machine, you are like a child. The government or the capitalists are necessary to take care of you.[4] Consider the social security system. A few generations still believe that you can have lifetime careers at a single company. You may also think that the government should take care of you when you retire. Where did all this co-dependence come from? Are we not capable individuals seeking freedom? Where did the concept of control over your own life go? Does your success depend on someone else or yourself?

Here's a simple test of the glass ceiling—do you believe in retirement? Consider the following—does the concept of retirement exists in a knowledge economy, as opposed to the labor intensive world that created the concept? Is all the fear about social security and retirement just a way to construct a solid glass ceiling within your mind? Living outside this mentality defines freedom. Retirement does not exist in a knowledge economy since it's brain power that companies value. With brain power, you can work less and earn significantly more. You're not a machine that has a linear potential. As a human knowledge creation organism, retirement of the brain doesn't exist. Imagine doing what you love for a few hours each week and earning more than what you're making currently. This is the reality that you can choose to live.

YOU HAVE 100 PERCENT CONTROL OF
YOUR FUTURE AS AN ENTREPRENEUR

Imagine this: you're in some comfortable clothes, walking under the summer sun, and enjoying a light breeze. The temperature is perfect as you stroll along the narrow path in the wilderness. The scent of some fresh flowers catches your nose around the turn of the trail. It smells tropical but somewhat subdued. "What could give the scent of tropical flowers in the middle of the woods?" you think to yourself. Your curiosity leads you to walk toward the scent. Before you know it, around the turn of the path is a cemetery. Someone had just laid some fresh flowers on a loved one's grave. Standing close to the headstone, you read, "Here lies the memories of John. He lived for 1 year. Rest in peace." You feel a sense of sorrow for John. As you continue to walk through the cemetery, a large tombstone catches your eyes. This stone had to be someone with quite a few dollars, filled with beautiful engravings and decorations. It reads, "Here lies the memories of Robert. Loved by many, he built an empire. He lived 6 months. Rest in peace." It strikes you a bit odd that all of these people only lived for such a short time. You start to feel hollow in your gut as you continue to walk. You read a few more others, "Jane . . . 2 years"; "Peter . . . 4 months"; "William . . . 2 years 2 months." None of this makes sense. What kind of cemetery is this?

You see a groundskeeper in the distance. Your curiosity drives you to approach him. He appears to be a man with gray hair. You hope that he possesses some good explanations for this weird place. "What is this place? How can all the tombstones reflect such short times of life?" you ask. The man first looks directly into your eyes and smiles. He had a piercing look, as if you'd known him for a long time. Speaking like a grandfather with all the knowledge and time in the world, he responds, "You are correct in your observations. These people lived a very short time. Although their lives are just like your own, the time on the stones only represent the combined time of true happiness."

You think to yourself, "What the heck does that mean? Why didn't they put their actual years of life down?"

The groundskeeper acknowledges your puzzled expression with a soft smile and continues, "When was the last time you were truly happy? When everything was going perfectly, as you desired? If you were to put those times together, how much life would you have? These people lived a full life. They were engineers, business owners, computer programmers, project managers, painters, and other professionals. Many were married and had kids. Yet in all this time, they were too busy working for happiness; they never slowed down enough to simply *be happy*. There was always something else to do or distracting thoughts that violates their inner peace. The tombstones represent the duration they lived a life worth living."

What feelings are you experiencing right now? The perfect moments exercise below is designed to bring a new level of awareness into your life. This exercise is intended to give you insight while helping you make conscious decisions to what you should let into your life.

Perfect Moments Exercise

You will need about 10–15 minutes for this exercise. Make sure you have a place where you will not be interrupted. This is for you to see only, no one else will have to know. Take some time to think through the moments where you had perfect happiness in your life — where everything was just perfect.

1. Take out a blank piece of paper and make three columns.
2. Label the first column "perfect moments." Label the second column "duration." Label the final column "violations."
3. For the first column, think back to a moment of perfect happiness. What was it like? What were you doing? This should be one of those moments where everything was just perfect. You forgot that the world existed and it was just you, and perhaps some others, floating on a cloud. Write it down in the first column.
4. In the second column, write down the length time of that moment. How long did it last? Was it minutes, hours? Be very specific on the duration — seconds, minutes, hours, and so on.
5. In the third column, remember what happened to take you out of that moment. Possibly, there was a phone call or a concern that came into your mind. What was the event that took you back into the concerns of your life? How did reality settle back in?
6. Repeat steps 2–4 to get as many perfect moments as you can remember.
7. Total up the time in column two. What do you have?

You've just walked through your life as the groundskeeper described. What did you end up on your tombstone? Do you have months, years? How does that make you feel?

Thinking back to the federalist days, when character was the measure of success, these perfect moments occurred more often in the company of loved ones. Without all the distracting forms of electronic entertainment, entrepreneurs lived a simpler life, filled with perfect moments. In today's age, time seems to grow scarcer. Many of the electronic entertainment options take away the opportunity to connect to another person. Can you remember when you had a perfect moment of happiness when watching TV or closing a business deal? If so, how long did it last? Did you make the time to enjoy your triumph?

Too often, the busy-ness of entrepreneurs steals more time away for business, while leaving the most important things behind. For the sake of making a living, the life you're working for is slipping away.

How many precious moments have you missed? Does time seem to fly by you?

In today's busy life, we all have more and more things to do. There is never enough time to do it all. Studies have found that over the past decade, Americans have increased hours worked by 20 percent. That's more than any other industrialized nation. Comparatively, France (−23.5 percent), Germany (−17.1 percent), and Japan (−16.6 percent) all have *reduced* the number of hours worked.[10] Myths about the need to multitask are driving the population toward a lack of focus. The more you try to do, the less you get done. As a result, the majority of the population is time poor. How often have you heard the excuse "I'm too busy" or "I just don't have the time." As an entrepreneur, you take control of your own time. By learning what's the most effective, you will master your life. This book will provide some basic analysis tools to see where you're spending your time. You can also engage in the exercises that will eliminate the wasteful activities so you will be time rich. Taking control of your time makes you an entrepreneur—someone who is independent and possesses freedom.

There are other definitions of being an entrepreneur. If you own a business with fewer than 500 employees, you are an entrepreneur as defined by the U.S. Small Business Administration. You took a risk at some point in life to gain control of your own future by starting your own business.

Whether it was passed down from family members, you started it on your own, or you purchased it from someone else, if you are a small business owner/ manager, then you are an entrepreneur. Recent research evolves around knowledge and behaviors of people just like you.

If you work for someone else as an employee, could you be an entrepreneur? According to popular textbook, you are an entrepreneur if you exhibit behaviors

---

Quick Tip: For any of the moments you identified in the Perfect Moments exercise that involved someone else, make sure to share it with that person and thank them. Let them know how rare the moment was and that you cherish them greatly.

> Quick Tip: If you want your children to be extraordinary, help them design a business card. Go to the nearest office supply store or print shop and; print a bunch of business cards for your children. On the card, make sure to have president or CEO as the title. Teach them self-worth. On the fun side, imagine how cool it is for a child to have his own card that says: Johnny Smith, President of Johnny Enterprises.
>
> You can expand on that to have a family mission statement or a tag line if you like, and update it regularly. This will give your child a focus on the finish line. Do it for yourself as well.

that include (a) taking initiative, (b) accepting risks or failure, and (c) combining resources, materials, and labor to create value for the customers.[11] If your company hasn't told you to be more creative and innovative or behave like an entrepreneur, they will or else they will not be in business for long. Regardless of what someone else believes, the time of safety in a lifelong career with a single company is over. Globalization of economies has forced an incredible speed of adaptation that drives change. Even if you work for someone else, you need to start thinking like an entrepreneur. You need to learn to market yourself and make sales pitches for potential buyers/employers for advancement. You need to produce a valued product. You have to do your own accounting/taxes each year for your most intimate organization—your family. You cannot depend on someone else to take care of things for you in all aspects of your life. Your mindset is what creates your worth to a customer (your company, wife, husband, children, clients, etc.) as well as your own future.

An entrepreneur is someone who takes control of his or her own future. By producing a product/service that others value, entrepreneurs have responsibilities to themselves as well as other people to be successful.

The pursuit of the American dream is one of entrepreneurialism—having independence and control of one's own future, and the sky is the limit.

What doesn't work is the current educational system. Here's a bit of a reality check.

- According to the latest research, 99 percent of all businesses in the United States are small businesses.[1]
- Between 50 percent to 80 percent of small business fail within the first three to five years of startup.[1,12]
- Millions are laid off unexpectedly each year by major corporations.
- Many Americans are suffering from a high level of anxiety and depression with symptoms like obesity, sleep disorders, impaired memory, suppressed immune function, and heart disease.[13]

Breaking out of the childlike or machine mentality, you need to think like an entrepreneur to live more than a few years of true happiness as in the tombstone story. Don't you deserve a life with a lot more than a few years of what the grounds keeper quantified as life worth living? An entrepreneur learns and applies new knowledge each and every day. This book was designed to change your reality by affecting your belief systems with simple exercises of self-discovery.

REFERENCES

1. *Small Business Administration* (1999). The state of small business: A report of the president, 1998. Washington DC: United States Printing Office. Also, Small Business Administration (2001). The state of small business: A report of the president, 1999–2001. Washington DC: United States Printing Office. These reports are produced by the Small Business Administration and illustrate statistical information and analysis of the small business environment.

2. S. Dawson (2004, April). Balancing self-interest and altruism: corporate governance alone is not enough. *Corporate Governance: An International Review* 12(2), 130–34. This article discussed the importance of having an entrepreneurial attitude/mentality in any organization. For organizations to survive, leaders need to engage in the self-interest of individual as well as getting everyone to see the larger picture.

3. R. Jacques (1996). *Manufacturing the employee: Management knowledge from the 19th to 21st centuries.* Thousand Oaks, CA: Sage Publications. This is a great book concerning the history of management theory. It starts with the federalist days where entrepreneurs were without large corporations. It moves through history to illustrate the demise of the entrepreneurial spirit during the Industrial Revolution.

4. T. V. DiBacco (1987). *Made in the U.S.A.: The history of American business.* New York: Harper and Row. This is another historical account of major entrepreneurs who made a significant impact to American history, such as Henry Ford and Alexander Graham Bell.

5. R. C. Paige and M. A. Littrell (2002, October). Craft retailers' criteria for success and associated business strategies. *Journal of Small Business Management* 40(4), 314–32. This study was out of Iowa State University. The authors included aspects of success when studying craft retailers' view of success and specific factors that impacted that success. The study validated the importance of a balance of various dimensions of success, including an intangible measure such as happiness.

6. D. F. Kuratko, J. S. Hornsby, and D. W. Naffziger (1997, January). An examination of owner's goals in sustaining entrepreneurship. *Journal of Small Business Management*, 35(1), 24–33. This study reports that entrepreneurs are not motivated only by financial measures. The motivations of security and autonomy for their families play a major role in the effort they make in their businesses.

7. B. M. Bass (1990). *Bass & Stogdill's Handbook of Leadership*, 3rd ed. New York: Free Press. A great resource for obtaining a high-level overview of leadership theories from the beginning of humankind to today's global economy. Although it is a bit on the technical side with ample historical references, it covers most dominant leadership theories and styles.

8. A. C. Cooper and W. C. Si Dunkelberg (1986). Entrepreneurship and paths to business ownership. *Strategic Management Journal* 7, 53–68. A study that looked at 1,756 owner-managers and the process they went through to own a business.

9. M. Weber (1954). *Max Weber on law in economy and society*. Cambridge, MA: Harvard University Press. Weber offered some of the traditional assumptions concerning organizational theory. Within his theory, Weber believed that organizations and people acted rationally. Scientific methods of production looked to maximize production while minimizing the effort. The human element of production did not receive much consideration.

10. G. Ip (2004, July 8). U.S. wealth tied more to work than productivity, report says. *Wall Street Journal*. This article illustrated the increasing hours of work exhibited by Americans over the years of 1970 to 2002. Americans were working over 20 percent harder, whereas other industrialized nations began to reduce the number of hours worked (i.e., France had a reduction of 23.5 percent, and Germany had a reduction of 17.1 percent).

11. R. H. Hisrich and M. O. Peters (1992). *Entrepreneurship: Starting, developing, and managing a new enterprise*. Boston, MA: Irwin. A commonly recognized entrepreneurship textbook that focus on specific skills one must possess for success.

12. R. Monk (2000, July/August). Why small businesses fail. *CMA Management* 74(6), 12–13. This article highlighted the 80 percent failure rate of small business owners with their first five years of operation. It also provided some interesting rationales for these failures. The most significant is the inability for entrepreneurs to implement essential business and management practices.

13. J. Schwartz (2004, September 5). Always on the job, employees pay with health. *New York Times*. This article discussed the various illnesses that Americans suffer from workplace stress. Some of the most common were obesity, impaired memory, suppressed immune function, and heart disease (such as hardening of arteries).

CHAPTER TWO

How to Read This Book

At the core of any kind of success, the ability to learn is crucial. Learning is a conscious effort. Yet the art of learning is often lost in most educational systems. Countless Americans read many books each year. But with each passing year, they face the same problems over and over again, only with different names and places. Not much changes, except for the level of frustration and stress that keeps in increasing. Think back to your New Year's resolution for the past five years. How different are they?

The journey in this book is one of self-discovery. This book intends to help you first obtain a deeper understanding of who you are as a leader and an entrepreneur. This is what I call the art of *being*. Like Brad Sugars of Action International once said, "You are all human beings, not human doings." You are a leader with great potential. To realize that potential, this book will not just tell you what to do. The various exercises focus on your beliefs and values first, to help you redefine your state of being. My intention is for you to create change at the root of who you are so that you can achieve sustainable success in life no matter what you get involved with.

Let's talk about learning for a second. What does learning consist of? How do you learn?

Defining Learning Exercise

1. Take out a piece of blank paper.
2. Jot down what learning means to you, as explicitly as you can.

   a. First, define it as a personal model of learning — how do you learn the skills required to have good personal relationships with people?
   b. Second, define it with respect to your work — how do you learn at work?

3. For each definition, think of how you exhibit these qualities in your life.
4. Ask yourself: Are my definitions consistent with my actions?

If we were in a workshop right now, we'd discuss this in much more detail and design a plan to update your definition of learning. For now, if you are consistent, that's a great start. If you're not consistent with the ideals of learning in your mind and your actions, you need to look deeper to understand this question about yourself. What scares you about learning?

When I was growing up, I was pushed to learn to read. Due to the pressures of reading, I developed a hatred for it, like many other children do. I used to be proud that I got through my undergraduate degree in engineering without reading one book. I simply did the exercises that gave me a good understanding of the theories and never read the text itself. Reading was like voodoo to me. Having avoided reading all throughout my primary schools, my reading speed was rather slow. A fear developed in me and I was afraid to let people know that I was so slow at reading. I thought people might think of me as stupid. I did not want that image. Therefore, I hid that fear quite well. It was not until I got into a doctorate program that I realized the fun in reading. I was able to overcome my fear of reading in some incredibly challenging subjects like epistemology and systems thinking. Today, I read quite often, and it is usually the beginning of my learning process.

If your actions are not consistent with your definitions of learning, dig deep and come to understand it. Use your incredible intellect to see that the fears of learning are groundless. Visualize how much fun it is to learn and embrace it with conscious acts of learning.

A shift in belief about learning marks the initiation of finding the courage to overcome fear. Based on my experiences working with hundreds of business leaders and professionals, the definition of learning is illusive. Countless people model learning after the educational system which often promote regurgitation of material. Learning is much more than summarizing information. Learning, under conventional wisdom, means to study hard and get good grades or performance reviews. In other words, if you digest the information I give you, I get to tell you whether you're a "good" student or worker. We all know how poorly that works. How much do you remember from your high school education? Most people use little of what they learned from the first 12 years in school. Furthermore, studies have found that less than 15 percent of your life achievement is learned from formal education. Over 85 percent of your life's accomplishments are based on your experiential learning.[1]

You are reading this book because you're looking to create a better future for you and your family. With the sky as the limit, you can achieve anything you desire. First, you'll need to redefine learning. Consider this definition: (1) the constant acquisition of knowledge, (2) the application of that knowledge, and (3) the measurement of its impact, thus creating new knowledge.

1. *The Mind of a Child*. You need to have the mindset of a child—someone who does not judge and is open to the acquisition of knowledge. As adults, the more education we get, the less open we tend to be to new information, especially from those who don't agree with us. Much research has been done on this subject. For example, Harvard Business School professor Chris Argyris found that the more successful the individual, the less experience they have with failure. In the fear of the failure itself, they tend to be poor learners. Most close their minds. They'd have to face that fear first, and many avoid it.[2] It's one reason that so many professors and educated people are viewed as stuck-up or closed-minded. The first rule of keeping an open mind is your language. A franchise (Action International) I used to own had a great concept—when you catch yourself saying "I know," stop yourself and say "that's interesting" instead. In my studies, the basic human psychology closes the door to the acquisition of knowledge when you believe you already know it. With a closed mind, you will not learn. That is a fatal mistake!

Let's look at the theory of knowledge—What *is* knowledge? How do you come to have knowledge? How does knowledge enhance your chances of success?[3] Questions like these have been debated since the days of Plato in 427–347 BCE. The questions about knowledge have historically focused on a few common themes: Are human beings capable of reasoning? What is the difference between knowledge and belief? Is knowledge innate?[3] From classical times to postmodernism, it has been generally agreed that knowledge is a crucial aspect of leadership and success in any organization.[3,4,5]

Knowledge is not information; information is not knowledge. Information is the stuff you read and hear and see. It goes in one ear and out the other. Information has no meaning associated. Knowledge, on the other hand, has emotional associations from the application or implementation. Most of what you read here will be information. Although valuable with proven results, it will never be your own knowledge until you take action on it. Your knowledge comes from your actions.

Knowledge is crucial to the success of the entrepreneur. It is the result of the accumulation of information by an individual who chooses to create meaning and take action.[5] If you stopped taking in new knowledge, the changing world will leave you behind to fail. Lack of learning is the ultimate point of failure for any entrepreneur. If you catch yourself closing off your mind with statements like "I know," transition your mindset to be that of a child. Say, "that's interesting." This practice also takes away the judgment of someone else's knowledge.

2. *Experiential Knowledge*. The application of knowledge is one of the most crucial aspects of learning. It is often lost in the early years of education. Throughout the primary educational system, you studied math, science, history, English, and many other subjects. Yet how much of it do you retain today? You

might barely remember the names of the teachers, much less the knowledge in those thick textbooks.

To get the most out of learning and being successful in life, you must be competent at applying new knowledge. Learning and real life are tightly integrated aspects of your road to success. Entrepreneurs have the power and ability to immediately take action on new information. For every one of the behaviors you'll read about in the following chapters, take notes on what you find meaningful and give yourself assignments to apply the knowledge. For each chapter, you should be conducting a number of exercises to learn about yourself. Integrate the knowledge to be useful in your daily life. Only then will you truly learn and transform yourself into the being you desire.

The application of knowledge is much easier said than done. As I was facilitating the collection of data on my dissertation, I noticed a very common thread. Many entrepreneurs saw the survey questions and said, "Yeah, I should be doing that." In reality, many were not. After performing the statistical analysis on the data, a fascinating conclusion was found. I separated the data into two groups. The first group had survived well beyond the five-year mark and was deemed successful in their business. The second group was under the five-year mark, which placed them in the statistics for an 80 percent failure rate. The first group had a 77 percent correlation between what they believed they should do and what they were actually doing. These successful entrepreneurs took action on their knowledge of what was important. In contrast, the data in the second group only found a 58.4 percent correlation. This meant that they only did what they felt was important a little more than half the time. What does that tell you about the criticality of knowledge application?

3. *Learning Metrics.* The final piece about learning is the measurement of it. According to Garvin, a respected professor and business leader, "If you can't measure it, you can't manage it."[6] This is true in countless businesses, small and large. You must measure what's important.

Think about your commute to work. What do you see? Do you remember the turns, the cars you pass, the lights you hit? Most of us have many unconscious competences. We've gotten so good at doing certain things that we don't even have to think about them. As a newborn baby, the only unconscious competence we had was breathing. As we grew older, new sensations became old hat. What was once a new taste is now something familiar. This is when learning stops.

Now think back to the last time you drove to work using a different route. How many miles was it? How many minutes did it save you or cost you? What did you notice as you drove to work? The awakening of your unconscious competence is often a simple but deliberate task. The awareness of measurement will often improve your performance. Try this—the next time when you play a game of any kind, don't keep score. See what happens to your mind. As an entrepreneur, your relationships are crucial—what if you measured them? Only when you measure them do you become aware of the impact the change has made. Thus, you'll be creating meaningful knowledge, rather than information in one ear and out the other.

Learning is at the core of success. It is also the foundation of human evolution. By being better at learning, you'll easily evolve at a rate higher than that of others. One way to determine the type of learning that's in your life is through the relationships you have. Ask yourself or others around you these questions: How do you feel about feedback from others? What do you do with it? Are you engaged in challenging relationships that build you up? Do you have friends who are going faster in life than you? One of the basic lessons I learned is that you need to have plenty of friends who are faster than you. By *faster*, I mean they have more knowledge, they learn better, they are highly involved in various groups you'd like to be part of, and they advance in their careers faster than most people. These individuals can pull you out of your comfort zone and challenge you to be like them. I refer to these friends as the intellectuals, mentors, and surrogate parents in my life. Of course, we also need other types of friends for functional purposes. Those that share my love for ballroom dancing, tennis, volleyball, diving, and other activities are all part of my circle of friends. The key is to create a balance between the different types of friends that help you learn different lessons.

As you work on your being, you'll find that you'll start to engage at multiple levels with each activity. For example, I play in a doubles tennis league where four people are placed on a court and play with each of the three others in a doubles game. Tennis is a very physical sport, but it is also a chess match of four minds. One game stood out in my mind. As you play with four people, you can learn a great deal about how they play and the constant strategy they use. The key to winning is not necessarily your ability to hit the ball, but rather the mind to maneuver through another's predictable strategy. There was one player who was not having a good game. He was by far the weakest player in the group. As I observed him, I made a choice to partner with him last. This allowed me time to learn from the other players and see how to beat them. I also realized that by the time I got him as a partner, he would have a very negative mindset, having lost badly in the first two sets. When I got this poor player as my partner in the last game, I made one simple suggestion to him—move close to the net and put his racket up. It doesn't take much skill at all to move closer to the net. By doing so, we jumped out and surprised our opponents. All of a sudden, there was a different player facing them. They failed to adjust their strategy and kept on hitting the ball into the net or out of the court. Seeing the first two games, most people could have never predicted a win for that man. But by learning and adapting, skill and luck had absolutely no choice but to step aside. We won convincingly at 6–3.

The integration of your knowledge and actions within a set time frame can yield surprising success. In business or in your personal life, the game is always the same—the one who learns the fastest and is able to take action will win.

To start understanding the person you are, let's examine the interactions you engage in currently. This is not meant to be a definitive measure of your relationships; rather, it's meant to give you some direction on where you'd like to consciously create some relationships.

Interaction Measures Exercise

Here's a simple measurement you could do for fun to determine the depth of your interactions with other people in your life.

1. On a small note pad, make four columns.
2. Label the columns as follows: Deep, Somewhat Deep, Casual, and Superficial.
3. Each column represents the level of depth in the communication you receive from people. For each email, phone call, or contact you get from a colleague or a friend, make a tick under the appropriate column. I'm deliberately not defining the meanings of these columns because they are only meaningful to you and based on your judgment of what a level of communication might be. This is merely a count of how many people you communicate with and the levels of depth. You could also classify each with the medium as well and see a further difference between emails, phone call, or person-to-person contact at work or outside of work.

   For example, if you get an email that says, "Hi, how are you? Let's go out tonight," that may be a mark in the Casual column. Make sure to use *your* definition of casual, because your definitions are the only ones that matter! Be honest with yourself, and try this for a few days. It'll reveal some interesting things about your relationship. As you measure these incoming emails and phone calls, your awareness of where you'd like to connect with people will also be raised. You may choose to engage at different levels consciously—which is the entire point of this exercise. Choosing a conscious level of relating to others is a crucial part state of being—to be conscious! Measure what you care the most about in your life and your business; the pure act of measuring will make you better at the task.

4. Depending on your level of computer proficiency, you can choose to make a table or chart of what this looks like (see Table 2-1). As you do this, remember not to judge on any specifics. This is purely intended to give some indications.

TABLE 2-1. An Example of Various Interactions throughout a Week

	Deep	Somewhat Deep	Casual	Superficial	Medium Totals
Emails	4	1	2	1	8
Phone calls	2	5	9	14	30
In person at work	5	4	2	1	12
In person outside of work	10	7	1	1	19
Category totals	21	17	14	16	69

As you can see in Table 2-1, this individual had 69 total conversations over a week that was recorded. Out of these conversations, the majority were very deep and transforming. What level of satisfaction do you think this person has in his or her life?

Taking these numbers a bit further into a percentage table (see Table 2-2), you can see the following trends.

The percentages in the columns of Table 2-2 are calculated by dividing the original count by the medium totals on the right side. From these data, you can tell that this person does not have deep conversations on the phone. Most of the deep conversations come from in-person interactions. The number percentages of conversations that are deep at work and outside of work are fairly similar. This could be an indicator that this individual enjoys work and is engaged with it.

Now that we've revisited what learning is, here's a quick overview of the book.

Part One includes the foundations of this book and the basis of understanding who you are and what you're seeking to accomplish. Transforming your being is like folding your future into the present. If you are ever to reach success, you must know where the finish line is and what it looks like.

TABLE 2-2. An Example Breakdown of the Different Types of Interactions Experienced by Entrepreneurs

	Deep	Somewhat Deep	Casual	Superficial
Emails	50%	13%	25%	13%
Phone calls	7%	17%	30%	47%
In person at work	42%	33%	17%	8%
In person outside of work	53%	37%	5%	5%
Category percentages	30%	25%	20%	25%

Parts Two through Four of the book cover the core successful behaviors and principles found in research. Although the word *behavior* is in the very title of the book, no behavior is sustainable unless basic beliefs of principles agree. Therefore, some of the behaviors resemble principles or mental states, rather than a simple surface behavior. The research encapsulates research over a 3-year period with hundreds of entrepreneurs and 17 years of entrepreneurship experiences. In each of the behaviors, specific foundations of knowledge are discussed to further your understanding of a behavior. Exercises within each chapter develop a deeper level of understanding and then challenge your beliefs as well as obtain alignment between behaviors and beliefs so that changes are sustainable.

Part Five summarizes the key aspects of successful entrepreneurial principles and behaviors. It includes a new leadership model for achieving balance in your life. This internalized leadership model offers a multidisciplinary approach that combines knowledge from both business and psychology literature.

The most important aspect of reading this book is applying the knowledge to your life and work. I strongly encourage you to not only read this book but take part in the exercises of self-discovery. After each chapter, take a moment to write down what you learned and how it applies to your life. There is a tremendous amount of information here, so don't try to digest it all in one sitting. Take the time to transform your reality to achieve your wildest dreams. I recommend that you read a chapter each week. Create multiple actions plans and measure them. One such plan could be the experimental stage where you embrace a belief in a safe environment. That way, it'll give you time to digest the information, develop a deep understanding of its foundations, participate in the exercises, apply the new knowledge gained, and measure the impact of knowledge application. Then develop another action plan that places a tested belief into your being in business. Feel free to revisit the book as often as you like. The various challenges that you face in life will shift and thus give new meanings and interpretations for each chapter. Enjoy the journey!

REFERENCES

1. S. B. Merriam and P. M. Cunningham (1989). *Handbook of adult and continuing education*. San Francisco: Jossey-Bass. This text provides some great research on adult education and learning. One of the most fascinating findings is that the majority of success is attributed from experiential learning (up to 85 percent).

2. C. Argyris (2002). Teaching smart people how to learn. *Reflections: The SOL Journal* 4(2), 4–16. (Retrieved January 14, 2004, from EBSCO Research Database.) This article was published by a very well-known Harvard University professor. In his research and studies, smart people are those who have achieved a certain level of success. Yet due to that success, they've not felt the impact of failure or how it can be valuable. This lack of experience creates an enormous amount of fear for failure that prevent them from exploring alternative viewpoints.

3. P. K. Moser and A. Vander Nat (1995). *Human knowledge: Classical and contem-*

porary approaches. New York: Oxford University Press. This is very heavy reading on the theory of knowledge. It provides an historical account of theories in epistemology from Plato to contemporary theorists. The overall theme of the text is to illustrate the vulnerability of human logic in what we think we know. For humanity to move forward, we must derive a fluid definition of knowledge, rather than an absolute that proves someone else wrong.

4. R. H. Hisrich and M. O. Peters (1992). *Entrepreneurship: Starting, developing, and managing a new enterprise.* Boston: Irwin. This is a standard textbook used by entrepreneurial courses in universities. It covers all the various aspects of running a small business from a high level.

5. I. Nonaka and H. Takeuchi (1995). *The knowledge-creating company: How Japanese companies create the dynamics of innovation.* New York: Oxford University Press. This is one of my favorite books on the topic of a knowledge creation at all levels of an organization. Based on studies of successful Japanese companies, the book clearly defines the intricate aspects of a knowledge creation spiral. It outlines a process that translates tacit knowledge to explicit knowledge. A system of knowledge transfer moves explicit knowledge throughout the organization. Application of that knowledge creates new tacit knowledge for the spiral to continue to grow organizational knowledge.

6. D. A. Garvin (1993, July/August). Building a learning organization. *Harvard Business Review* 71(4). (Retrieved November 15, 2003, from EBSCO Research Database.) Garvin's work expands Drucker's concept of a knowledge worker toward acquiring knowledge on an organizational level. One of the major principles in his theory is that understanding your strengths and weaknesses is only the start of learning. By measuring the impact of learning, you can really get to know what the organization values and how to improve on it. This process of measuring sets the path for individual/group learning.

CHAPTER THREE

Theoretical Foundations

From an academic perspective, this chapter is a section on the previous research conducted on a subject. From a realistic perspective, this can be a tedious chapter to read. Yet as part of the constant need to make sense of what we take in, theoretical foundations challenge what you think you may know about success, entrepreneurship, and leadership. Is your thinking consistent with conventional wisdom, or is it considered "out-of-the-box" thinking? If you believe in the existence of a box for thought, perhaps you're only creating another box, when you're thinking outside the box. Why do we have a box that contains our thinking in the first place? These are the fundamental questions that fail to reach most people's awareness. In the journey to discover the survival tactics, we make an attempt to throw out that box.

ARE YOU INSIDE A BOX?

Before throwing out the box, consider some of the common boxed thinking (some may call it a myth or a false belief) in current practices. Two dominant boxes continue to confuse entrepreneurs: the education of entrepreneurs and certain popular books on entrepreneurship.

From the educational systems, entrepreneurship texts still focuses on a number of skills and tasks a business owner must be competent in.[1,2] Although many books note the lack of knowledge as the reason for failure, they continue to teach the same specific competencies such as operations, marketing, and management over a short time period of a single course.[1] These might be basic skills to know, but most human beings fail to acquire those skills in the period of a semester or quarter. According to the *Handbook of Adult and Continuing Education*,[3] formal education only accounts for 15 percent of the variation in lifetime earnings. So why do the same if you desire a different outcome? Consider Albert Einstein's definition of insanity—doing the same thing over and over again and

Quick Tip: Thinking and believing in the box creates mediocrity. See if you can throw out the box entirely to create new a different thought process.

Think back to your childhood. At what age did you stop dancing just because you felt like it? Think about the last wedding you went to. How old were the kids dancing in the middle of the floor when no one else was out there? At what age does the box begin to contain your desires?

When you hear a good song you like, regardless of place, just let your body go. If it's in a supermarket, move your body to the music down the aisles. Break out of the box. See how it feels to eliminate the box, even if it's just for a few seconds.

expecting different results.[4] Because formal education fails to yield successful entrepreneurs consistently, what new strategies have you invented? How will you stop the insanity of doing the same things and expecting different results?

The second box consists of the popular notion of quick fixes. Conventional wisdom tells people to do what other successful people have done. If they can do it, why can't you? Research on entrepreneurial books found many strategies and skills. Many of these books contain specific behaviors that created the success for the authors. But where's the research? Can you really live in someone else's box of behaviors? In statistics, a single data point represents nothing. A minimum of 30 data points begin to provide evidence of scientific information. Thus, copying what someone else has done may not yield definitive results, nor will it offer you the comfort of being congruent with who you are. There are no quick fixes to being a successful entrepreneur! No specific box will ever contain the thoughts and actions of all successful entrepreneurs.

Every aspect of entrepreneurial success is a constant journey of learning and growing. Although many of your experiences have validity, a fixed theory will not have the impact it did on its inception. Consider the box that creates the context of your thought patterns. For example, how do you see a traditional salesperson? Often, we tend to think of a salesman as someone who knocks on doors or a telemarketer who calls during dinner. Worse yet, we always laugh at the jokes about the car salesman. The connotations associated with salespeople are not the most glorious, which is one box of thought. As an entrepreneur, selling yourself and your company is a core aspect of success. Does that make you a salesperson?

In a leadership program that I facilitated, one individual did not enjoy the selling aspects of her job in a family business. She didn't want to push the products onto customers or make phone calls soliciting clients. Yet is it really the action of selling or the context of thought that prevents her from being an effective seller? In further conversations, I discovered that she had a negative connotation toward the concept of salesperson. To enable this individual to love her job, the box about being a salesperson needed to be eliminated. Rather than looking at the sale of a product, she started to see the process as the start of a relationship with the client. This relationship can manifest in many ways based on sincerity and trust. By focusing on the relationship, rather than the money or contract, a context of inspiration lifted the dreadful thought of being a salesperson for this individual.

Out-of-the-box thinking calls for understanding the premise of the box. Once the context of the box is identified, like your connotations of a salesperson, then you're open to the possibility of a different reality. Yet this reality is far from perfect. To live with no box to contain your thoughts, you must reinvent yourself on a regular basis. Rather than focus on what you're doing or ways to improve, ask yourself—who are you being?

RESEARCH THAT BUILDS FOUNDATION

The research process used to define survival tactics here is one method to achieve that reinvention. The research lasted over three years and included hundreds of entrepreneurs. Starting with my 19 years of entrepreneurial experience, focus groups were used to further define the areas of focus for success; many major companies have such study groups to determine consumer trends and tastes. Based on the analysis of the focus groups, 104 successful entrepreneurs participated by taking the resulting survey instrument. Statistical analysis indicated specific behaviors toward success.

The extensive research initiated with focus groups. These groups consisted of up to 24 CEOs and business owners. For example, one group is the CEO Brain Trust. This group consisted of 29 CEOs/small business owners who met on a monthly basis. These meetings facilitated sharing and learning from an executive perspective. Using groups like those, the research determined the key areas of focus on what makes entrepreneurs successful. Within each focus group, entrepreneurs answered each question to the best of their knowledge. The Exploring Your Knowledge exercise contains the key questions asked during the focus groups. Feel free to explore these questions on your own; then compare your answers with what the research found.

Exploring Your Knowledge Exercise

Take a moment and answer these questions to be the best of your knowledge or experience.

1. What motivated you to start your own business?
2. Why did you pick the type of business that you're in?
3. Have the reasons for owning your own business changed since you initially started?
4. Please take 10 minutes to jot down your answers to the following questions.

a. What skills do you think are necessary for an entrepreneur to become successful? For example, what skills helped you become successful? List five or more.
b. What knowledge do you think one must have to create sustainable success? List at least five areas of knowledge.
c. What are some strategies that you've implemented that have given you the success you enjoy today? List five or more.
d. What is the biggest challenge you face as a business owner working in your business?
e. What gives you the greatest personal satisfaction from your business?

The focus group analysis yielded fascinating indications of success. A standard pie chart was used to illustrate the frequency of each area of interest (see Figure 3-1). Inductively, I determined the underlying major themes and subthemes, in addition to comparisons and contrasts with existing literature on entrepreneurship and leadership. The research and literature review yielded 10 areas of knowledge, skill, and strategies, many of which overlapped: people

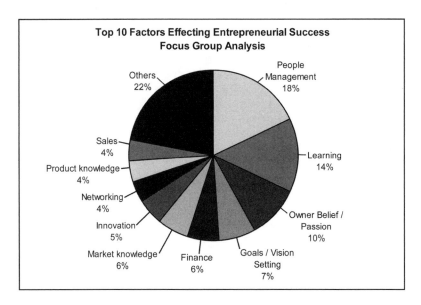

FIGURE 3-1. Top 10 factors affecting entrepreneurial success. This pie chart depicts the various areas of knowledge that identified by the exploratory research. A small focus group of successful entrepreneurs defined the knowledge areas that are most important for success. They listed the areas of significance for entrepreneurial success on a blank sheet of paper.

management, learning, owner belief/passion, planning/goals/vision, finance, market knowledge, innovation, networking, and product knowledge and sales. Ironically, traditional entrepreneurial texts pay limited attention to the top three areas of interest discovered. Could these texts be missing something?

These categories served as the baseline along with information gleaned from the literature review in establishing the overall survey design and specific categories of questions. The literature review included 172 books, texts, articles, and research papers. On the completion of the survey design, a pilot study established statistical validation and reliability. Over a period of six weeks, successful entrepreneurs took an online survey. On average, these entrepreneurs built their business well over six years and had a significant level of financial and personal success. The analysis of these fascinating data discovered the top 11 behaviors in the following chapters.

REFERENCES

1. R. H. Hisrich and M. O. Peters (1992). *Entrepreneurship: Starting, developing, and managing a new enterprise*. Boston, MA: Irwin. A commonly recognized entrepreneurship textbook that focus on specific "skills" one must possess for success.

2. T. S. Hatten (2006). *Small business management: Entrepreneurship and beyond.* New York: Houghton Mifflin. Another common text used for entrepreneurship courses at universities. Much of the book focus on specific functions such as financial and legal management. It does contain a small section on leadership as it pertains to small businesses.

3. S. B. Merriam and P. M. Cunningham (1989). *Handbook of adult and continuing education*. San Francisco: Jossey-Bass. This text presents research and concepts for adult learning.

4. Quotation from Albert Einstein—retrieved on May 16, 2006 from www.wisdom quotes.com/002899.html. This site by J. J. Lewis contains some interesting quotes from famous figures in our history.

CHAPTER FOUR

What Does Success Mean to You?

Success as an entrepreneur is not as simple as a balance sheet to accountants. With ever-increasing costs for all organizations, success can manifest in finances as well as personal welfare that includes free time away from work. Some of the latest entrepreneurial studies suggest that in addition to traditional elements of success such as profitability and personal net worth,[1] success also includes intangible measures such as personal happiness and freedom from work.[2,3]

Think about a successful individual—do they have a huge income? Or are they simply happy with the amount of free time they can spend without interruptions from work? One of the trickiest concepts to measure is success in terms of entrepreneurship. Some of the most brilliant entrepreneurs rarely show a profit; yet they are able to afford luxuries of life. As I started to apply for college, one of the fascinating concepts that puzzled me was my ability to get financial aid. Many middle-class families had limited access to grants and funding, and my parents rarely showed much in the way of an income. For entrepreneurs, personal income is not often a direct correlation to success. Although my parents owned a restaurant, their actual income through the business was low; this allowed me to get financial aid that many friends were not able to receive. If you can't see the success on tax forms, how do you determine that success?

One study included two aspects of entrepreneurial success: traditional measures and intangible measures. The traditional measures were profitability and return on investment.[1] Intangible measures of success included self-evaluations concerning levels of personal happiness and fulfillment, independence and control over one's life, satisfaction of ownership, and personal gratification.[2] There was also an overall measure of success that took into account the perceived success of the entrepreneur in life. Based on these views of success, where would you rate yourself?

Evaluate Your Success Exercise

> Although this might be a challenge, be as honest with yourself as you can. From a scale of 1 to 5, with 5 being the highest level of success, how would you rate your own level of success in these categories? See Table 4-1 for a chart.
>
> Once you've rated yourself, average your scores. Items 1 and 2 are traditional success. Items 3, 4, and 5 are nontraditional success. In which category did you score higher? Did any of the categories make you think further? Were you uncomfortable in what you might have scored?

Within the context of the study, two separate windows viewed success of entrepreneurs. Aside from the separation of traditional and nontraditional measures, the importance of a specific category determined the individual relevance of a measure. This is a missing element in many surveys. Imagine asking people about a specific skill or success attribute. Would their response matter if they felt that the skill or attribute is worthless? For example, if I asked you about your preferred color and size of a motorcycle, your answer would depend on whether you actually cared about having a motorcycle. If you didn't care about having one, your response will be indicative of the importance of that motorcycle. Therefore, when asking questions about the level of success, the carefully constructed survey determined if successful entrepreneurs cared about certain dimensions of success.

In the Table 4-2, a significant difference between traditional and nontraditional success exists. The study found that successful entrepreneurs focused significantly more on the nontraditional dimensions of success than traditional ones. This is consistent with other studies that clearly define the endpoint of projects, rather than a focus on the means to get there.[4] Which basket do your eggs lie in? The traditional one or the nontraditional one? Or perhaps both?

Looking at the levels of personal achievement, successful entrepreneurs achieve slightly more in the nontraditional dimension of success. How does that compare with your numbers in the above exercise?

TABLE 4-1. A Chart Similar to the Survey that Seeks a Better Understanding of Entrepreneurial Success

Success Category	How Successful Do You Feel? (Rate 1–5)
1. Net profit/income	_____
2. Personal net worth	_____
3. Personal happiness and fulfillment	_____
4. Complete independence and control over life	_____
5. Personal gratification from work	_____

TABLE 4-2. Success Levels of Entrepreneurs with Respect to Two Types of Success. Traditional Success is the Typical Financial Measures of Success; Nontraditional Success is Emotions Attached to the Business and Self

	Average Perceived Importance	Average Personal Achievement
Traditional Success	3.43	4.2
Nontraditional Success	4.27	4.56

DIFFERENCES BETWEEN MEN AND WOMEN

According to the Center for Women's Business Research,[6] female-owned businesses grew more than the national averages. In terms of employment, these businesses grew more than twice the rate of the national average (24.2 percent for female-owned businesses and 11.6 percent for the national average). They also led in revenues by 5.8 percent compared with the national average over the years from 1997 to 2004. What does that say about success differences between genders?

In general, psychologists agree that men and women think differently. In one of the most widely studied subjects—IQ assessment—men and women have shown differences in specific areas of intelligence.[7] Do these differences attribute to success?

The study found a fascinating fact that successful female entrepreneurs have a significantly higher focus on the nontraditional views of success than traditional measures. Successful male entrepreneurs have a slightly higher focus on the traditional measures of success (3.46) compared to the focus exhibited by females (3.35). That difference is larger when looking at nontraditional measures with males at 4.13 and females at 4.62 (see Table 4-3). Could this difference in focus be one reason for the higher revenues and employee growth by female entrepreneurs?

When looking at a level of personal achievement, numbers are reflective of the level of importance. Because male entrepreneurs perceived a greater degree of importance in the traditional measures of success, they rated 2 percent higher

TABLE 4-3. Comparison of Perceived Importance by Male and Female Entrepreneurs' View of Success

	Males	Females
Traditional Success	3.46	3.37
Nontraditional Success	4.13	4.62

TABLE 4-4. Comparison of Personal
Achievement by Male and Female
Entrepreneurs' View of Success

	Males	Females
Traditional Success	4.23	4.13
Nontraditional Success	4.47	4.76

than females. Females rated 7 percent higher in nontraditional success than males (Table 4-4).

Aside from the male/female analysis, a fundamental difference in belief exists between male and female entrepreneurs. This leads to significantly different behaviors. An individual focused on the financial outcome may miss the lesson. A recent study by Seijts and Latham from the Richard Ivey School of Business discussed the difference between learning goals and outcome goals.[5] Because the tangible measures of success are outcome-based goals, individuals must possess the skills required to achieve the goal. Otherwise, a narrow focus on the outcome greatly limits the learning required to achieve it. On the other hand, as female entrepreneurs focus more on the nontraditional measures of success, emotions become the focus, rather than an end state. This creates more room for entrepreneurs to find their own way through learning and building relationships. This fundamental belief on the type of success can lead toward considerable differences in behaviors. These behaviors eventually lead any entrepreneur toward the success they desire.

TIME RICH

In most measures of success, time is not typically part of the equation. Although it's not part of a balance sheet, it is often a significant intrinsic motivation for entrepreneurs owning their own business. According to the *Wall Street Journal*, Americans are working 20 percent more hours when a simple comparison is made of work time from 1970 to 2002. Yet, most of our industrialized trading partners, such as Japan, France, and United Kingdom, have decreased their working hours by as much as 23.5 percent.[9] Apply this research toward yourself: how many more hours did you work last month compared to a monthly average from the prior year? Are you really making the effort to measure your time as part of success?

Learning to work smarter is a basic measure of success. Many popular authors and speakers discuss the concept of time as one of the most crucial and valuable resources one could have.[8] Unlike money or property, this is one resource you cannot save. Each day, you're given 1,440 minutes to spend. How you spend them is a direct reflection of your values and your level of success. Let's take a moment to quantify this measure.

Time Rich or Poor Exercise

Over the next few days, jot down how much time you spend on work, family, education, hobbies, and any other activity you engage in. Just take a simple note card and write down the category and time spent for each category.

On a separate sheet of paper, write down the top five values you hold along with a short and simple sentence describing that value. Keep in mind that an action/verb is not a value. Money, which is only a means to get something, is also not a value. Make sure you label the values in order of importance and fill out the corresponding chart.

This exercise is a simple indicator of where you spend most of your time. How does it reflect your values? In many workshops over the past several years, I've found that most people fail to reflect their time allocations toward their value system.

The wealth of time is not a simple concept. Part of a basic mental shift requires you to look at the impact of their time, rather than the total of time spent. Unless the output is of value, endless hours spent on a specific activity do not generate revenue. Let's look at a simple example of an experiment you can conduct in your relationships. One of my clients was a mother. She spent 30 minutes with her son just playing with him (being fully present). The next day, she spent 30 minutes watching TV, a passive activity. On the surface, it appears to be the same 30 minutes spent at the same time of the day. After 30 minutes of actively playing with her son, she was free to go anything she needed to. On the contrary, after 30 minutes of passive activity, her son refused to let her Mom go, asking for more time and attention. Time is not a linear concept! You cannot manage time like a machine, since full presence of your mind can

TABLE 4-5. A Worksheet to Determine the Amount of Time You Spend on Each Activity and How They Align with Your Values

Personal Values	Time Spent in Value over 2 Days	Percentage of Total Time (Divide the Hours by 48)
1. _____	_____	_____
2. _____	_____	_____
3. _____	_____	_____
4. _____	_____	_____
5. _____	_____	_____

make a dramatic impact to relationships. Just as the Mother found the difference between active and passive engagement, successful entrepreneurs don't focus on the quantity of time. Instead, they focus on being fully present with other people. They fully engage, especially with their staff. As the growth progression of a business develops, entrepreneurs can spend more time on developing systems that can be sustainable without their physical presence. Specific tasks such production, maintenance, and record-keeping should decrease as a business grows.[8] More important, measure the time you spend against your personal values and those of the organization. A constant measurement will increase the awareness of that success factor.

REFERENCES

1. K. H. Chadwick (1998). *An empirical analysis of the relationships among entrepreneurial orientation, organizational culture and firm performance.* ProQuest Digital Dissertations (UMI No. 9840688). Chadwick's study was based out of Louisiana Tech University. He looked at the various type of entrepreneurial behavior and its impact on the firm's performance using only the tangible measures of performance, such as profitability and return on investment.

2. R. C. Paige (1999). *Craft retail entrepreneurs' perceptions of success and factors effecting success.* ProQuest Digital Dissertations (UMI No. 9950110). Paige's study was out of Iowa State University. She included other aspects of success when studying craft retailers' views of success and specific factors that impacted that success. Her work validated the importance of a balance various dimension of success including the intangible success measure such as happiness.

3. T. Sun (2004, May). *Knowledge required to achieve entrepreneurial success.* ProQuest Dissertations (ISBN: 0–496-83341–5). This study is the foundation of this text. A balanced view of success considered both the tangible and intangible aspects of success as well as an overall measure of success in life.

4. J. C. Collins (2001). *Good to great: Why some companies make the leap . . . and others don't.* New York: Harper Collins. One of the primary principles of the research found people matter more than the objects such as projects or finances. Collins's principle, first who, then what, clearly looks at the people focus, rather than the traditional focus on profits. When you have the right people, the work will get done and the profits will be a result.

5. G. H. Seijts and G. P. Latham (2005) Learning versus performance goals: When should each be used? *Academy of Management Executive* 19(1), 124–31. This research article refuted the conventional wisdom of outcome-based goals. Though it creates competition and unnecessary fears on individuals, outcome-based goals are not appropriate in many organizational settings. The authors propose learning goals as an alternative, focusing on individual experimentation of new knowledge.

6. Center for Women's Business Research (2004). Privately-held, 50% or more women-owned businesses in the United States. Retrieved on June 26, 2006 from http://www.womensbusinessresearch.org/freepublications/USFiftyPercentorMore-Owned.pdf. This resource provides some descriptive data on trends of women-owned businesses and compares them to the national averages.

7. R. J. Cohen and M. E. Swerdlik (2004). *Psychological testing and assessment: An*

introduction to tests and measurement (6th ed.). Mountain View, CA: Mayfield. This psychology text covers the different aspects of psychological testing, including IQ and personality assessments. The various differences between gender and culture are included in the interpretation of these tests.

8. A. McCarthy, D. A. Krueger, and T. A. Schoenecker (1990, Winter). Changes in the time allocation patterns of entrepreneurs. *Entrepreneurship: Theory and Practice* 15(2), 7–18. This is a study that looked at the time allocation of entrepreneurs as the business grew. Because all entrepreneurs have a limited amount of time to perform specific duties, the division of time to specific tasks is crucial to success. The study found some interesting trends on the potential lack of time management by entrepreneurs surveyed.

9. G. Ip (2004, July 8). U.S. wealth tied more to work than productivity, report says. *Wall Street Journal*. This article provided some basic statistics on how much more time Americans are working. People place too much of a focus on time put toward work rather than on the actual outcome of that work.

PART II

SELF-LEADERSHIP

Three distinctive themes divide the remaining part of the book. Based on the four statistical analysis methods, the results formed three distinct groups: self-leadership, interpersonal leadership, and planning/systems management. The self-leadership behaviors are those that concentrate on the entrepreneur. Unlike many leadership myths that focus on what you should do to be a leader for others, the self-leadership behaviors seek growth from within (i.e., intellectual or emotional awareness). The significance of self-leadership was a bit of a surprise to me. Based on previous research, the surveys contained the least amount of questions on self-leadership and significantly more questions on interpersonal leadership and planning/systems management. Yet after analysis, my study found more critical success factors in the area of self-leadership than in any other category. In the norms of American society, we spend a lot of time investing in stocks, mutual funds, bonds, and so on. Very little if any conscious effort is spent on continuous self-development. Could this be a root cause for the 80 percent failure rate of entrepreneurs—a lack of conscious focus toward the development of self?

Self-leadership is another name for *reflective or internalized leadership*. Although others have used the term as a means to reflect on one's personal behaviors to understanding how they affect the behaviors of others, reflective leadership is internal to the entrepreneur. It does not involve anyone else. The various forms of intelligences are the start of thought patterns within the leader. The exhibited behaviors are only a reflection of those thought patterns. The impacts of those behaviors are influenced by those behaviors. To get to the root of understanding one's business, one must focus on the self. All events that occur within any business/organization are merely a reflection of the internal self. If an individual does not have a well-rounded awareness and development of self, external successes are temporary and purely circumstantial.

The following self-leadership behaviors are the fundamental parts of entrepreneurial success: constant learning, technical proficiency, self-confidence, codependence, risk taking, and reactivity.

CHAPTER FIVE

Behavior 1: Constant Learning

Have you ever wondered why it's rare to have a sports team consistently win? For example, very few teams have ever repeated a Super Bowl or World Cup championship. Even fewer individuals have repeated Olympic gold medals. What makes it so tough to stay at the top?

The answer is the ability to constantly reinvent oneself from a learning perspective. Typically entrepreneurs and leaders start a business at the top of their game. Their passion for the work makes them a rare commodity. Their courage to go out on their own makes them a force to be reckoned with. The difference between those that continue to stay at the top of their game and those that fail in their business is *constant learning*. As the first behavior of self-leadership, your ability to learn sustains any success you desire, regardless of the state of the economy, competition, or globalization.

LEARNING AND EGO

Change is constant! Especially in a global economy where your competitors, suppliers, and customers can come from any part of the world, change is part of every business. If you choose not to change, you'll be extinct within a matter of years, sometimes even months. In the beauty of change, you have choices. Although conventional wisdom might suggest that you change just to keep up, consider how you might lead change. Imagine the possibilities of your business and life when you're always leading change, instead of just following it. What would that look like? How would it feel to always be ahead of the competition, never having to worry about them? What will the newspapers print as your business exemplifies tremendous success year after year?

To achieve that level of success, monitor your ego from month to month, if not more frequently. The ego is a fascinating aspect of humanity. It has caused wars between countries while crumbling empires within the human race. With every achievement, the ego increases its need for more. For some people, too much success can cause the ego to be out of balance with humility.

In studies on learning and ego, many of the smartest people in the top professions are poor learners.[1,2] When people at the top of their game reach a certain level of knowledge, new learning becomes more difficult. After all, if a set of knowledge helped reach a goal, why not use it all the time? With this myth, one assumption fails to hold true. The context of situations is constantly changing. There is very little chance that the environment will be the same as it was when the first achievement occurred. This entrenched knowledge becomes frozen knowledge.[3] Rather than being open to new ideas, a successful person's pride in knowledge keeps him or her from learning.[1]

From a psychological perspective, I use a simple concept called the "I know" syndrome to describe this mentality. Think of how often you use the word *but* and the context of how you may have used it. For example, when you're late to a meeting, you may find yourself saying, "I apologize for being late, but [some reasons] kept me from being on time." This is part of our left brain interpreter that makes sense out of everything that happens to make us feel like we're in control of our environment.[4] For every action, you'll have reasons to think that your actions are justified. If you allow your ego to dominate your thoughts, your reasons are always perfect and better than other people's. This behavior causes higher order thought to be nonexistent. You've basically shut the door to the possibility of seeing another perspective.

Here's a fun little experiment you can conduct to see how much learning happens when ego is dominating.

The Ego Check

> This exercise illustrates how much learning occurs when one's ego is engaged. People have these conversations on a regular basis; all we're doing here is seeing it from a different context.
>
> 1. Think of a few successful or smart people in your life. This could be a co-worker, a partner, or even a fellow entrepreneur.
> 2. Schedule a half hour with them to engage in a topic of your choice that they care about. Play the role of a devil's advocate and choose to disagree with them.
> 3. Notice how much they defend their position with reasons. Compare that with the effort being made to ask you about your perspective.
>
>   a. Keep a mental count of the reasons they may give you.
>   b. Count the number of questions they ask.
>
> 4. On completion of the conversation, take a few minutes and reflect on the following questions.

a. How much did they learn about you? If anything, what do you think they learned?

b. Do you feel like you were heard in the conversation?

From a leadership perspective, we all understand the importance of listening to others and learning about what they need and desire. Yet when the ego is engaged, very little learning occurs, other than the validation of self. In the process of defending the ego to prove its absolute perfection, the most brilliant minds become disabled in learning.

Learning requires humility in addition to pride of success. It's easy to look at other people and see how they might be driven by the ego; the difficult part is to see it in yourself. Ego is part of human nature. It has its place in your life along with the success you've achieved. Yet in the reinvention of yourself, the ego needs to be balanced with humility. One method to keeping your ego in check is to understand and recognize your motivations for an activity or decision. If you're extrinsically motivated by some external factors, such as revenue or an award, your ego may be doing the driving. Part of the ego is saying that you need recognition to validate yourself. From another perspective, how much would you like to be controlled by someone else? The ego is easily manipulated and is often used to entice people to perform activities that they might not choose to do otherwise. Consider the common business world—if bosses wanted an employee to perform a task or take on a project, more money often makes it acceptable. The society we live in loves extrinsic motivation. You may often find reminders from just about everyone around you on how important it is to get good grades in school or get certain jobs or make specific levels of income.[5] The higher the external focus, the more controlled the population becomes and the less self-aware they are. Are you willing to allow someone to control you through the engagement of your ego?

To create a balance, consider what intrinsic motivations you might have for decisions and actions. A good question to ask yourself is: Would I make the same choice if the external award were not present? Your willingness to make decisions without external consequences reveals a deeper level of self-awareness. It also allows humility to perpetuate through everyday decisions and actions. A willingness to act provides an internal peace that opens the door for learning. Intrinsic motivation creates optimal learning as well as a self-regulated learning process.[5]

REDEFINE LEARNING

When you think of learning, what is the image that comes to mind? How does it feel to have homework? Homework usually has negative connotations. Unfortunately, the current hierarchical methods of education often misrepresent the idea of learning. Before going forward to discuss how you can reinvent yourself by learning, we need to reorient your assumptions and beliefs about learning.

While I was visiting Oxford University in England, presenting my paper on meaningful learning methodologies, a fascinating discovery occurred in a rather heated debate. The context of the conversation happened within a group of professors from around the world at the Global Conference for Business and Economics. I presented my research on educational methodologies, and one of the principles provided for students' input into their grade. It made sense to me because the knowledge learned in class was only useful if the students found a way to apply it in their own lives. The success of that application was foreign to the professors, because they have little or no knowledge of the pressures the students face at work or the projects they have on their plate. Nor could professors truly grasp the impact of that application within the students' environment. I recommended that learning should have a significantly higher assessment by the students. This caused a few members of the audience, who were all well-published professors, to jump out of their seats. One stated, "How does the student know if they've learned it properly? We're the ones who are experts." I challenged the audience back with another question: "Are we really the experts of their lives? Sure, we get to see them on a regular basis for a few hours each week; does that make us the real experts?"

Unfortunately, that individual's remarks represent a common mentality with many educators. Part of that conversation goes back to the ego and mentality of education—a pedagogical perspective that students are dependent on teachers and their experiences are of little value.[6] If you're always being told how good a student or worker you are, you're not able to voice your own thoughts. Can you truly learn in such an environment?

One of the dominant forces in education as well as society is behaviorism. Behaviorism states that external stimulus induces human behaviors such as learning.[5] The stimulus-response relationship is easily visible with animals as we train them to perform certain tasks for a treat. Some of the assumptions under that theory fail to truly predict the complexity of humanity. For example, one of the assumptions is that human behaviors change largely as a result of a change in the environment. This assumption fails to account for the creative nature of the mind. Some behavioral changes occur because of a shift in thought, not of the environment. Another assumption is that learning involves a behavioral change with a direct relationship to the stimulus. This occurs in many organizations.

At a major company, projects were not being completed on time and information between team members was not shared. To change this behavior, management attempted to add a stimulus, such as financial incentives to timely completion of project. Even without knowing the details, you might think this stimulus makes sense for a materialistic environment. In reality, it had no impact. The real issue at hand was job security. When previous workers completed their projects and shared information, they were let go for lack of projects. Thus, no one was willing to share information or complete projects on time in fear of termination.

The human mind is much more complex than that of animals, especially when it comes to learning. Human beings should not be trained like animals to perform tasks with stimulus. From a cognitive perspective, reinforcement of a certain behavior has no guarantee that it will work next time or if the visible behavior is directly related to the stimulus given.

From a physical perspective, the human brain contains significantly higher level thinking than animals. The size of one's brain is not significant to intelligence, instead, the important part is the percentage of the cortex (the frontal part of the brain responsible for higher level thought) compared to the entire mass of the brain. For example, most mammals likes cats and dogs have less than 10 percent of their brain mass in the cortex, whereas human beings have more than 20 percent.[5] This presents clear evidence that thought must also be part of learning, not just observable behaviors. Based on the latest educational psychology literature, consider this definition of learning: "relative permanent change, due to experience, either in behavior or in mental representations or associations; something that lasts for a period of time."[5]

Based on this definition, it's perfectly fine to do nothing, because we're not "human doings," but rather "human beings." For the learner, part of learning process happens internally. Learning doesn't have to be for someone else to review or grade. It has to have meaning and some level of fun and curiosity. As the most vital principle to any success at all levels of organizations, your ability to learn conquers any material placed before you.

STRATEGIES FOR LEARNING

Keeping this definition of learning in mind, the following strategies create a learning system based on some of the relatively new theories of learning such as cognitive psychology,[5] constructivism[5,6] and meaningful learning.[5,7]

Relating Information in a Meaningful Way

You are a meaning-making machine. For any information to become knowledge that has a relative permanent recall, you must attach personal meaning to it. Today's world is full of information. No matter where you go, an enormous amount of information stimulates your vision, hearing, and feelings. On average, a human brain processes over 400 billion bits of information per second. Yet a mere 2,000 is within some level of awareness to us.[9] As an entrepreneur, how much vital information can you afford to miss?

Think back to commercials you remember the most, whether they were on television, the Web, or radio. Which ones do you remember right now? The ones that draw on your ability to make sense of them are those you remember.

Mortgage commercials are abundant in advertising. Yet most of us don't remember them, unless we're in the market to buy or refinance a home. When we attach meaning to new information, we have significantly more retention of that information. More important, if we use that service, the permanence is dramatically increased. A study by Cornell University revealed the importance of meaning attachment to new information. They found that on average, the human retention of new information is within 5 percent to 10 percent when just reading or listening. Yet the retention rate increases up to 75 percent when we use what we received within a short time period.[10]

To maximize learning, use the new information immediately after you've acquired it. The following are a few of the basic methods to maximize your learning.

- Elaborate on the information with friends and colleagues.[5]
- Make an accountability structure with friends to apply the knowledge and share it. An accountability structure is fairly simple—tell a friend/colleague that you're going to complete a specific task in a specific time frame. Ask that person to hold you accountable. We're more likely to complete a task if other people are involved.
- Periodically check on the new information and investigate its relevance. This is a process for new knowledge creation and drives innovation.[5]
- Be very active in your own learning. Don't learn something just because someone else tells you to. Learn what interests *you*. No one else knows exactly what you desire or need.[5]

Create a Conscious Learning System

Because the success of your business and life is a mere reflection of your internal growth, design a learning system that is ideal for your schedule and challenging. This learning process should always push beyond your comfort level, into an area where you're not the expert. Whether the system uses the technical expertise or certain types of communication skills such as body language or leadership characteristics and beliefs, the learning system you design will help you reinvent yourself and lead the pack in any business. Rather than the conventional wisdom of keeping up with change, you can easily lead change, while others are following your leadership.

Your learning system is multidimensional. From a time perspective, creating a time block of at least a few hours each week will enable learning. From the study of successful entrepreneurs, a few of the top growing business owners were taking entire weekends to read up on the latest research and news concerning their industry. A few others read development books and journals on a daily basis for half an hour each day while planning new activities based on the information. To obtain the maximum return on investment, this time block is most effective in the morning when your mind is fresh and open to new ideas.

If you schedule this in the evening, you may find that concerns of the day or tomorrow may not allow you to create that focus.

From a content perspective, make sure the knowledge you gain is validated research and vital to your business. Many people read the news. As current as that might be in today's media delivery systems, it's still information on things that have already happened, causing you to follow. Rather than reading the news (or in addition to it), take time to read up on studies of various interests. For example, one area of interest for entrepreneurs is leadership—how to lead or develop worthy relationships with customers, vendors, partners, and so on. The appropriate content for this learning is self-development information such as emotional intelligence, leadership theories, and communication skills. All of the information required for such development does not come from the news. Some are in the form of books; the latest information is often in academic or industry journals.

From a contextual perspective, the learning system needs to have a balance of your various intelligences.[11] Organize your learning into different intelligences, such as emotional intelligence, systems consciousness/spiritual intelligence, somatic awareness, and so on. Consider for a moment that life is not filled with ups and downs—it's relatively flat. Yet rather than having a round wheel that takes us on our journey, our dramatically different levels of competence creates the ups and downs. As shown in Figure 5-1, you can see that IQ development is very high for most entrepreneurs. Analytically, we are the masters of our work. Yet in some of the other areas of intelligence we do not have the same capacity or we have very limited education. The lack of balance in our internal wheel of development causes the ups and downs of life in any business.

To establish the balance, your learning time can focus on each of your areas of weakness as well as strength.

Another crucial contextual piece to self-development is to reflect on the fear of failure. As studies have shown, the fear of failure haunts many successful people to the point of creating a huge ego.[1] One of the primary causes of this fear is the perceived endpoint of any task. In this focus on outcome, there are only two choices—either you fail or you succeed. In the context of learning, neither hold true on a systemic level. You may find that doing the same in similar situations may result in both failures and successes. Such a duality of outcome often builds immense anxiety that may not be conducive to learning.[12]

When visiting a client recently, I stopped to talk to a project manager who was responsible for the company's annual conference. Angela is a very passionate and capable individual, and her knowledge of the products and services is well known. Yet when I walked by her desk, I saw stress and anxiety all over her face. I casually asked, "What are you working on?" Angela replied, "I'm working on the program for the annual conference. There's so much information I have to consider; it has to be perfect."

At just one level below the owner and a nationwide conference to plan, Angela was carrying a huge amount of weight on her shoulders. Can you imag-

Wheel of Development for Entrepreneurs

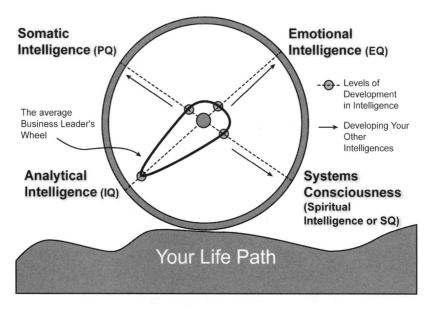

FIGURE 5-1. Wheel of development for entrepreneurs. Human beings have more than a single dimension of intelligence. Each of the spokes of the wheel represent a dimension of intelligence, including somatic awareness, emotional intelligence (EQ), analytical intelligence (IQ), and spiritual intelligence (SQ).

ine the stress and pressures of making sure the conference was perfect? The fear of failure was creating much discomfort in a workplace that focuses on wellness. I planted a seed in her mind: "What if there was no such thing as failure? What if you *could not* fail? Being that this is a huge event, it's a journey for everyone involved to learn about the challenges of organizing and planning. Every mistake is only a valuable lesson worth attention. Every success is only an acknowledgment that you're doing something well this time. The actual outcome will be perfect in its journey, irrelevant to external judgment".

"I knew I needed to spend more time with you," Angela replied. "I can have fun learning about the process and continue to improve. No such thing as failure! That really takes the weight off."

Instead of focusing on the endpoint/outcome of any task or project, focus on the journey. Create process goals that deal with learning.[12] For example, you may want to build better relationships with others. An outcome goal may be the revenue you generate from these relationships. But that's only a result of the depth of relationship. Process goals deal with the relationships themselves. You can seek to understand trust while learning to improve that trust with various

> Quick Tip: The world is loaded with judgment. To rise above it, focus on learning when other people are involved. When someone criticizes your actions or decisions, consciously choose to seek the wisdom of others (whatever shape it comes in) by asking, "what would you do in my place?" or "what would you recommend?" Both questions puts ownership on the one giving the critique while allowing you to see the brilliance of others and create respectful relationships.

promises and follow-through actions. A process goal could be the number of communications in which you made a commitment and followed through to completion. The journey you're on as an entrepreneur is loaded with countless invaluable lessons. If you can't fail, egos can stay seated and watch on the sidelines. Your inner child, which is a brilliant learner because it has no judgment on anything, can enter the learning system to absorb all types of fascinating lessons that help you lead change.

The learning strategies you create have two ultimate goals. The first is to increase your self-efficacy, a belief that you're capable of learning anything or reach any impossible goals. As you move forward to improve your various intelligences, you'll find an enormous amount of abundance in knowledge and your abilities. As an entrepreneur, you need that self-belief.

The second goal is to silence the ego. Leaders who create sustainable business successes are not interested in being right.[13] The same principle applies to entrepreneurship. Top leaders are focused on the process and the organization, rather than on self-validation or outcomes. They are capable of creating an environment that focuses on learning for both self and the business. Top leaders often have multiple levels of mentors and coaches to guide them. Their humility is as powerful as their pride, and they are always striving for continued growth. They often create self-imposed contingencies to push the learning envelope.[5] As long as you're focused on growing, you cannot fail in entrepreneurship. The evidence in the research clearly shows that constant and systematic learning is a core practice for successful entrepreneurs.

REFERENCES

1. C. Argyris (2002). Teaching smart people how to learn. *Reflections: The SOL Journal* 4(2), 4–16. This article was published by a very well-known Harvard University professor. In his research and studies, smart people are those who have achieved a certain level of success. Yet due to that success, they've not felt the impact of failure or how it can be valuable. This lack of experience creates an enormous amount of fear of failure that prevent them from exploring alternative viewpoints.

2. C. Argyris and D. A. Schon (1978). *Organizational learning*. Reading, MA: Addison-Wesley. This book discusses learning from an organizational perspective. Learning is defined as one of the most crucial aspects to organizational growth and survival.

3. R. Jacques (1996). Manufacturing the employee: Management knowledge from the 19th to 21st centuries. Thousand Oaks, CA: Sage Publications. This is one of my favorite readings because it clearly reveals the historical evidence of how principles of learning created the concepts of management and why they do not work for today's economy.

4. M. S. Gazzaniga (1998). *The mind's past.* Berkeley: University of California Press. This book provides a detailed description of the mind and how it functions. It offers neuron-biological studies that illustrate the brilliance of the left brain interpreter, which is always manufacturing reasons to make us feel like we're in control.

5. J. E. Ormrod (2006). *Educational psychology: Developing learners* (5th ed.). Upper Saddle River, NJ: Prentice Hall. This book covers many theories of adult learning as well as measurements. It is rather technical from an educator's perspective, but provides the latest research knowledge on learning.

6. M. K. Smith (2002). Malcolm Knowles, informal adult education, self-direction and andragogy. Encyclopedia of informal education, available online at www.infed.org/thinkers/et-knowl.htm. This article discusses the differences between traditional learning foundations and the more recent beliefs in adult learning (andragogy). If you're looking to teach/mentor people at any point in life, this article is a good place to evaluate your personal beliefs about your role as the teacher and that of the student.

7. L. Abbeduto (2006). *Taking sides: Clashing views in educational psychology* (4th ed.). Dubuque, IA: McGraw-Hill. This book offers some fascinating discussions on how adults learn and what needs to be considered. Arguments from both conventional wisdom and the latest research offer multiple viewpoints.

8. T. Sun (2005). Meaningful learning: An effective methodology that yields tremendous leaders today. Conference Proceedings on Global Conference on Business and Economics, Oxford, England. This is a paper I wrote on creating effective methods for learning with adult learners. It offers research validation for methods used.

9. *What the #&*! do we (k)now!?* (2004). 20th Century Fox Home Entertainment. This movie is about quantum physics. It reveals some incredible insight on what we perceive as reality versus what we create in our own mind. In reality, the brain can't tell the difference between what is really in its environment and what it remembers.

10. Cornell University (2004). National Resources Conservation Service, USDA, "Instructional Systems Design (ISD)—Developing Performance Measurements." Retrieved from http://www.nedc.nrcs.usda.gov/isd/isd6.html. This site illustrates the results of the study on human retention. The rates of retention increases as application of new information occurs. The following rates of retention were found: lecture = 5 percent; reading = 10 percent; discussion group = 50 percent; practice by doing = 75 percent; immediate use of learning = 90 percent.

11. H. Gardner (1993). *Multiple intelligences: The theory in practice.* New York: Basic Books. This book was revolutionary in thought. It introduced the complexity of human intelligence with multiple dimensions that are interconnected and work in concert to help us achieve our goals. Gardner introduced seven different forms of intelligence.

12. G. H. Seijts and G. P. Latham (2005). Learning versus performance goals: When should each be used? *Academy of Management Executive* 19(1), 124–31. This research article refused the conventional wisdom of outcome-based goals. While it creates competition and unnecessary fears on individuals, outcome-based goals are not appropriate in many organizational settings. The authors propose learning goals as an alternative, focusing on individual experimentation of new knowledge.

13. J. C. Collins (2001). *Good to great: Why some companies make the leap . . . and others don't*. New York: HarperCollins. This very popular book reveals many leadership qualities based on Collins's research. From his studies, real leaders strive to create sustainable organizations through systems, rather than create codependent relationships that caused failure once they depart.

CHAPTER SIX

Behavior 2: Technical Proficiency

Being an expert in your field is a foundation for success. This sounds like basic common sense, but it is a huge pitfall for many people. How can it be both a competitive advantage and a disadvantage? What is the real technical expertise? Is it an expertise in leading people, a product, or leading yourself?

High technical proficiency is a snapshot in current time, nothing more! If you believe otherwise, consider this true story.

While I was in high school, my parents owned and operated a restaurant. Both my father and mother were excellent chefs in authentic Chinese cuisine and developed incredible entrees for the customers. They had a profound technical expertise in making great food. I, along with the countless repeat customers, thoroughly enjoyed their dishes. Many even followed them through the selling and purchasing of larger dining establishments. Although this gave a promising start to a business, it also trapped my parents at work. The labor-intensive business required the physical presence of that technical expertise approximately 72 hours each week, not including all the administrative requirements of owning a business. Imagine working 12 hours every day for 6 days every week. How would you feel? Are you really working as an entrepreneur or are you a slave to your business? Although providing great startup success, this technical expertise limited the growth potential of the business. For a small business to increase its customer base, owners must be able to produce the products/services to match. Because my parents were crucial to production, additional growth would have required additional production time. Would you be willing to give up that single day off for another 12 hours of work? Consider Figure 6-1.

On the family front, growing up in with entrepreneurial parents had its difficulties. Although I was able to treat certain girlfriends to fantastic meals cooked to their desires, I was also often left to fend for myself. While my parents were working 12+ hours each day, I learned to be very independent at a young age. Certainly, independence is part of being a leader; it also had an adverse effect

FIGURE 6-1.   The typical view of an entrepreneur who has maintained technical competence without sharing knowledge. He is often stuck doing all the work, wearing many hats that he cannot let go of. If he does let go, the business will fall. In this behavior, entrepreneurs' families lose much family time.

on the parental relationship. I grew to be independent of my parents as well, with limited emotional connection. I bet that no one sets out to be an entrepreneur to decrease their family ties. Even after years of research in entrepreneurialism to understand the events of my childhood, I continue to work on developing the relationship with my parents.

Technical expertise needs to further develop as the business grows. If left alone, that expertise will become the ball and chain that makes an entrepreneur a slave to the business. Transferring the entrepreneur's technical expertise to the people within the organization on a systemic level yields the freedom that entrepreneurs desire. Once the system for transfer is created, you'll have the time to expand that expertise in new dimensions, such as leadership.

TECHNICAL PROFICIENCY TRANSFER

Free time was rare for my parents. The technical expertise they exhibited gave a great foundation for the start of the business, but it also trapped them inside it. This cannot be the primary production driver as the business grows. If you're the only one who knows how to perform a specific task, your life will be slowly consumed by the business as it grows. To avoid this trap, the transfer of individual technical expertise toward organizational knowledge is a minimum requirement. This expertise in knowledge transfer requires two basic elements. The first is a development skill—a good understanding of knowledge transfer practices and theories.[1] The second is a crucial belief of abundance over fear.[2]

Many studies and books have documented knowledge transfer practices and principles.[1,3,4] The basic premise is to create a learning system in which technical expertise is passed from one individual to the next. Tacit knowledge of the industry and its processes enable the creation of the business. Yet that tacit knowledge can only go so far. Successful entrepreneurs understand the importance of transferring that expertise to others by making the knowledge explicit and developing systems that get others in the organization to embody that knowledge.

Figure 6-2 is a simplified overview of the organizational learning system. In practice, this model moves the organization forward by relieving the entrepreneur from being the sole knowledge expert and empowers the employees of the organization to lead the production. The system provides the entrepreneur time to increase technical proficiency in a global economy. As long as the entrepreneur is constantly growing in technical expertise and passing it on to the organi-

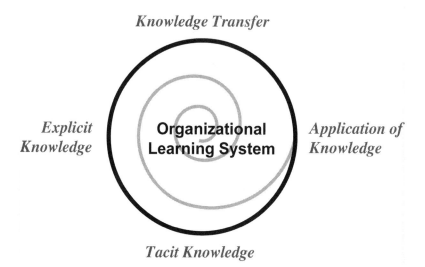

Organizational Learning System

Knowledge Transfer

Explicit Knowledge — **Organizational Learning System** — *Application of Knowledge*

Tacit Knowledge

FIGURE 6-2. Organizational learning system transforms individual knowledge toward organizational knowledge. (This figure is adapted from *The Knowledge-Creating Company*.[1])

zation, success is only a matter of time. This learning system deals with taking tacit technical expertise and moving it toward organizational knowledge. A typical process would incorporate the following steps in an organizational setting. As you read through these basic steps, you'll find that substantial attention is placed on creating the context for learning and not the transfer itself.

1. Establish Key Metrics for Learning

Drucker introduced the concept of the knowledge worker in 1968.[7] Since then, an incredible amount of literature and research has been conducted on the subject of knowledge, learning, and the individual's role in the economy.[1,3,4,6,8,9] One of the basic established principles in the theory is measurement. Many believe that to manage learning, one must be able to effectively measure it.[8,9] Yet in our society, measuring outcome dominates most organizations, whereas measuring learning is neglected.[10]

One owner and CEO of a struggling business had the measurement principles down pat—at least that's what he thought. In our first meeting, he showed me all the documentation he had for measuring the enterprise from an individual level all the way up to the whole of the business. All of the measurements had an outcome focus. As a service-based business, the owner created measures such as weekly individual service calls, average dollars earned per service call, and weekly revenue generated by each worker. Each individual in the organization knew exactly what he needed to do to keep the business profitable. In the break room, a board listing the weekly outcomes of every person illustrated the health of the organization from an outcome perspective. Employees knew exactly how many calls they made compared to others. They knew who was making the numbers and who was not. Although these types of measurements made logical sense, it also created certain levels of anxiety, fear, and competition within the company. Just imagine if you were in the bottom of the numbers for a few weeks. How would you feel? What would you have learned by being in the bottom? What would you need to learn to get higher results? Well, if you look at the well-researched cases at Lucent Technologies, this type of management by the numbers taught managers to distort the numbers so that they'd appear to be doing their job. When managing by outcome-based measurements without a balance in learning goals, natural human tendencies move individuals toward extreme behaviors. Those making the outcome goals would thrive, and the lower group's behaviors could be detrimental to the organization. So where is the balance?

According to research, learning goals are most appropriate when the individual(s) may not possess the knowledge or the skills to perform the specific tasks.[10] In a constantly changing environment, isn't this always the case? You can never have all the knowledge or the ideal skills to achieve sustainable greatness at what you do. In reality, the outcome of any business is always a reflection of the learning that occurred inside the business, just as the success of your life is often an outcome of your growth. As you start the process of creating learning measures, make no assumptions concerning what you believe your people might know. Such an assumption can be demoralizing. Think back to a time when your parent/supervisor/manager required you to take a class on a subject you already knew. What did you learn from the experience other than a negative experience of how that parent/supervisor/manager had no idea what you knew or appreciated who you were? To maintain a high level of respect and fairness from your people, conduct the measure before any knowledge transfer begins. This is like the trust you may have with your doctor, who'd never prescribe medication before diagnosing your condition. Use these measures as regular checkups to see how successful your knowledge transfer system is.

The ideal learning goals focus on creating an organizational context for growth. They build the roads that move your people toward the desired outcome. The primary reason why the Roman Empire was one of the greatest of humanity was that they built roads to reach their goals of conquest. Today, your small business can be significantly greater in size than any Roman empire could ever imagine. Today, the roads for that global conquest are made of knowledge and innovation. Learning goals build knowledge. For example, customer service is a key development skill for most small businesses. A typical outcome measurement would be to track customer retention or repeat business. A learning measure would focus on the skills required for great customer service. One measure might break down the process to initial greeting, follow-through with promises (or be consistent with integrity), or how well one can get to know the customers. Each of these learning goals is a game where every person can play with how they greet the customer to capture attention or to keep a running tab on promises given to a customer and its respective follow-through (an accountability structure). All of these measures focus on the process of customer service, thus laying exactly the skills required to reach great customer service.

2. Discover Motivation for Learning

Once you've created the measurement, you may find that your people may not be motivated to learn. A common myth about motivation continues to thrive in the industry of motivational speakers. Do you think you can motivate another individual? Many believe that money is an all-powerful motivator; if so, why are well-paid employees ethically challenged in many organizations? How many do you personally know who fit that image?

Motivation starts intrinsically. People can't speak to you about your motivation unless they listen and discover what your motivations are first. We all have different motivations based on life experiences and present needs. Knowing how to influence people based on their personal motivations is one of the hidden competencies of an effective entrepreneur or great leader. To do that, one must take the time and effort to ask the simple but complex question—what motivates you? What are you most passionate about? Then take the time to listen with an open mind. People's answers usually fall into these two common theories: McClelland's acquired-needs theory and Maslow's hierarchy of needs.

McClelland's acquired-needs theory breaks motivation down to three basic needs.[11]

- *The need for achievement.* This form of motivation is an individual's drive to excel and achieve in relation to a set of standards. Sometimes this form of motivation may appear as competition, because it has a specific set of standards for one to achieve a certain level of success. For example, Benjamin Franklin was driven by achievement. He wore countless hats in many professions and made significant contributions to our country. He was constantly looking to improve himself in various skills and habits.
- *The need for power.* This kind of motivation thrives in political arenas or highly political business cultures. Individuals with this type of motivation have a basic need to make others behave in a way they would not have behaved otherwise. You may all know someone who's on a power trip, looking to influence people to behave in a certain way. You may all have had teachers who wanted you to write or think or follow the exact way *they* wanted. From a historical perspective, Adolf Hitler is an ideal example of a need for power taken to the extreme.
- *The need for affiliation.* This is a dominant motivation for many people who choose to be in the service industry. These individuals desire friends and close interpersonal relationships. You may know someone who knows everyone else around you. Especially with technology, these individuals may have extremely high links within a network.

Maslow's needs hierarchy is another popular motivational theory.[11] It is different from McClelland's theory in that it has five needs instead of three. Furthermore, Maslow created an order for meeting these psychological needs. He felt that for Benjamin Franklin to get to the top level of motivation (self-actualization), the lower needs must be satisfied first.

1. *Physiological needs.* As the basic and most primitive need, individuals seek to sustain life, find shelter, and satiate hunger and thirst.
2. *Safety needs.* This form of motivation is concerned with the need for security and stability. It includes basic health issues such as illness, pain, and mental/physical threats. While working in this domain, the primal brain is engaged.[2] People living in this reality tend to perceive fear that may not be real. They will take illogical actions without any consideration for the consequences. For example, when a few leaders at Lucent felt their safety to be threatened, they simply acted in a way that they thought would protect their safety. They acted accordingly to protect their jobs and families over the needs of the organization. The primal brain dominates human behavior when physiological and safety needs appear to be

a challenge. Regardless of how "smart" an individual may be, once basic safety needs are in a perceived jeopardy, primal instincts take over in a "struggle" to survive.

3. *Belonging.* One of the worst punishments for a human being to endure is complete solitude. As a species, humans have an innate need to socialize. This motivation focuses on the need for acceptance and love. Interactions between people dominate the rationale for behaviors (It is very similar to McClelland's need for affiliation.). People with significant influence of belonging needs will likely be networkers. They desire constant involvement at every level of every group. While they make great friends, their need for attention may cause codependent relationships. These people may avoid conflict to maintain a surface cohesion.

4. *Esteem.* The final two needs are usually considered growth motivations that engage the higher order brain functions. Through personal achievement, individuals greatly enjoy recognition from others as well as the respect of peers. While people at this level are interested in self-development, they continue to have a need for recognition from others.

5. *Self-actualization.* This is the top of the motivational pyramid. A very small number of people can maintain this level of confidence. Individuals in this group fully realize their potential. They're clear on the purpose of their life and how to reach that purpose. They're also incredibly confident individuals who command influence with their mere presence.

Check Out the Motivation of Others

Now that you've had a quick overview of motivations, it's time to put your new knowledge into practice.

1. Think of three people you believe you know well. Write their names in the first column of Table 6-1.
2. Next, jot down what you think they're motivated by. Use one column for McClelland's theory and one for Maslow's theory.

TABLE 6-1. Worksheet to Get a Better Understanding of the People Around You as Well as Test How Well You Know Them

Names	Your Perceived Motivation (McClelland)	Your Perceived Motivation (Maslow)	Discovered Motivation (McClelland)	Discovered Motivation (Maslow)
1.				
2.				
3.				

3. Here's the fun part. Now you'll have a conversation with those individuals on their motivation. Start with the questions "What are you most passionate about?" and "What motivates you the most?" Although these might to be simple questions, the answers are complex. Often, you'll need to dig deep and ask more questions about the responses. At different times during the day, responses may be different. So try this in different contexts, such as at work or during lunch away from work.

Ironically, among the hundreds of graduate MBA students I've taught around the world, I have yet to find one student whose supervisor/manager asked them about their motivations or aspirations. Imagine how people would look at you if you did nothing else but ask the question and have a conversation that highlights the core of that human being. Once you get an understanding of the individual motivations in your organization, you can start to make the connection between motivation and learning. Once your people have the desire to learn that technical expertise, the learning potential increases dramatically.[5]

Another roadblock to ponder on before learning can happen is our personal history, which some tend to call our baggage. We've all had personal experiences with education, whether it was positive or negative. The concept of education or training is often a loaded statement. To some, education may have a negative connotation because they were told what to do as a child. To another, education may be the lift they needed to get out of a lower economic status. Carefully choose the words you use to associate with the learning activity.

Recently, I was leading a discussion in a business formation meeting with a number of leadership experts. The group was looking to find a neutral term that described the educational division of the business. One member felt that "to teach" was appropriate, and another thought "to train" was better. Although both may have similar definitions, the connotation based on the audience can be drastically different. I asked the group, "How many of you enjoyed being taught in school—thinking back to your elementary or high schools?" I then asked the question, "How many of you believe that training is effective in the workplace?" Both of the questions lead to a majority of negative answers. Most people do not enjoy having another individual pushing information at them.[12] In my personal experience working with people, the term *homework* often gets a quiet moan from leaders. As you're looking for your people to embrace the transfer of expertise, use neutral terms like *development* or *self-improvement*.

3. Systemically Create Learning Time
for Every Individual

Now that you've got some metrics for learning and understand the individual motivations involved, the last contextual construction of the system is time. This is a crucial piece often forgotten by countless organizations as they put employees through training classes and miraculously expect the training to flow into established work habits.[5] Imagine that you've just completed a course on your favorite subject or a crucial skill you've wanted to learn. You were taking the course for the last few hours, and you're returning to your work knowing that there's a build-up of voicemails and emails needing your response. Although you had planned on taking some time to reflect on what you've learned and place that new information into some new actions, the need to take care of the waiting communication is too strong. So like any rational technical expert, you address the more immediate needs of those voicemails and emails. Before you know it, your day is at an end as your hunger for food drives you home for dinner. The phrase "honeymoon effect" describes this situation perfectly.[13] Although most people have honorable intentions to apply the new information, the pressures of existing tasks and responsibilities allow limited time to implement new actions. Studies have shown that when students only have lecture as the basis of learning, average retention rates rests at a mere 5 percent. Yet if immediate time is given for applying the new information, retention of new information drastically increases up to 90 percent.[14]

Learning does not happen in the classroom alone. For people to retain new information, the attachment of emotional bonds transforms information into knowledge. The emotional bond is strongest when immediate application occurs and the impact is measured. So if you want your people to retain a very high level of your technical expertise, create an environment where they have the time to experiment and apply the new information as soon as possible.

4. Define the Technical Expertise

This step in the process is often trivial, but requires depth of thought. For a technical expert, actions and behaviors are often unconscious. The more of an expert you are at what you do, the tougher it will be for you to slow down enough to make your knowledge explicit. I learned this lesson back in high school where Mrs. Warye, an English teacher, asked us to write a directions paper on a common competence. Because simplicity and efficiency was in the mind of most high school students in terms of homework assignments, I picked the simple action of putting on a jacket. Others picked putting on lipstick, painting their nails, and putting on shoes. These papers provided the content for one of the most memorable classes of all time. As we each turned our work in, Mrs. Warye asked a different student to read aloud the directions written in the paper. Another student (victim) sat in front of the class and performed the stated directions with no assumptions about the task. We quickly learned that even though we were the experts at these activities, writing them down into a set of clear directions was tougher than we thought. Each of us made countless assumptions that yielded hilarious outcomes. The lipstick directions painted the face of a student like that of a clown. The nail-painting directions failed to even open the bottle. My putting-on-a-jacket directions covered another student's head, rather than his body. No one succeeded in writing down an expertise in such a way that another student was able to perform it successfully.

Do you have the attention to detail to make this work? Test it out on someone. Start with a simple activity, such as brushing your teeth, and then move to a more complicated one, like how to build stronger relationships when major conflict occurs.

When taking tacit knowledge/technical proficiency into explicit forms, a vital consideration is to make *no* assumptions. Slow down your thought processes as you capture your wisdom in writing. Make no assumptions about your audience. Today, I use this exercise in many workshops to illustrate the challenges of communication and learning. Very few participants had the sense to truly succeed in the simplest of tasks. Yet after the workshop, leaders have a higher awareness of their assumptions. This empowers them to write with deeper thought.

5. Share the Knowledge

Once the technical expertise is defined, top entrepreneurs create regular workshops, classes, and meetings that share this knowledge. Although some may prefer to pass out a written version first and discuss later, others prefer to explain it first and demonstrate. This step initiates the actual transfer of expertise. Depending on the type of business or environment, the frequency of these learning sessions can vary between weekly to monthly. As you start, allow the frequency to fluctuate with human needs (i.e., measure and consider current work load and learning rates). At certain times of the year, people within an organization can be effective learners, because the workload allows time to learn and experiment. At other times, such as tax season, many organizations become madhouses working 10–12 hours a day. During these times, flexibility would be wise. Within each business, there are cycles. The brilliant entrepreneurs know how to embed the learning system into the cycle so that the required skills are at their top proficiency during the busy times, while the maximum individual experimentation happens on the off-seasons.

6. Create an Environment for Application and Failure

One of the companies in the study had an interesting policy: if you don't fail, you're fired. This entrepreneur understood the basic need for sustainable change in the economy. Requiring his people to fail as part of their job, he pushed them to take on new activities and constantly learn. This step is also missing in much of today's education.[5,11] With every piece of new information, an individual needs to apply that information on a personal level. This is also called *innovation*. Though the same information is given to different people, the applications of it can be vastly different. Imagine transforming every person in your organization into innovators. Some are innovators of products; others innovate processes that make you incredibly efficient. Within the concept of a learning organization,[4] every individual has the creativity and wisdom to identify problems and create solutions based on new information.

Out of the many methods that I've employed and tested, one stands out from the rest. As Jeffery Ford, a professor at The Ohio State University, once stated, "Talk is the blood of organizations." Transforming talking to lead people can be very powerful. Visualize an environment where people didn't always go around saying, "Hi, how are you?" as you walk by each other. Instead, your initial greetings incorporated the following question: "Hi, what have you learned today? What will you do differently next time?" These simple questions effectively transform organizations toward constant learning. It works in almost every organization. Especially for many e-businesses, these questions have significantly more power. Rather than responding immediately as if you would in person, the recipient would ponder the question further. Sometimes, it might even take actions to learn something so that they can answer responsibly. How fun of an environment would that be?

7. The Knowledge We Possess Is Alive

Because people are living creatures, our knowledge is alive. We're constantly creating a reality that makes us feel positive about ourselves. This organizational learning system is an endless cycle that sustains success for small businesses. When an individual innovates a new idea based on new learning, successful entrepreneurs capture that innovation immediately by cycling it back into step one of the process.

In the study of many successful entrepreneurs and organizations, the owners and presidents have the freedom to take a few weeks to go on vacation or attend a conference within the industry.

A friend of mine owns a health education organization; she has two doctorates in the field to establish her technical expertise. Her business began in the basement of her home as she taught health classes to people who wanted to know the truth about their foods. Due to her vast knowledge of the field, her

---

Quick Tip: Outsourcing and globalization are strong trends taking over economies. Yet what's often missing in most outsourced processes/production is knowledge transfer. Few organizations are able to understand and practice these concepts so that outsourced units continue to add to the organizational knowledge. If you're looking for a new career that will prosper into the next decade, consider becoming a knowledge transfer expert. You can work in any industry and in any country of your choice by teaching companies how to capture organizational knowledge in a globally competitive marketplace.

business grew quickly. Within a few years, she added a production facility to provide nutritional foods as well as a national distribution center. Her activities yielded a multimillion-dollar operation. But before she was able to grow the business exponentially, she learned to pass her knowledge on to many other facilitators. Through their system of learning, the technical expertise of the owner became the organization's knowledge base. Many employees have the opportunity to learn as much as they'd like. The day-to-day operations of the company are in the capable hands of the employees, while the owner takes time to continually advance her personal technical expertise, which her capable staff will systematically learn. Currently, her operation spans the United States. Yet she has the time to take month-long vacations or attend international conferences without any negative impact to her business.

Testing Your Knowledge Transfer System Exercise

Whether you own a business or are working for someone else, much of your success and advancement depends on the ability to be recognized by your expertise and how to transfer it. This exercise will help you clarify your responsibilities as well as see if others see the same view.

1. Write a detailed job description about what you do every day. You can take a few days to list your activities and categorize them into meaningful groups. What you do and how you go about doing it clearly demonstrates your technical expertise. Create a table called "My Job Description" (see Table 6-2).
2. Ask a few co-workers or even family members to do the same for your job description. They can make a similar table. See if they come up with the same items and descriptions you've written down. How does your view of what you do differ with those around you? Do people truly see you?

TABLE 6-2.   My Job Description Worksheet

Responsibilities	Description
1. Chief innovator (as an example)	I'm constantly learning new ways of doing my job and creating new processes to enhance the lives of the people I work with. A weekly innovation is a minimum requirement.
2.	
3.	
4.	

3. Take a moment to look at your current job description (if you don't have one, make one). How does it compare with what you wrote down? How does it differ? Why does it differ? Many job descriptions in organizations were written as frozen documents, rather than being treated as living entities. The description might be true when it was initially written, but the tacit knowledge of the position changes monthly, sometimes even weekly.

Consider this: if people around you don't know what you do, how will they value you? Sometimes, this also gets into the concept of codependence (further defined in Chapter 8). If people have little idea of what you do, they'll always need you. Although it's nice to be needed, it does not create the independence for you to live freely.

Feel free to conduct the exercise with yourself and others from time to time (perhaps a six-month period). If you're successful at transferring technical expertise, your version of your job description will match what others believe your role is.

ABUNDANCE INSTEAD OF FEAR

Understanding the principles of the organizational learning system requires a fundamental shift belief. A few of you may have already asked the question while reading about organizational learning—if you make your technical expertise/competitive advantage public to every employee, won't competitors steal it easily? Consider this: what would happen if your people didn't learn from you? Are you willing to be the bottleneck and a slave to your business? The fear and protection mentality also leaves out a basic assumption: your technical expertise or competitive advantage is stagnant. In a world of constant change, technology and innovation are moving faster than what most organizations can adopt. Depending on the industry, technology can make your current processes and system obsolete within six months to a few years. So if your competitors do steal your expertise from yesterday, aren't they a bit behind the curve because you've gotten new innovations today?

Fear of the competition may be one of the highest motivators in organizations.[2] Many large companies spend millions of dollars on protecting their intellectual property, and a fraction is spent on innovation. Take a moment to look at your organizations—how many rules and policies are there about protection? Compare that with rules and policies about learning and innovation. This lack of balance creates a heavy focus on activities that are limiting, rather than growth oriented. As an entrepreneur, you cannot afford to spend the time or money on protecting your technical expertise. Growth does not come from perceived protection. As long as building that expertise is a conscious effort, no competitor will ever be able to keep up. Abundance above fear builds sustainable technical expertise that exudes success.

The journey of an entrepreneur starts as technical proficiency in a specific field. That type of expertise needs to shift if you intend to keep a healthy balance between business, personal well-being, and family. To grow the business, that technical proficiency translates into a mastery of organizational learning and people development. This form of leadership takes time to build; it is not at all a quick fix like many leaders like to believe. The fruits will yield endless success in the continued growth of every individual within the organization.

REFERENCES

1. I. Nonaka, and H. Takeuchi (1995). *The knowledge-creating company: How Japanese companies create the dynamics of innovation.* New York: Oxford University Press. This is one of the most well-known books on knowledge creation and the management of organizational knowledge. It used traditional theories on epistemology and combined it with new methods of managing and growing knowledge with research on successful Japanese companies who used the methods.

2. D. Baker, C. Greenberg, and C. Hemingway (2006). *What happy companies know: how the new science of happiness can change your company for the better.* Upper Saddle River, NJ: Pearson Prentice Hall. The initial chapters of this text talks in detail how many companies are driven by fear in the majority of their behaviors. Baker then provides research data on how some companies are driven by a happiness model that engages the higher order mind of the human brain.

3. N. Dixon (2000). *Common knowledge: How companies thrive by sharing what they know.* Boston, MA: Harvard Business School Press. This research article presents methods on how companies can share their knowledge. Many of these practices build a foundation for proven success.

4. Harvard business review on knowledge management. (1998). Boston, MA: Harvard Business School Press. A collection of peer-reviewed articles on the subject of knowledge managed within an organizational setting. A number of organizational learning processes are discussed in this text.

5. D. Goleman, R. Boyatzis and A. McKee (2002). Primal leadership: Realizing the power of emotional intelligence. Boston, Massachusetts: Harvard Business School Press. This text covered emotional intelligence and its significance to leadership. A crucial aspect of leadership is learning. Goleman presents interesting data on why corporate training does not work often and the frustration that HR departments face.

6. B. Presnell (1999). *Small business managers and adult learning: A study of how small business managers acquire the knowledge necessary for success.* ProQuest Digital Dissertations (UMI No. 9939298). Presnell's study was a doctoral dissertation that focused on the learning methods of a group of entrepreneurs. As a case study, her in-depth discussions with entrepreneurs discovered a wide range of learning activities that were informal.

7. P. F. Drucker (1968). *The age of discontinuity.* New York: Harper & Row. This is a well-known text that introduced the concept of a knowledge-worker. Well ahead of its time, this text took the traditional concept of a labor worker into that of a knowledge-worker.

8. D. A. Garvin (1993, July/August). Building a learning organization. *Harvard Business Review*, 71(4). Retrieved November 15, 2003, from EBSCO Research Database.

Garvin's work furthers Drucker's concept of a knowledge-worker toward acquiring that knowledge on an organizational level. One of the major principles in his theory is that understanding your strengths and weaknesses is only the start of learning. By measuring the impact of learning, you can really get to know what the organization values and how to improve on it. This process of measuring sets the path for individual/group learning.

9. J. Stack (1992). *The great game of business.* New York: Doubleday/Currency. All great sports teams have the ability to manage every player by their numbers. In doing so, they're able to achieve incredible results. Yet, in business, not everyone knows the stats about how their work is being perceived and its value to the organization. This text covered a method on making work into a game where everything the company values is measured to the nth degree.

10. G. H. Seijts and G. P. Latham (2005) Learning versus performance goals: When should each be used? *Academy of Management Executive,* 19(1), 124–131. This research article refused the conventional wisdom of outcome-based goals. While it creates competition and unnecessary fears on individuals, outcome-based goals are not appropriate in many organizational settings. The authors propose learning goals as an alternative, focusing on individual experimentation of new knowledge.

11. S. McShane and M. A. Von Glinow (2002). *Organizational Behaviour* (2nd Ed.), The McGraw-Hill Companies. A common text on organizational behavior used in business schools. The text covers the major theories on motivation such as Maslow and McClelland.

12. R. Jacques (1996). *Manufacturing the employee: Management knowledge from the 19th to 21st centuries.* Thousand Oaks, CA: Sage Publications. A text that provides a historical view of the purpose of the existing education system. Takes education from the pre-industrialized era through current educational methods.

13. J. P. Campbell, M. D. Dunnette, E. E. Lawler III and K. W. Weick (1970). *Managerial behavior, performance and effectiveness.* New York: McGraw Hill. First defined the honeymoon effect with many training programs as few provided time to implement new information.

14. Cornell University, 2004. National Resources Conservation Service, USDA, "Instructional Systems Design (ISD)—Developing Performance Measurements." Retrieved from: http://www.nedc.nrcs.usda.gov/isd/isd6.html. This study clearly illustrates the importance of application based on new information gathered. When people are left with traditional lecture alone as their classroom learning, retention is a mere 5%. Using various strategies to increase learning created the optimal retention.

CHAPTER SEVEN

Behavior 3: Self-Confidence

Do you believe that people who are confident are more likely to achieve the desired future? In fact, many psychology and leadership experts see self-confidence as one of the most important determining factors to success, whether it's in the workplace or in life in general.[1-4] Depending on the context, the terms *self-confidence*, *self-esteem*, *self-efficacy*, and *self-worth* are used to describe one's view of self and the belief in one's abilities. More specifically, entrepreneurs with high self-confidence and self-efficacy have a belief that they are capable of achieving high levels of performance and acquiring specific behaviors.[1] On the other hand, self-esteem relates to one's perception of self-worth.[5] It is also a measure of how comfortable we are with ourselves. Based on previous studies, many other psychological factors have a direct relationship to self-esteem.[4] Of course, self-confidence is not an actual behavior. Yet it lies at the core foundation for many behaviors that are significant. It's a crucial part of entrepreneurial success.

From a leadership perspective evidence suggests that self-confidence is a significant factor in many types of successes in both small and large businesses.[6] Individuals with high self-confidence are less anxious in the face of uncertainty. Rather than running from the unknown, they tend to welcome it with open arms. These individuals are less likely to be depressed or irritable with the difficulties of life. When it comes to relationships with other people, self-confident individuals are often a magnet for others due to their accepting nature. Because they are authentically content with themselves, self-confident people tend to bring out the best in the people around them. Their optimistic view can be a light in the worst of moments.

From an entrepreneurial perspective, self-confidence creates a solid foundation for the business. Employees can depend on confident leaders to always be there, no matter what the situation. When you have it, it's an amazing feeling of inner peace.

Let's examine the case study of John, a successful entrepreneur who was facing a horrific challenge of entanglement. He had bought a franchise a few years before and had been working as one of the franchise owners. Being with this particular franchise consumed much of his life. As he grew his business, he realized that the franchise was changing in a direction that was not congruent with who he was. During that time, like most franchise owners, he was paying monthly fees in the thousands. When he recognized the lack of congruence, he spoke with the franchisers about leaving. Not willing to give up the money, the franchiser only offered a walk-away option with no refund of any franchise fees. This represented a huge dilemma for John, because the investment to purchase the franchise was significant. Being a confident man, he chose not to fight the options and clean up the entanglement by simply leaving. Within that week, he signed the documents and walked away from the franchise, leaving many thousands of dollars on the table. One of the concluding remarks from John exemplified his confidence: "Money comes and goes. I'm not willing to sacrifice my values to try and get more money. Fighting them would only increase the entanglement. I'd much rather be in peace knowing that I can make all of it back."

How many of you are willing to leave lots of money on the table to maintain your congruence? This action is just one of many incredible acts of self-confident entrepreneurs from the study. These people don't get caught up in the scarcity mentality. They tend not to fight or flee. They don't have a need to lie or to be a fake with anyone.[2] Self-confident people are safe to be around, because they have no desire to manipulate and control others.[3] More important, self-confidence is a characteristic that is the foundation for countless leadership behaviors. It transcends any economic environment, and its presence welcomes success.

So let's see how self-confident you are. Be as truthful as you can be. There is no right or wrong in the following exercise. This mini-instrument is only a marker of where you stand today. It is not a determinant of who you are or who you will be. One of the flaws in many assessments is that people tend to use them to categorize people into groups. In considering the reality of assessments, they're only a snapshot of a particular moment, nothing more. You will change in time. What's more interesting is to test yourself with the same assessment with specific time frames in between (three months' duration, for example). This will reveal your development and present meaningful information.

The Self-Confidence Test

This mini-instrument provides a quick snapshot of your self-confidence. It's short so that you can do it quickly without having too much anxiety. I highly recommend you take this assessment more than once to determine your progress. A one-time average is meaningless, as every person has their own path and beliefs about what success can be.

TABLE 7-1. A Short Survey to Determine Your Self-Esteem. Scoring: average the scores of all eight questions. List them below in Table 7-2

Some Basic Questions about You	Not at All	Moderately	Extremely
1. I am well respected by people of all ages.	1 .... 2.........3 .... 4.........5 .... 6.........7		
2. I love being my age.	1 .... 2.........3 .... 4.........5 .... 6.........7		
3. I am a lot of fun to be with.	1 .... 2.........3 .... 4.........5 .... 6.........7		
4. I am content with my life.	1 .... 2.........3 .... 4.........5 .... 6.........7		
5. I lead others with my ideas.	1 .... 2.........3 .... 4.........5 .... 6.........7		
6. I relate well with others of the opposite sex.	1 .... 2.........3 .... 4.........5 .... 6.........7		
7. My work is always my best.	1 .... 2.........3 .... 4.........5 .... 6.........7		
8. I have the determination to complete any task I choose.	1 .... 2.........3 .... 4.........5 .... 6.........7		

After you've taken the assessment over a six- to nine-month period, put the numbers into a chart (using a spreadsheet program). See how you're progressing. Then consider the various high points and low points. If we were in a workshop setting, we would discuss these trends and seek to understand the various events that increased or decreased your confidence. We would then design specific outcomes to further develop your self-confidence. For now, ask yourself these questions to get a better understanding of you. What events or accomplishments increased to decrease your self-confidence? How do I design more of this confidence into my life? You may choose to seek out those events/accomplishments that increased your self-confidence and engage in them more often.

This instrument selected questions that were adopted from Toney's work in traits of goal achieving leaders and Ryden's work with self-esteem inventories.[6,7] The original instruments had limited scales. In addition to the change in scale, these questions incorporate theories from leadership, psychology, and emotional intelligence and make leaders their target audience.

TABLE 7-2. Scoring Matrix for Self-Esteem Development over a Selected Period

Assessment Count (Every 1–3 Months or Quarters)	Average Self-Confidence Score
1st month/quarter	_____
2nd month/quarter	_____
3rd month/quarter	_____
4th month/quarter	_____

The concept of self-confidence begins to develop when we were children. It grows and develops as you encounter various situations and outcomes. One of the differentiating attributes of humanity is the awareness of self due to higher order thinking. We also have the ability to deliberately change our self-confidence with various strategies. Before moving toward these strategies, developing a basic understanding of why many people do not have the confidence to walk away from entanglements like John did in the above story identifies the pathways for understanding our own limitations. In a technical society built on materialism, what often defines success is the amount of tangible objects one might have, or even the pieces of paper, such as awards and diplomas. When thinking of goals, people usually state material objects like owning a large home, having a great job, or being debt-free. Yet the goals often change. For example, when you graduated from college, what was your goal? A common goal at that time to get a good-paying job. The minute you got the job, you were off to another goal. Maybe it was to buy a house or get more responsibilities for a promotion. Sometimes, a good job means it's time to settle down and get married. Once you get that dream house or that promotion, you move on to wanting a bigger home or the next promotion. In essence, this mentality has you trapped in the endless chase of a moving target. How often have you stopped to smell the roses? In a recent poll among a leadership group, the following question was asked, "How many of you have taken the time to really slow down and go for a walk in the park with no worries or a relaxing drive with no destination to explore nature?" Out of a group of 26 leaders from various small businesses and civic organizations, no one could raise their hands to confirm. As we're in a constant state of motion trying to reach a goal, the acknowledgment of past or present successes are short-lived.

What if the real goal is not even tangible? When I was part of an international business coaching organization led by Brad Sugars (a very successful entrepreneur), a profound statement weaved its way through the organization. Brad believed that we are human beings for a reason, not human doings or human having. Yet when looking at many people's goals, you'll notice that they are all about something to have or something to do. Where is the *being* in goals? If you look at your current goals for the month or year, how many of them are a state of being?

The transition from the endless chase to a state of being is a shift in your current goals. Imagine if you were able to live in that goal you desire. How much self-confidence would you gain when you believe that you *already* have the goal accomplished?

Living Within Your Goals Exercise

Let's see how you shift your goals into a state of being. On a blank sheet of paper, create four columns. Execute the following steps for each column. This exercise is only effective when you execute each step in order as you read it. Read each step, execute it, and then move to the next step.

1. List your goals in the first column. Be specific — in what time frame, amount, and so on.
2. In the second column, list the challenges that face you in accomplishing the goal.
3. In the third column, design the actions you're taking to overcome these challenges in the second column.
4. In the last column, write down what you will feel when you've accomplished the goals in step 1 by executing the actions in step 3 to overcome the challenges in step 2. Make sure this is a feeling/emotion.

When you've finished all four columns with all the goals you currently have, take a careful look at the entire exercise. Which column is your *real* goal?

Imagine being in a race. Could you finish the race if you had no idea where the finish line was? Would you finish it if the finish line constantly moved? This exercise illustrates your current goals from a tangible perspective. It also reveals the misdirection of the goal. Consider the emotions in the fourth column to be your true goal. Human beings use emotions, justified by logic, to make the majority of our decisions. When you see that emotions are the actual goal as a state of being, you have the ability to live within that emotion this moment. The endless pursuit of goals sustains the desired emotion. You don't have to constantly chase, just *be*.

A brilliant woman named Carol Coffey shared the initial version of this exercise in a seminar in 2002. Since then, I've been able to build on the foundation of this exercise with theories from emotional intelligence and leadership.

The foregoing exercise is a fun process that has lit many light bulbs in the minds of leaders. It has defined the finish line that's been elusive for many years. Furthermore, this finish line is created by you, not by someone else or some organization. When you have a focus on the actual finish of a race, it is within your power to reach out and cross that line.

Self-confidence comes from repeating emotions that validate your abilities. To greatly increase the likelihood of achieving success in all aspects of business leadership and ownership, self-confidence must be part of your mental state. To maintain and nurture self-confidence, you'll need to carefully consider the activities you engage in and the people around you. They both have a tremendous impact on your self-confidence.

The activities you engage in can increase or decrease your confidence level. Some confidence builders are superficial, whereas others have a profound effect on your core beliefs. I'm going to discuss a few strategies that build on your core beliefs about who you are and what you can accomplish. These strategies include designing doable task lists and journaling.[1,8]

Building a doable task list might sound easy at first. But a number of considerations for building confidence need your attention. Under conventional wisdom, we're all taught to constantly create goals that are challenging to us. Yet if you're constantly challenged with stretch goals, when is there time to breathe or slow down enough to learn? Although challenging activities enhance cognitive development, a balance of simple tasks helps solidify confidence. One method is to conduct a task analysis each morning, after you've written down the tasks you would like to accomplish in the day. Aside from the traditional prioritization you may be familiar with, make several reviews of your task list and analyze their respective value. Read through each of those tasks and consider them in the following areas.

1. How challenging is this task? How realistic is it? Top entrepreneurs do not stress themselves out every day with very difficult tasks. Each day has a balance of easy and challenging tasks. This mixture is tailored to your level of confidence and your current environment. For example, if you're in optimal health on a relatively calm day with nothing pressing, you might choose a few more challenging tasks. On the same note, if you're not feeling well or have pressing issues, do not load the list with many difficult tasks. This would only lead to increased anxiety and unnecessary stress.

2. Define the tasks in terms of skills you're looking to build. Each task offers a wide variety of skills development. As Einstein stated, "Insanity is doing the same thing over and over again and expecting different results." For every task you take on, look at the different skills required to improve on it with full consideration of environmental changes. For example, a simple trip to the grocery store can yield higher profits (in terms of time). When we view a basic task with the concept of time, consider how much time most people spend in line waiting or walking to their cars. What if you didn't shop when everyone else was shopping? What if you shopped in the middle of the day, when everyone else was working? You would carve out an extra 10 or even maybe 20 minutes with less traffic, no time waiting in line, and reduced stress, and you'd get the best parking space up front. When looking at tasks, the worst possibility is to sleep-walk through it and not think about it. Consciously allow yourself greater insight with a careful view of skills development.

3. How does each task align with who I am? The most brilliant and successful entrepreneurs know when to engage and when to remove themselves from activities. Too often, I see many people get in the habit of problem solving. Although it's a good skill to have, many of the problems solved provide very little value in terms of the business and the entrepreneur. It's simply food for one's ego. You always have a choice not to engage. In

the story of John with his franchise dilemma, the choice not to engage gave him a sense of ownership and peace. Although his situation of losing money is rationale for a fight, he simply chose not to engage with people who did not share his values. When you see that a task does not contribute to your growth, consider whether it's necessary to complete it.

With a balanced task list, check off every task you complete. Although it might sound basic, the physical act of checking off a list makes a mental impression of accomplishment. As the end of the day gets near, seeing a number of checks on your list tells your brain that you've made an impact. Repeating this sense of satisfaction and accomplishment builds self-confidence, especially when you've purposefully designed the list to have both easy and challenging tasks. At the end of the day or the next morning, reviewing your list of completed tasks is like giving yourself a pat on the back.

Journaling about these experiences from the day provide further validation. A journal can be a great reflection tool. It helps entrepreneurs capture the moments of excitement when challenging tasks are completed. Other times, journaling is an analysis tool, assisting entrepreneurs in the breakdown of events on paper. Aside from the psychological and emotional support, it helps entrepreneurs work through tough situations. Journaling is also a tool for learning. When you write experiences in your journal, you may find that the reflection process offers many insights of what you should or should not do next time.[9]

Aside from careful design in your activities, the people you surround yourself with also play a crucial role in building your confidence. One of the fascinating points of interest in the study was the network of successful entrepreneurs. Those who are successful always kept an eye out for someone who could challenge and inspire them to be more so. Often, I found groups of successful entrepreneurs sharing, supporting, and challenging each other in regular monthly meetings. These enriching relationships become a sounding board as well as a self-validation experience. For a moment, picture yourself as a car. You're driving along at 50 mph; to go faster, you need other cars that are driving at that or faster than you. Those that are going slower will slow you down if you get stuck behind them. Slowly, you realize that the more cars driving faster than 50 mph you engaged with, the faster you're able to increase your speed.

The same applies to the relationships you have. How many people around you are conscious about *your* growth, and how many people need you? People who are aware of your growth will provide constructive feedback. They may ask you, "Could you tell me why you chose that?" or "What would you do next time?" Confidence requires validation. As much as you might think you can do it on your own, confidence needs the validation of other people. The more the people around you are consciously aware of your development, the greater impact they'll have on enhancing your self-confidence.

On the other side of the spectrum, you may also find people who are not as confident as you are. The sad part is that when you begin to move in a direction away from their place, they may unconsciously attempt to hold you back. It may appear to be a legitimate disagreement or a difference of opinion. In reality, the person is going through a form of withdrawal. The further you move toward being more confident, the greater the difference between the two of you. The recognition of that difference creates an incredible fear that you are leaving that person behind. I've seen this happen often when working with clients. As entrepreneurs move to a place of inner peace, the relationships of need are no longer required. The people on the other side of the relationship will react. In rare occasions, I've seen the brilliance of people recognize the difference and willingly accept it. In most cases, this difference causes a bit of drama.

Self-confidence takes time to build. There is no overnight fix. Successful entrepreneurs make the conscious choices in activities and relationships that sustain success. These choices are often tough to make and even risky, but they yield great fruit. Your willingness to let go of what was comfortable in the past will determine the room you create for those who can build your confidence.

REFERENCES

1. J. E. Ormrod (2006). *Educational psychology: Developing learners* (5th ed.). Upper Saddle River, NJ: Prentice Hall. This book covers many theories of adult learning. Self-confidence, self-esteem, and self-efficacy are all crucial aspects to sustainable success.

2. S. R. Covey (1989). *The 7 habits of highly effective people: Powerful lessons in personal change.* New York: Simon & Schuster. Coveys refers to a principled center that cannot be moved regardless of the situation. This solid center is the core of self-confidence.

3. D. Chopra (2003). *The spontaneous fulfillment of desire: Harnessing the infinite power of coincidence.* New York: Harmony Books. This book focuses on one's ability to bring forth the desired future into the present by changing one's beliefs about self and the world.

4. L. Janda (1996). *The psychologist's book of self-tests.* New York: Berkley Publishing Group. This book offers a great tool for self-assessment. It provides a general overview of many different psychological factors along with some basic self-scored assessments.

5. M. G. Aamodt (2004). *Applied industrial/organizational psychology.* Belmount, CA: Thomson Wadsworth. This is a great textbook on organizational psychology with many specific factors that impact the overall wellness of an organization.

6. F. Toney (1995). *A research study to determine: Traits, actions, and backgrounds of leaders that result in goal achievement.* ProQuest Digital Dissertations (UMI No. 9608646). A study conducted on top organizational leaders using various attributes, including self-confidence, found that it plays a significant role in a leaders' abilities.

7. M. B. Ryden (1978). An adult version of the Coopersmith Self-Esteem inventory: Test-retest reliability and social desirability. *Psychological Reports*, 43, 1189–1190. Ryden enhanced the original version of the Coopersmith measure of self-esteem in children for adults. This version included 58 questions. Only a number of those questions were adopted for use in this book.

8. T. Buchoff (1990). Attention deficit disorder: Help for the classroom teacher. *Childhood Education* 67, 86–90. Although this article was targeted for increasing the self-confidence of children, many of the principles apply to adults as well. Often, adults create impossible tasks and goals to look good or challenge themselves. In reality, simpler tasks are needed to build up to challenging goals. The use of journals and doable task lists can improve one's self-confidence.

9. K. Adams (1990). *Journal to the self: Twenty-two paths to personal growth.* New York: Warner Books. This is an excellent read for those interested in learning more about techniques for journaling. It also provides some great reasons why journaling is effective and how it can help people grow.

CHAPTER EIGHT

Behavior 4: Co-dependence

Do you feel like you're working too many hours? Wasn't the goal of being an entrepreneur to have the independence and freedom that you want for you and your family? Isn't freedom what America is all about? If you're working more than what you'd like to, you have a co-dependent business! According to the *New York Times*, the United States had the highest percentage change in hours worked per capita, from 1970 to 2002 at +20 percent, whereas the rest of the industrialized nations, such as France and Japan, lowered their hours worked by 23.5 percent and 16.6 percent, respectively.[1] What's that telling you about co-dependence? Are we learning to work smarter as a nation? Probably not! We as working people cannot just put our head down to work. You cannot expect better results if you're not changing how you go about doing the work. As the world becomes more complicated with globalization and technology, this behavior will strip you of any independence you had in mind and force you into the institution of a job or ball and chain.

The concept of co-dependence is usually discussed in terms of alcoholism or drug abuse. In the context of an entrepreneur, co-dependence is between you and your work. In other words, your involvement is required at all times. Studies have found that many entrepreneurs have a difficulty delegating and thus make themselves indispensable within their work.[2] Ask yourself: if you left your role or function for a month-long vacation, what would become of your business? Would you be replaced or would your business be dead? What would be the impact to your income if you left for a month?

Let's consider a case study. Ron (not his real name) had lived a good life with a loving wife and a few kids. He had built his firm along with a partner and was looking for the next step in life. Trained as a mechanical engineer, Ron had lived a very analytical life. When we met about a year before his unexpected death, he was having trouble thinking outside the box with respect to the shrinking manufacturing marketplace. We were part of a CEO brain trust group, and we discussed the opportunities available to him. After hours of tossing around various ideas from successful leaders, Ron could not realize any of them. He was simply stuck seeing the reasons why the options would not work.

Ron and I sat down and discussed the process of thinking outside the box. Rather than put forth more ideas that he'd just shoot down, I took a different approach. Ron needed a shift in the way he thought. After talking for about an hour and getting a good understanding of who he was, I gave him a simple exercise. You may try this as well,

Waking Your Mind Exercise

Most people go through life at an unconscious level. They do the same things that they've always done and then complain about the lack of success. If you truly want a different life, you cannot just do a few things differently. Success comes from being awake and conscious. This exercise brings forth a new level of consciousness in something that each of us do so unconsciously.

1. Write down at this very moment what you experience when you were going to your present physical location. You may be at home or at work; so think about your drive or ride getting there. What do you remember about it?
2. Take one day a week and drive to work using a route that you have not taken before or haven't taken in a while.
3. After arriving, write down what you've noticed. Realize the difference in your consciousness — what was the color of the trees, the grass, and the cars you passed? How many traffic lights were there? Did you see any nice houses along the way? Any parks with people in them?

Through this activity, you'll start to realize how much you don't pay attention to because you're so unconsciously competent with something.

Before passing away, Ron took the time to try this exercise a few times. In an email, he wrote: "I have taken a different route to the office a few times, but more importantly, I've been changing (ever so slightly) my patterns for other 'routine' activities. It's an interesting process." As much as I would have liked to see Ron continue the process, he only did this exercise a few times and went back to his old ways. A year later, the brain trust group was discussing business plans and the topic of how to dream. This might be odd to fathom, but when it got to be Ron's turn, he wanted to pass. "I don't have one! When I dream, all I see is black," Ron stated.

Ron was so inundated with the day-to-day operations of his business that he couldn't see beyond today's problems. He had a co-dependent business that drained his creativity and eventually his life. As an engineer, he had a great ability to be able to focus on today's challenges. As an entrepreneur, Ron's firm could not live without him. With every passing day, new and reoccurring problems consumed him.

On a Saturday shortly after the brain trust meeting on dreaming and planning, Ron passed away at his home unexpectedly. There was no warning whatsoever. Due to the co-dependence of the business, it did not survive without him. Within the same week, the business had cut down the five-day work schedule to four-day work schedule. Shortly after, the business was no more. Can you imagine the impact to his family as well as all the employees at Ron's manufacturing firm? First death and then layoffs?

Take some time to really think about this. What would happen if you left for a month or stopped being around? What would happen to your family? Are they taken care of? What would happen to your business and all those who work for you? Where would they go? What happens to your legacy? Do you want people to say, "It was a great company to work for; but when he died, he took it all with him. I was left without income to support my family"?

Co-dependence thrives in an unconscious life. The way you think brings forth the reality of what you receive. As many philosophers believed, our senses cannot truly experience reality. There are many perspectives on any given situation. With every event, we throw our baggage and judgments from the past into a given situation. Through our consciousness we can begin to see the difference between the event itself and an interpretation of it. This provides the opportunity to keep codependence out of our lives.

According to hundreds of successful entrepreneurs in one survey, co-dependence is a serious threat to their success. They were asked to assess the truth of the following statement: "My business cannot survive without me, since I am responsible for producing products and services." Three different types of analysis (frequency analysis, correlational analysis, multiple regression analysis) were conducted on the data to determine the impact of co-dependence. All three analyses found that successful entrepreneurs rejected the co-dependence behavior. Being physically present in their business took away their ability to achieve success, especially when it came to spending time with family. Because entrepreneurship is about independence, being able to detach themselves from the business for long periods was an important factor.

To be able to depart the business, there must be a systematization of your role. This means that you need to have what you do in the business written down and train a few others to handle issues. Here's an exercise to get you started.

Business Systematization Exercise

In this exercise, you'll start to identify what your role should be and what should be passed on so that your business does not depend solely on you. When doing this exercise, you'll need 5–10-second increments with some diligence over two to three days. The results of this exercise will fascinate you and reveal the life you're living. This exercise is worth your persistence!

1. Get a small note pad that you can carry with you everywhere.
2. For each activity you engage in, jot down the activity and the present time. By the end of the day, you'll have a list of all the activities you've engaged in. Make sure to note down every phone call and interruption.
3. Conduct this exercise over a period of two to four days, depending on how repetitive your days are.
4. Analysis #1: Take a look at the trend of the activities. Do you see yourself rather focused with a specific set of activities through specific time periods? Or do your activities seem to be all over the place? If they are, no wonder it's impossible for anyone to do what you do! You've just made yourself irreplaceable, and thus, you have a co-dependent business.
5. Analysis #2: Create the matrix as you see in Figure 8-1. Above the top column, the horizontal axis is labeled Business Impor-

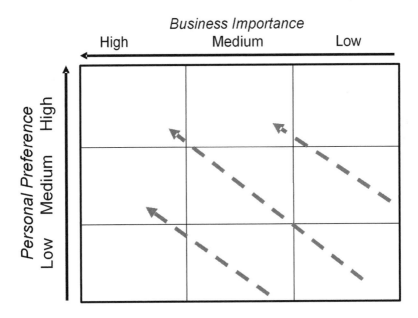

FIGURE 8-1. Task movement matrix. This task movement matrix illustrates how an entrepreneur needs to shift their tasks from low to high in terms of business importance and personal preferences. As entrepreneurs learn to maximize the number of tasks associated with success, they'll have an abundance of time.

tance. On the side, the vertical axis is labeled Personal Preference (how much you like doing this activity).

For each of the tasks from your list, place them into the appropriate box. For example, opening the mail; you may not like doing that much, and it's of low importance to the business. You may choose to place it on the bottom right square. Other activities, such as establishing vendor relationships, you may enjoy doing, so it'll be at the top left-hand box.

6. Once you've filled your tasks into the matrix, take the activities from the bottom right square and either delegate them or systematize them. Give the activity away to someone or something else. Think of how much you're worth an hour — let's say $100/hour. If you're opening letters that's worth $8/hour, you're throwing away $92 each hour. If you add up all the hours you throw away, how much is that in a day? Why are you doing it? Get rid of that task.

7. Slowly, you'll work your way up to only working in one box — the box that is of high importance to the business and something that you enjoy doing very much.

This exercise takes some time to develop. Some of my top clients got almost all of their activities into the top left box within three or four months. But that's some serious work! Yet the result is invaluable. They work significantly less than they used to and enjoy the peace and freedom in their dreams. Some even take vacations on a monthly basis. Imagine what your life would be like if you could take a vacation once a month or do something you really wanted without anything or anyone holding you down. Where would you choose to go? What would you like to see?

This exercise is only the first step toward complete independence from your business. You have a choice when to work and when to engage in activities. You'll need diligence to get through it. When you have completed this process, you'll have an abundance of free time on your hands and have minimized the co-dependence of your business. I strongly recommend that you revisit this exercise yearly. With each year, your desires and life situations will change. As your business grows to be more successful, you need to reposition your role as an entrepreneur on a conscious level.

Co-dependence is also said to be an unconscious agreement.[3] It gives you excuses to take a victim mentality when something bad happens. Your behavior is completely dependent on someone else. For example, when I was working in my parents' family restaurant, co-dependence played a major role in my life. One day, when one of the cooks didn't show up for work, one of my parents would be forced to go back and do the cooking. The excuse was an irresponsible cook. There was always that irresponsible person at work that "made" you work more. Someone had to be involved with the production of the products. It's easy to blame the invisible person who didn't show up. Sure, it's entirely their fault, and you end up paying the price for it. How does that relate to your independence?

When you have a co-dependent relationship with your work, you have an ugly entanglement in which you get to be the victim. Sure, there will always be emergencies that pop up, but what are you doing to ensure that the next time, you're not needed? Getting out of this situation requires a new level of awareness. You need to be conscious of the decisions you make on the activities that require your valuable time. So the next time someone asks for your help or requires your attention, make a conscious effort to choose the engagement. Ask yourself the following questions.

1. Is this activity/situation worth my time?
2. Could I schedule it at a later time while keeping my focus on my current task?
3. Is there anyone else who can come close to solving it? (There's always someone else, you just have to think harder and trust them.)
4. If I have to get involved, how do I systematize this engagement so that I will never have to do it again?

This process requires you to *slow down*. By slowing down enough to choose what you engage your time in, you've made a conscious choice for a better life.

REFERENCES

1. G. Ip (2004, July 8). U.S. wealth tied more to work than productivity, report says. *Wall Street Journal*, p. A4. This article discussed the increasing trend of Americans working more compared to other industrialized trading partners.

2. K. H. Chadwick (1998). *An empirical analysis of the relationships among entrepreneurial orientation, organizational culture and firm performance.* ProQuest Digital Dissertations (UMI No. 9840688). This is a dissertation that studied various attributes that relates to performance. One of the crucial findings illustrated the lack of ability for entrepreneurs to delegate tasks to free themselves up for more important activities.

3. J. G. Covin and D. P. Slevin (1989). Strategic management of small firms in hostile and benign environments. *Strategic Management Journal* 10, 75–87. Entrepreneurs are not often aware of the unconscious agreement they make when managing a business. Many actions may appear to be justified, but the context often suggests codependence with others.

CHAPTER NINE

Behavior 5: Risk Taking

Are you a risk taker? How would you define *risk*? Is it determined by society norms, the stock market, or something that is personally felt?

One of the common myths of entrepreneurs is that they take risks. In reality, what many may deem as risky is simply normal for entrepreneurs. The study found the definition of risk to be dependent on perception. Successful entrepreneurs do not like to take risks. From an epistemological perspective, how you define *risk* determines your likelihood of respective behaviors.

DEFINING RISK

Risk is often viewed as a game of chance. For some, it is a situation with a degree of uncertainty. Such a situation offers an individual some degree of control with respect to the possible outcomes. Although this might sound like a simple definition, the perception of control varies greatly among individuals.[1] This perception is directly related to one's self-confidence, and it often becomes a self-fulfilling prophecy. If you believe you have some degree of control and you have faith in your abilities, the actions you take move you closer toward the desired outcome. If your self-confidence is low, you may not see yourself as a capable individual. Therefore, self-confidence is a strong indicator of entrepreneurial success. The more you take charge of your self-confidence, the more perceived control you have. With that perception, you'll be more likely to take actions that move you toward the intended outcome.

From a scarcity mentality, risk is often about the potential losses. The significance of such losses and the uncertainty that comes with them are all part of the consideration.[2] The magnitude and lack of certainty to a specific outcome define risk.[3] Furthermore, the individual's current state of need also plays a role in defining the risk. In some situations, an individual chooses to maintain status quo in an effort to remain comfortable. For example, one of the study participant's business was growing fast (I'll call her Donna). With a growing national enterprise, the norm is to update the marketing materials to reflect the multimillion-dollar business. Some hire professional designers and marketers to create a new image. Yet Donna chose to stay with the "homemade-looking" marketing materials for their image. Regardless of the rationale behind the decision, the choice to maintain the current process eliminated the thought of possible risks. In other situations, external forces drive individuals to take risks that they might otherwise avoid. A few entrepreneurs studied started their own business after unforeseen layoffs. After spending a significant amount of time and energy doing a great job, being laid off by one's organization sends many people into emotional resentment. As a result, the risk of starting a business becomes minimal compared to the desire to never let someone else control their fate.

ENTREPRENEURSHIP AND RISK

According to the *Oxford English Dictionary* and *Webster's Dictionary*, an entrepreneur is a person who owns and manages one or more businesses. Furthermore, these dictionaries state that an entrepreneur is a person who takes on or assumes the risks thereof. Other texts on entrepreneurship also support this definition. For example, the word *entrepreneur* was originally a French noun meaning one who assumes and manages the risks of a business.[4] In today's entrepreneurial research (i.e., entrepreneurial orientation: risk-taking)[5] and education (entrepreneurs accept risks or failure),[6] the concept of risk taking is common. Yet few stop to consider the perception of risk from a psychological standpoint as opposed to the observable financial and mathematical perspective.

Two general categories define risk—financial risk and psychological risk. Although both involve a level of uncertainty, the surface issues of risk lie within the financial measures and statistical probabilities.[7] From this logical premise, risk increases as the potential outcome increases in range or expected loss.[8] From a different field of study in neuron-biological studies, the need for the appearance of logic is a dominant feature within the human brain. As we've seen with many companies, the manipulation of financial measures for the "right" reasons is within the abilities of any person. The core piece of risk is not at the surface of financial or statistical measures. Instead, it is the psychological desire to feel like you're in control as dictated by the left brain interpreter.[9]

When an individual faces a risk, the emotional content/drive or one's gut/spirit makes a quick decision. Although this might be at a subconscious level, your logic goes to work to find all the reasons why this decision makes sense. For example, think back to when you had your first crush on someone in high school. For a brief period, didn't that person seem perfect? Every activity he or she engaged in, he or she was great at it. The way the person walked, talked, and smiled were all perfect.

Risk perception functions in a similar manner. Society norms may perceive a specific risk based on specific models of logic, such as financial measures by

Quick Tip: Life is full of countless growth opportunities. The more you see it as a growth opportunity, the greater the depth in your concept of risk. Think about the next immediate decision you're about to make, and take your initial instinct as the decision. Take action on that instinct and then measure the outcome of that risk. Don't just measure it from a tangible outcome perspective; also see it from a contextual basis in the lesson(s) you will learn from this decision. Have fun with this — life is full of fun and exciting risks.

the stock market; an entrepreneur perceives a different level or type of risk. Some may even see it as a great opportunity. Research has often indicated that when entrepreneurs take on risk, they may possess some knowledge or experience that other people don't have.[10] This knowledge is intangible. External entities such as books or research articles do not contain this knowledge. It lies within you—self-confidence or self-efficacy. When you believe in your abilities to master any challenge, your innate sense will push you to take on the risk. The rest of the logic that comes after will only prove that you are in control. Perhaps you can conduct the quick experiment suggested in the boxed tip. When faced with your next decision, go with your first gut instinct. See what happens when you silence the mind and take a risk. Regardless of the outcome of that decision, you'll grow in experience and knowledge. Entrepreneurs who possess such risk behaviors master their organizational effectiveness.[11]

RISK DIFFERENCES

Regardless of your propensity toward risk, you can change it. Studies have shown that risk perceptions differ by age, achievement, and environment.[12,13] Gender, on the other hand, has no significant impact on risk-taking or risk-avoiding behaviors.[12] Depending on the stage of life or the environment, people can choose to take on more risk. For example, in an environment with a high need for achievement, people are significantly willing to take more risks. Higher levels of education have also been attributed to willingness for taking risks. Other studies have shown that age and seniority is inversely related to risk-taking. As managers increase in age or move up in the organizations, they tend to be more risk-averse.[12] Although there is continual research concerning risk behaviors, you can influence the risks you and your people take. By getting more education and creating an environment for higher achievement, risky behaviors are more likely. If you wanted to decrease risky behaviors, you could either hire older people or add additional responsibilities and titles for your people. Regardless of your preferences, keep in mind that reaction to risk is often a fear-based strategy. Today's management texts talks about risk mitigation and planning, minimizing risk, and finding all necessary information about potential gains and losses. But do you, as an entrepreneur, want to be driven by the fear of some event? Or would you rather be driven by the possibility of growth and learning? Risk is a selection of a path. Whether it's high or low, each risk offers invaluable lessons. For you to win at the game of business, having both feet on the court allows you to stay in the game. Perhaps your perception of risk can take on a new paradigm. Nothing worthwhile is gained without risk. Risk is a mere step in life loaded with lessons.

Let's take a look at where you stand with risk.

Understanding Risk: The Moving Target Exercise

In this exercise, you'll define what risk means to you in a chronological perspective. You'll draw from your personal experiences and get a better understanding of how you've changed the way to perceive risk and the resulting actions that come afterward.

Using the Table 9-1, fill in each of the rows as specifically as you can. Each row should be completed before moving onto the next row.

1. In the first column, describe a risk you took in the specific time period in your life. What was it? How did it feel to take on that risk? It could be a decision about different events/situations (a relationship decision, a decision about a job, a choice concerning a major project, or maybe an action required to move your family forward).

2. In the second column, define the risk based on what you thought at the time. Remember your mindset at that choice. Think about the mentality you had at the specific time when you had

TABLE 9-1. Worksheet Depicting the Various Perspectives of Risk as You Develop

Time Period	Describe the Perceived Risk	Risk Rating (1–7)	Resulting Impact of Action Taken	Using Today's Concept of Risk, Was This a Risk?
5 years ago				
1 year ago				
Present				Future concept of risk:
Future			N/A	Future concept of risk:

to take on the risk. Make a quantum leap in time to that exact moment. Give the risk a rating, with 1 being the least risky and 7 being the most risky.

3. In the third column, write the result of the risk. How did it turn out? Was it what you expected? Would you do it again? What did you learn from taking the risk?

4. In the forth and final column, remove yourself from the past. You're back in present time. Looking back at that risk, with all of the wisdom and knowledge you currently possess, how risky does it seem now? If the same risk occurred today, would you make the same decision with more ease?

5. Repeat steps 1–4 for time periods of five years ago, one year ago, and the present.

6. In the last row with a present risk, consider your growth path. Considering how you've grown in knowledge and experience, picture yourself with that wisdom a year from now. Look back at the current day's risk with that wisdom. How does it look now?

7. In the future row, consider a risk you'll be taking within the next year. Describe and rate the risk as before. In the final column, do the same as you've done in step 6, except with a further projection of your wisdom of an additional year. You are now two years in the future. With all the wisdom of these two years, describe the risk at hand.

Look at the risk descriptions and rating of the time period and compare that with the present or future concept of that risk. What do you see? Even within yourself, the definition of risk changes as you grow. During certain aspects of your life, food and shelter (and having a job to pay for them) is a huge risk. For some, as you journey with growing wisdom, the risk of losing basic necessities decreases in time. Other risky decisions become more apparent, such as entrepreneurship. Perceive your journey in the concept of risk. This is a great mirror to observe the growth of your wisdom and maturity as a leader.

How have you grown in how you view risks? For most successful entrepreneurs, the risks they took a year ago (or sometimes even within the last month) often seem to be minuscule. The cognitive development of the human mind is often the best tool for risk mitigation. Moving from the logic of risks, successful entrepreneurs have a propensity toward risk that is deemed dangerous by others.[14] The key to understanding your risk behaviors is the cognitive interpretation of certain events that influence your decisions. At times, these interpretations may be a reflection of internal fears, rather than reality itself.[1]

THE THREE F's OF RISK

Entrepreneurs have the options to deem risks as failure, fear, or freedom. Failure (the first F) is a common motivation in many people who never get their dreams started. In a materialistic world, failure means a loss of material goods or status. So what if you lost all the material goods? Doesn't that mean you just opened the doors for start again? But this time, you can do it better and faster, having learned from the previous mistakes. Failure in entrepreneurship only exists if you discontinue the journey. I find it ironic for the U.S. Small Business Administration and other entrepreneurial sources measure the success of a small business in terms of financial gains and longevity. Some of the most successful entrepreneurs in the study were ones that failed a few times (some even went into bankruptcy), learned from their mistakes, and reinvented themselves to have multimillion-dollar businesses. Why not determine for yourself what success and what failure are? Why follow the numbers dictated by some external source as a determinant of entrepreneurial success? Consider this thought for a moment: what if the risk you're facing has no potential to fail? You can either succeed wildly or learn an incredible lesson that ensures future successes. What would you do? Failure does not have to exist in the way it does today.

With every risk you face, there will always be an element of fear (the second F). The fear may rear its face in what others may think of you or it may stare you down based on past traumatic events. Ask yourself this question: is this fear *real*? If you're concerned about what others may think of you, do you believe that people have ample time to make judgments about others around them on a regular basis? Even if they did, are they aware of your perspectives? People probably do not judge or are not aware. In reality, being an entrepreneur already makes a statement that you are different from the rest of the population. You take chances that others may deem risky. That is the normal expectation. Now imagine what others will think of you if you didn't take the risk. Looking at the historical context may introduce fear, but the reality of the last similar situation is rarely the same as today's situation. With every passing day, your experiences and knowledge add to your wisdom. Even if you were in exactly the same situation, environment, and the same people, you're a lot wiser than you were in the past. If a situation occurs within the risk, you'll have additional insights and abilities to create the desired outcome. Fear is a natural emotional state. It is part of who you are. Embrace it and see the valuable information it offers. Yet fear stops there. It does not get to dictate your future actions. This is where courage enters the picture. You cannot have courage if fear does not exist. Find the courage inside to embrace fear and do something different.

The final F of risk is *freedom*. One of the founding principles of the United States and many other nations is freedom. Entrepreneurs are the living symbols of that freedom. Within this freedom, a heightened sense of risks exists along with the courage to face the inherent fears. Being risk-averse removes the freedom of choice. To enhance freedom, successful entrepreneurs possess a high degree of self-efficacy. This magic bullet is a precursor to much success from making decisions deemed risky by others.[12] Effective entrepreneurs are not threatened by failure or fear. They see both as a tool for growth. A good friend of mine, Alan, owns a technology company. He had a sense that he could do anything he wanted. Once he read in a scientific magazine about a gravity-defying device. Within the week, he built a small model with wood and magnets to prove its validity. Alan's sense of self-efficacy helped him be extremely powerful as an entrepreneur. He saw risks as part of the journey and full of opportunities. As he saw the global trend in business and teleconferencing, he took huge risks to invest in the development of data/video compression and streaming technologies. Even as wireless companies are entering into the video streaming markets, for months, Alan was able to view television from across the world using his streaming technology. While wireless companies provide limited video streams of sports and video, Alan's service provides worldwide entertainment with no limitations.

Let's look at this from an opposing point of view. If you choose to be risk-averse, what are you saying about your self-worth? Entrepreneurs who are not successful are those who disengaged themselves from risks. They often do not engage in aspiring goals because they judge themselves incapable of reaching such goals. As these choices build, the business eventually shrivels up. From a number of focus group discussions, I often saw many entrepreneurs fear audacious goals. In their daily actions, ample excuses dominated any plans to accomplish the tasks required for the business. One client, Joe (not his real name), had a lot of excitement for the business. He owned a restaurant type of business that was thriving when he initially opened. Each week, we looked at the different tasks he needed to complete with varying degrees of risk. As a commitment at the end of each meeting to move toward the desired outcome, Joe promised to complete these tasks within the week. When the following week came around, he chose not to do the tasks due to the lack of time. Yet each week, he would have a lot of knowledge on local current events, such as elections or the gossip in the city. If you wanted to know anything about the country or the city, Joe was the man to see. That was his safety net. The news he saw on television or read in the newspaper couldn't hurt him. But the actions he took in business could, if he perceived failure. Eventually, what started as a brilliant business concept with great success diminished into the sale of the business at a huge discount. Without a sense of self-efficacy in taking on risks, his lack of action destroyed all of Joe's dreams.

So which entrepreneur would you like to be—Alan or Joe? Both had incredible dreams. What makes the difference is their tendency to embrace risk and fear. What most people deem as risky is part of Alan's passion for life.

Here's a few strategies you can take to assess the reality of risks and the possible respective decisions.

1. Is the risk real? Is there a historical significance to it? How am I projecting the past into the future? Evaluate the risk from both a tangible and psychological perspective. Remember that many of the reasons for acceptance or avoidance of risk is manufactured in your left brain interpreter.
2. Who are the stakeholders involved in the risk? Make sure you are aware and involve other people affected by the decision. Even with home businesses, decisions impact multiple levels of customers to vendors. Often, the risks you take as an entrepreneur also affects your family. To obtain their support, involve them in the decision before making a choice.
3. What are your intentions for taking on the risk? For some people, accepting a risk means a chance to prove themselves. This may not be the ideal intent, because taking on a risk for the sake of achievement will reduce limited resources. Check to ensure that your motivations involve your well-being as well as that of your business and family. Also make sure that the risk moves you toward the purpose and mission of your business.
4. What measurements do I need to constantly measure the risk? Risks often transform from their initial inceptions. To ensure that it is a worthy journey, measurements should illustrate the value of the risk. These risks should have a balance of tangible outcomes as well as intangible factors, such as the level of stress or conflict.
5. What would I do if I was a year wiser? Most people have a higher cognitive ability to project themselves into the future. I've often guided leaders toward empowering themselves by asking them, "What would you do as a great leader?" The same applies to you. You know that you will gain a significant amount of growth over the next year. You will gain in confidence as well as experience. As you saw in the exercise, use your future self-image to engage in greatness.

These are just a few strategies to consider as you seek to understand risks. Sustainable success often presents itself in the form of risks. As you grow with each passing experience, the risks change to reflect the growth you need. Learn to minimize the need to seek what others may deem risky, as most people have little idea concerning the tacit knowledge and experiences you possess and the abilities you have. You'll learn to empower yourself significantly by doing so. Risk is specific to you—it is what you choose to see and to accept. Embrace risk as part of the journey in entrepreneurship. By thinking forward with your mind, you'll be projecting yourself into the future to bring forth the success you desire.

REFERENCES

1. S. Williams and S. Narendran (1999, February). Determinants of managerial risk: Exploring personality and cultural influences. *Journal of Social Psychology* 139(1), 102–25. Solid research article that looked at various perspectives of risk from a cultural and

personality perspective. Two hundred eighty-five managers in India and Singapore provide some interesting traits for managers who are willing to take on risks.

2. J. F. Yates and E. R. Stone (1992). The risk construct. In J. F. Yates (ed.), *Risk-taking behavior* (pp. 1–26). Chichester, UK: Wiley. This book saw risk in terms of losses and the decisions that come about losses.

3. K. R. MacCrimmon and D. A. Wehrung (1986). *Taking risks: The management of uncertainty*. New York: Free Press. This book provides a generalized definition of risk and how to handle it.

4. R, Sobel and D. B. Sicilia (1986). *The entrepreneurs: An American adventure.* Boston: Houghton Mifflin. A fascinating text illustrating the historical progression of entrepreneurs.

5. G. T. Lumpkin and G. G. Dess (1996, January). Clarifying the entrepreneurial orientation construct and linking it to performance. *Academy of Management Review* 21(1), 135–73. A research article on entrepreneurial orientation as a framework for studying entrepreneurs. Risk-taking is one of the five dimensions of entrepreneurial ori-entation—innovativeness, proactiveness, risk-taking, autonomy, and competitive aggres-siveness.

6. R. H. Hisrich and M. O. Peters (1992). *Entrepreneurship: Starting, developing, and managing a new enterprise*. Boston: Irwin. This is a standard textbook used by entrepreneurial courses in universities. It covers all the various aspects of running a small business from a high level.

7. J. Jia, J. S. Dyer, and J. C. Butler (1999, April). Measures of perceived risk. *Management Science* 45(4), 519–33. A journal article that looked at the measurement of risk.

8. C. H. Coombs and P. E. Lehner (1981). An evaluation of two alternative models for a theory of risk: Part 1. *Experimental Psychology, Human Perception and Perfor-mance* 7, 1110–23. An extended work by Coombs and Lehner further defining perceived risk. This is an academic article for the savvy reader.

9. M.S. Gazzaniga (1998). *The mind's past*. Berkeley: University of California Press. One of my favorite texts concerning neuron-biological studies and the human mind. Although it's a bit technical in language, the book reveals some incredible facets of how the human intellect functions to create a perception of control.

10. E. Bukszar (2003, Winter). Does overconfidence lead to poor decisions? A com-parison of decision making and judgment under uncertainty. *Journal of Business & Man-agement* 9(1), 33–44. A research-based article that examined the potential that entrepre-neurs possess different knowledge/experience that moves them toward taking on risks that others would not take.

11. T. Peters and R. Waterman (1982). *In search of excellence.* New York: Harper & Row. This text quantifies many behaviors for success. Risky behavior is one of the many that has an impact on organizational effectiveness.

12. G. Wyatt (1990, July). Risk-taking and risk-avoiding behavior: The impact of some dispositional and situational variables. *Journal of Psychology* 124(4), 437–48. Pro-vides some research on the why people take certain risks and the potential influences on risk, such as achievement levels and age.

13. L. L. Cummings, D. L. Harnett, and O. J. Stevens (1971). Risk, fate, conciliation, and trust: An international study of attitudinal differences among executives. *Academy of Management Journal* 14, 285–304. An interesting article that summarized a study

between different managers from different countries on risk behaviors. The study found people in certain countries possess more risk-averse tendencies than others.

14. S. B. Sitkin and A. L. Pablo (1992). Reconceptualizing the determinants of risk behavior. *Academy of Management Review* 17, 9–38. This article defines risk and its determinants. Various characteristics include one's risk propensity and risk perception.

CHAPTER TEN

Behavior 6: Reactive

Do you remember having a friend who called you excessively, always asking for something? Or a co-worker who needed something from you every other minute? How did you feel about those types of people?

When we see people who are constantly bothering us, we call them needy. That judgment is also an indication of our own ability to communicate our needs. We all know a few needy people. The tough question is: are *you* needy in some areas? Our study revealed evidence that this behavior has a significant negative impact on entrepreneurial success. This was the only behavior that had an impact on all types of success—financial, emotional, and overall success measures. Reactive behaviors inspire the tendency to respond to events without thinking through all the various impacts to the many stakeholders. For example, when a customer situation occurs, you run immediately to the person responsible for the situation. Being reactive can have a detrimental effect on your success.

IMPACT OF BEING REACTIVE

On a personal level, being reactive means that you're not spending time to critically think about decisions that lead to irritable actions toward others. Especially with the ease of technology (such as email, cell phones, text messaging, etc.), more people are reaching out simply whenever they get the urge to do so. Depending on the age of your recipient, this may or may not be an accepted behavior. Successful entrepreneurs take the time to make two considerations: the acceptance of interruptions and the impact on one's productivity.

One of my graduate students conducted a research project on the leadership desires and tendencies between different generations.[1] If you look at the business or organization you're working with, different age groups have different preferences on how they'd like to be treated. For example, the baby boomers (born between 1946 to 1964)[2] were a generation who grew up without a lot of technology. They tend to enjoy some regularity with their tasks while making a living. Part of the expectations of this generation was to work for one company for life and retire from it. Within the entrepreneurship world, baby boomers are looking for a family feel. Small businesses provide a sense of security that the larger corporations no longer offer. This desire for security also impacts negatively on constant interruptions. They prefer not to work with constantly changing priorities and tasks.

Going back to Joe's restaurant from Chapter 9, remember that it was an initially thriving business that went under within a few years. Joe was constantly reacting to changes in his environment. Regardless of how small or major the events, he always wanted to do something about it. In winter, shortly after a successful holiday season, news got to him that a large number of restaurants in the city went under at the beginning of the year. His reaction was to quickly review the numbers of his business and find a problem to solve. On the same day, in fear of the same fate, he chased down his front staff manager and his chef to review the numbers. His baby boomer chef did not take the conversation well. Under normal circumstances, this chef was a very composed individual who knew how to run the kitchen well. He barely showed emotions at work and was a steady leader. All of a sudden, ideas of new menus and food costs became a high priority. All of the plans from previous months had to change immediately to avoid failure at that moment. He was irate. This became one of the major tipping points for his resignation shortly after.

On the other hand, the front staff manager had quite the opposite reaction. Being a member of Generation X (born between 1960 and 1980),[2] Bill was used to constant change and adapted well. Like many Generation Xers, he carried a cell phone and accepted change as part of business. When Joe ran him down to have this urgent meeting on the numbers, Bill was much more accepting of the notion to change a few priorities. Although he did not care for the violation of space (the owner stepping all over his responsibilities), he reacted calmly. He took on some of the suggestions and implemented them with ease. Knowing that most of his staff was also of Generation X and Y, Bill understood that the immediate changes were a part of life for them.

The majority of the staff working on the front of the house (wait staff, cashiers, hostesses) for Joe's restaurant was composed of Generation Xers and Yers. (Generation Y was born between 1980 and 2000.)[2] These working adults tend to work to live, rather than the baby boomers, who tend to live to work. Generation Y grew up with technology and is used to all types of interruptions. This was also part of the challenge—keeping them focused on tasks. They are used to getting text messages and phone calls constantly regardless of where they are or what they're doing. One of the major challenges that Bill had was to keep them from being interrupted with personal phone calls at work. As the trickle-down effect of Joe's reactive behaviors hit the front house staff, they perceived it as a normal change. They understood that if they didn't like the change, they could leave and find another job.

Joe's reactive behaviors had debilitating consequences to his business. At the management level, his head chef, who started with a great deal of trust, left shortly after the incident. Both were blaming each other, and the business lacked leadership in the kitchen. The front of the house had very high turnover because of the constant reactive changes. Many of the younger folks working in those positions accepted the changes initially. But when Joe repeatedly got after them about a single customer complaint, they simply choose to not be facing the reactive entrepreneur. As with any restaurant, the front of the house is the face of the business, involved with greeting and serving customers on a daily basis. With countless facelifts, customers found a lack of consistency. Eventually, the business was sold for a fraction of its worth.

In addition to the human implications to reactive behaviors, productivity of the entrepreneur is also at stake. A recent study showed that close to 30 percent of human resource hours are spent without any meaningful productivity.[3] Take this into context of an entrepreneur who spends 50 hours (conservative estimate) each week at work, and this statistic reveals over 15 hours of unproductive work. How much would your family enjoy that extra 15 hours? Looking at the financial side, an estimated $600 billion is lost to unproductive work within the United States. Yet despite these appalling figures, more than 25 percent of American executives do not have a specific target to improve performance of their employees.[3] Are you going to be one of them? Without consciously creating a higher level of focus on productive work, the reactive behaviors of people in organizations are only going to further reduce productivity. Can you really afford to have that within a small business?

DISENGAGING YOUR TENDENCY
TO SLEEP WALK

The tendency to react dates back to the ancient times of prehistoric human beings. In those days, the need to react was crucial to survival. If you didn't run from a bear immediately, you'd be eaten! If you failed to fight and put a spear into a wild boar, your life is over. Being reactive is part of human nature. We all have those tendencies deep inside.[4]

But in today's world, do life-threatening situations occur that often? When I see people who are constantly in a battle with something or someone or people who are constantly fleeing from situations, I try to wake them up from their sleep walking. Part of being reactive is a form of sleep walking. When an entrepreneur is sleep walking, they're doing what they've always done to get by. They engage with everything that comes at them, without calculating the potential benefits/costs of the engagement. Sleep walkers rarely engage their higher brain functions and constantly react, as if their life is on the line.

Being awakened from sleep walking and reactive behaviors is a skill. Remember the last time you went on vacation? To go on the vacation, you had to finish many different projects and tasks. How much more were you able to accomplish the day or two before departing? In the short amount of time before a vacation, most people are able to accomplish two the three times as much as they normally do. The inspiration of a vacation drives people to make a list, plan out various strategies to accomplishing the tasks, and focus on completing each task. During that time, you might have noticed that you don't react to too many events. If unexpected events occur, you likely placed them in an existing time slot or put them off until after the vacation. This level of focus is the opposite of reactive behaviors. Imagine that passion and focus being present everyday. How much more work would you complete, in less time than you've ever imagined?

Time is a scarce resource for entrepreneurs if reactive behaviors are the norm. Three specific strategies to move away from that inefficiency are your environment, your plans, and your conscious higher order thought when faced with an emotionally challenging situation. The environment of an entrepreneur is often chaotic. You are the individual responsible for the business, and countless people are interested in your time. More often than not, time spent in the office is far from efficient. People can find you, call you, email you, and page you. Alone and focused time can be a conscious choice. Many entrepreneurs under my counsel have taken time away from the world each week to accomplish crucial work growing the business. For some, it means that they take their work into their basement, turning off the phones and having no connectivity to the outside world. For others, a flight on an airplane is a very productive time. Imagine how much focus you'll have if there were no emails, no cell phones, no one to disrupt your train of thought. In these moments, the isolated environment allows creativity to flow. Remember the last time you took a long flight on a business trip? How much work did you get done on the airplane (as long as you didn't sit next to someone who was always talking)? Moments alone are incredibly valuable for an entrepreneur. Some of the most successful business owners take entire weekends to be away from the busy-ness of their business. This helps them focus and produce some of the most amazing work that leads their industry.

The key skill of planning is a widely researched topic from entrepreneurship to executive management. Most entrepreneurs lack a formalized planning pro-

Quick Tip: Each week, actively create an environment where you are alone for a while. This should be a safe space where you can be completely disconnected from the rest of the world. Forward all phone calls to voicemail and turn off your cell phone (no emails or pagers either). The rest of the world will manage without you for those few hours. See how productive and creative you can be in the brilliance of alone time. Once you realize its power, increase the frequency of this environment to a few hours each day, if possible. Your business will thrive with a productive leader at the helm. Start creating alone time for your people as well.

cesses.[5,6] As a result, empirical studies have determined that reactive strategies without planning methods have a negative impact to success.[7] On the other hand, leaders who actively engage in planning performed far better than those who simply reacted to the environment.[8] This study also found similar results. All of the successful entrepreneurs spend a great deal of time planning their strategies and communicating their thoughts to their staff. Similar to the behaviors of transformational leadership, these entrepreneurs actively and effectively communicated plans, visions, and core values to their people.[9] Although there are many dimensions to planning (which we'll discuss on the Part IV of this book), a values-based approach is crucial to one's reactive behaviors.

Do you believe in the notion that if your heart is not in the game, you won't do well? In most instances, this is an accurate assessment. Because human beings are emotion-driven creatures, we must care about what we do to be fully engaged in the activity. This is another reason why many organizations that require people to go through training find that they have to repeat the training more than once. People only do well if their heart is in the game. This is especially true for entrepreneurs. As an entrepreneur moves through daily tasks, activities that are least favored will take more time, even if the tasks are simple. Reactive behaviors arise from the lack of congruence to your value system.

Task–Values Alignment Exercise

This exercise is intended to illustrate a new perspective that you may not have considered. While working through the exercise, be patient and refrain from judging yourself. This exercise is a reflective tool in your journey to be completed from time to time.

1. Over the next three days, jot down the different activities you're involved with using Table 10-1. Be as specific as you can. Start with waking up and end with going to sleep. Carry a small

TABLE 10-1. A Simple Worksheet for Looking at the Number of Interruptions that Enter Your Mind as You Attempt to Focus on a Task

Task	Starting Time
Task name & description . . .	
Interruptions:	
1.	
2.	

notebook with you and write down the task and the time. Break the page down into two columns.

If you are interrupted from a task, also write that down.

2. After you've compiled a list of actions you've taken over three days, calculate the total time you've spent on each task.

3. Go back to the top five values you've completed in Chapter 4 and list the top five values in Table 10-2.

4. For each of the values, write down what you think is the ideal amount of time you'd like to spend in this value, assuming that you have about 100 hours of awake time in a single week.

5. Next, group each one of the tasks into the specific value. While doing this, you'll also have tasks that do not fall into a value; place these into a miscellaneous group. Some tasks may fall into more than one values group; this is fine.

6. Total the actual time spent in each value in the final column. Then calculate the percentage of time by dividing the total amount of awake time over those three days.

TABLE 10-2. This Worksheet Seeks to Identify the Allocation of Task Time toward One's Value System. Percentage calculations present the likelihood of alignment between individual values and actual tasks

Top 5 Values	Ideal Time Spent in Each Value (out of 100 total hours)	Actual Task Time (over 3 days)	Total Actual Time Spent on All Tasks within a Value
Example Value: Family	20 hours	Cooking dinner—3 hours Eating together—3 hours Helping kids with homework—1 hour Reading to kids—2 hours (TV time is not included, because it is passive time with minimal engagement)	Total family time: 9 hours Out of a total of 48 hours of awake time in 3 days. Total percentage: 9 / 48 = 18.75%
#1			
#2			
#3			
#4			
#5			
Miscellaneous			

How does your actual activity time reflect with your ideal time spent on each value? You may find that you're not spending enough time in the most intimate values. You now have the opportunity to change that. As with any tool, use it to track your progress. The more alignment you have between your activities and your values, the more success and focus you'll enjoy.

I've had many entrepreneurs go through this exercise, and one of the side benefits that results is awareness of activities. Many entrepreneurs see a pattern emerge when they're writing down activities and interruptions. Once they recognize the pattern, they can choose to alter or enhance the activity for optimal productivity. This exercise is incredibly amazing to experience and observe. I'm sure you'll enjoy seeing yourself from a distance. In addition, you'll be more conscious of the activities you're taking on. When entrepreneurs are engaged in activities that are not reflective of their values, their performance is far from optimal. Just imagine you are cleaning a floor with a toothbrush (assuming that it would not be consistent with your crucial values). How easy would it be for you to get distracted?

Maintaining alignment with values creates higher focus. Just as in the vacation example, when you're truly inspired and driven, your ability to be productive can exponentially increase. Your likelihood of behaving reactively is minimized, and your core values will trump most immediate reactions.

The final strategy to minimizing reactive behaviors is empowering your higher order thought. No matter how well you plan, there will always be people and events that attempt to move you away from your focus. The news that affected Joe in his restaurant business about the high number of business failures is common. Typically, the media will report 50+ serious events that cause fear in just about any business leader on a weekly basis.[4] This doesn't include all the events that may impact entrepreneurs from the local environment, including your business. The key to not reacting is to engage and train your brain to engage in higher order thought. When building this skill, a simple principle can lead your thought. Put the following three questions on a sticky note.

1. What is the impact of this news/event to me and my people?
2. Does my initial reaction align with my values (look at your top five values)?
3. Does an immediate response change the outcome drastically?

Take the sticky note and place it on top of something you see often, such as your computer screen or office desk. This tactic that applies learning modalities; when you see it often, you'll be more likely to do it. I've used this approach with many personal growth skills as well as with countless entrepreneurs. For instance, one of the organizations I've worked with had a leader who lived "in the moment"; let's call her Jane.

Jane was a very friendly person whose top value was for everyone to get along. In alignment with this value, she always felt the need to keep connected. In this practice, being connected meant that communication was frequent. For every event that happened, Jane felt the need to communicate it immediately to the persons involved through email and phone calls. As you can imagine, working with such a reactive behavior can be very disruptive. As one of the people in the loop, Alex felt well informed but at the price of constant interruptions to his work. As much focus and planning that Alex achieved, Jane's behaviors found a way to break that focus. Alex realized that he had to train Jane so that she would collect her thoughts before coming to him. For himself, Alex made a conscious choice to disengage with Jane whenever she called or emailed. He constantly reviewed the three questions on his sticky note and placed her communications to be reviewed in a later time slot. He would also return many of her emails by listing and numbering each event. Regardless of how many messages Alex got, he always returned them in an orderly manner. Within about a month, Jane figured out that Alex wanted information that was ordered and listed. To be consistent with her value of getting along, she naturally took the hint to provide him with lists of events at the end of the day.

This "in the face" learning (the sticky note) enables your mind to engage in higher order thought. Successful entrepreneurs have control of their reactions, regardless of people or events that attempt to interrupt their focus. In the event of a crisis, successful entrepreneurs appear to slow down and make detailed plans to handle the crisis rather than react immediately. They understand the potential harm derived from reactive behaviors on both the business and the people in the business. When you learn to take the time to think, you'll realize a greater degree of self-confidence as well as a more successful business.

REFERENCES

1. D. S. Chan (2005, July). *Relationship between generation-responsive leadership behaviors and job satisfaction of generation X and Y professionals.* ProQuest Dissertations. Dr. Chan's study of leaders from different generations reveals the need to be adaptable with specific behaviors. Not only are cultures important to building relationships, the different age groups also need different ways to lead them.

2. R. Zemke, C. Raines, and B. Filipczak (2000). *Generations at work: Managing the clash of Veterans, Boomers, Xers, and Nexters in your workplace.* New York: American Management Association. This is a great book on the details of how to lead the various generations within a workplace. It clearly defines the different generations and their preferences.

3. M. Klempa (2006, October). Eliminating productivity roadblocks. *Financial Executive* 22(8), 32–35. This great article that provides some fascinating details on how unproductive many people are and how to maximize productivity through the use of planning.

4. D. Baker, C. Greenberg, and C. Hemingway (2006). *What happy companies know: How the new science of happiness can change your company for the better.* New York:

Prentice Hall. One of my favorite books that detail the effects of defining fear-based reactions that harms the organization.

5. R. C. Paige (1999). *Craft retail entrepreneurs' perceptions of success and factors effecting success.* ProQuest Digital Dissertations (UMI No. 9950110). This study looked at various factors that attributes to entrepreneurial success in the craft industry. One of the findings illustrated a lack of formalized planning.

6. P. R. Stephens (2000). *Small business and high performance management practices.* ProQuest Digital Dissertations (UMI No. 3040560). Another study on small business practices that impact organizational success. Planning is discussed as a key practice toward success that many entrepreneurs are not well equipped for.

7. M. Frese (2000). *Success and failure of microbusiness owners in Africa: a psychological approach.* Westport, CT: Quorum. A study that took a psychological approach toward business success. One of the findings that contributed to failure is reactive strategies without properly planning.

8. C. Snow and L. Hrebeniak (1980). Strategy, distinctive competence, and organizational performance. *Administrative Science Quarterly* 25, 317–36. This article discussed the impact of various strategies that impact organizational performance. Planning is among the most crucial strategies for organizational success.

9. B. M. Bass (1985). *Leadership and performance beyond expectations.* New York: Free Press. A great book on transformational leadership and some of the basic leadership behaviors that attribute to organizational success. One of the important behaviors is clear communication of key information, such as organizational vision, plans, and mission.

PART III

INTERPERSONAL LEADERSHIP

Congratulations on getting to this point of the book! I know it is much easier to focus your efforts on working with external behaviors with others than to work on yourself from an internal perspective. Through the internal growth inherent in reflective leadership, you are now more capable of transforming others around you, including your business and your personal organization. More important, you're also able to sustain leadership for the duration of any organization.

One of the primary factors for success as a leader is interpersonal intelligence.[1] How one applies it defines one's ability to lead within any organization. Some of the most popular leadership theories focused on the ability to lead others and the key characteristics that lead toward success. Although many of these theories have powerful concepts, this book collects these ideas and engineers them into the context of entrepreneurship. A few of the leadership theories applied are reflective leadership (conventional definition),[2] transformational leadership,[3] and servant leadership.[4]

Reflective leadership in its conventional definition is a process of reflection by leaders to analyze their behaviors to grasp its affects on other people.[2] In contrast, the definition I use has no relationship to external realities. When it comes to interpersonal leadership, some of the ideas behind the conventional reflective leadership have merit. Part of the theory includes a movement away from the "profitability-at-all-costs" mentality and toward the development of human beings. This style of reflective leadership promotes long-term planning for the integration of human intellect as a whole, rather than the traditional view of parts and pieces.[5] It has always seemed ironic to me that organizations have a high focus on profits without a balanced focus on people. If you really thought about it, who are the people who get you the profits? Why focus on something that is only a result of something else? From a scientific perspective, it is a bit odd to focus on the outcome rather than the actual variables that create that outcome. Focusing on the people of any business facilitates incredible profits.

When people in the organization grow, the undeniable reflection of that growth is in the profits, revenues, market share, and so on.

Transformational leadership is one of the most popular and comprehensive leadership theories in contemporary literature and research. The prerequisites to being a transformational leader require high self-esteem and a sense of purpose. Such a person is enthusiastic about the future and is tolerant of ambiguity.[3] As you've completed many of the activities in the self-leadership chapters of this book, you are that person (yes, *you*)! Once you have that self-belief, behaviors that influence others can begin to be a healthy focus. Transformational leadership is an ideal fit that seeks to transform followers from both a cognitive and emotional perspective. These leaders build the confidence of their people as well as provide meaning for each activity leading toward an authentic goal that has the commitment of every individual. According to studies, transformational leaders are able to form better relationships with people, compared to other forms of leadership such as transactional and laissez-faire. The followers also tend to expend significantly more effort for these leaders.[3]

Contemporary literature classifies transformational leadership with four specific factors: idealized influence/charismatic leadership, inspirational/motivational leadership, intellectual stimulation, and individualized consideration. Idealized influence describes a leader's ability to influence followers' feelings of identity and similarity to the leader. Followers often see themselves as people who have complete faith in the leader. An inspirational motivation factor is a leader's ability to articulate a clear communication of purpose and goals. These are often challenging messages, but they are in alignment with the values and beliefs of the followers. The third factor—intellectual stimulation—is one of the most crucial aspects of transformational leadership. In this factor, leaders push the mental capabilities of their followers while asking them to question existing beliefs and principles. This kind of stimulation provides incredible innovations. The final factor is individualized consideration. In many studies over the past few decades, effective leaders have always been able to connect individually with their followers. This individual relationship sustains the performance of an organization. Putting these four factors together, people within organizations are inspired to give their best, empowered to take action, and driven by their hearts to make a difference.[3]

Servant leadership is also a popular theory in practice. Originally defined by Robert Greenleaf, this leadership theory found its roots in a novel that portrayed a mythical trip titled *Journey to the East*. From the story of a group of people pursuing a spiritual quest, Greenleaf felt that true leadership transpires when the primary motivation is to serve other people. There are 10 specific characteristics of the servant leader; some are similar to reflective and transformational leadership. Listening is the top characteristic. Although contemporary wisdom may only perceive listening as a communication tool from one person to another, this characteristic encompasses self-communication. To listen within the context of servant leadership is to understand and accept one's own inner voice.[4] Daily or weekly self-reflection creates a doorway for understanding and acceptance.

Only when a leader hears him- or herself can he or she hear the thoughts and unspoken desires of other people. Transformational leadership confirms this characteristic because it requires leaders to be free of internal conflicts.[3]

Two other characteristics that have an element of self are healing and awareness. Servant leadership assumes that many people possess broken spirits from the emotional challenges in today's society. To transform followers, a leader must be able to heal self and others. Although the standard definition of servant leadership is to serve the highest priority of other people, three of the characteristics have a focus on the self.[4] The characteristic of awareness encompasses self-awareness as well as an awareness of systemic impact. On the general level, this awareness perceives organizations from a systemic perspective as something that lives within a web of relationships.[6] On an individual level, this awareness perceives people with tremendous inner peace, separate from the world. This separation allows leaders to be grounded in any crisis while remaining calm and collected as defined by transformational leadership.[3,6] These characteristics offer a solid balance between the importance of self and the desire to transform others. The importance of health (psychological, emotional, spiritual, social, and physical) as a successful entrepreneur comes before service to anyone else.

The rest of the characteristics in servant leadership focus on serving others. Empathy (the understanding and acceptance of others), persuasion (influence on decisions regardless of position or authority), conceptualization (seeing and communicating the big picture while balancing the tactical day-to-day tasks), foresight (connecting past lessons, present realities, and future possibilities in a connected understanding), stewardship (commitment to serving the needs of others), growth (focus on growth of every individual), and community (building a community in organizations) are the remaining seven traits.

Reflective, transformational, and servant leadership are just some of the commonly discussed theories. Countless other leadership theories, styles, and characteristics flood contemporary literature. Within the *Handbook of Leadership* alone, there are over 900 pages of leadership theories and studies citing over 7,000 studies/articles/texts.[3] Can you imagine if you were to collect all of these characteristics and attempt to behave using each of them? It would be nearly impossible to wrap a single mind around all of these theories.

My intent with this book is to engineer a meaningful and systematic way to break down leadership theories and characteristics into a set of tangible tactics crucial for entrepreneurship. To do so, eight different dimensions of interpersonal leadership composed the study. Each dimension covers a multiplicity of leadership theories and characteristics. After the data were analyzed, the study revealed two dominant influences to success: employee training and development and team-based decisions.

REFERENCES

1. H. Gardner (1993). *Multiple intelligences: The theory in practice*. New York: Basic Books. This groundbreaking work introduced the concept of multiple intelligences. Rather than seeing the human intellect as a single entity, Gardner was the first to break

human intelligence into distinct intelligences. Interpersonal intelligence is the one most relevant to relationships with other people.

2. S. Ollila (2000, September). Creativity and innovativeness through reflective project leadership. *Creativity & Innovation Management* 9(3), 195–201. This article defines the conventional definition of reflective leadership and its practice. The leadership context is placed on the project level.

3. B. M. Bass (1990). *Bass & Stogdill's Handbook of Leadership*, 3rd ed. New York: Free Press. This is a great resource for obtaining a high-level overview of leadership theories from the beginning of humankind to today's global economy. Although it is a bit on the technical side with ample historical references, it covers most dominant leadership theories and styles.

4. L. C. Spears and M. Lawrence (2002). *Focus on leadership: Servant leadership for the twenty-first century.* New York: Wiley. A collection of articles on leadership with a primary focus on servant leadership.

5. M. D. Looman (2003, Fall). Reflective leadership strategic planning from the heart and soul. *Consulting Psychology Journal: Practice & Research* 55(4), 215–21. A powerful article that speaks to the need to focus on human potential rather than profit within organizational settings.

6. F. Capra (1996). *The web of life.* New York: Doubleday. A great quick read on the connectivity of humanity. It clearly provides examples of how each person is connected to the world in an endless web of relationships. It also helps people see the trees from the forests and motivates one toward a holistic perspective, rather than an individual motivation.

CHAPTER ELEVEN

Behavior 7: Employee Training and Development

The development of people is a crucial aspect of running a solid organization. Regardless of the size of business—whether you're the only employee or if you have many people in your organization—how people develop and grow from working with and for you defines the success you'll have. Some companies have even gone as far as creating a position titled chief learning officer to ensure that the people constantly learn and grow.[1] Even if you don't have any employees, what your customers learn from you is the ultimate irreplaceable product.

Before moving further into this chapter, we need to eliminate and redefine a few basic concepts. The first is the common concept of employee training. Typically, employee training is done with single modules aimed at addressing an employee or organizational problem. These programs have minimal impact and do not address the root cause of any problems, which organizational processes and structures often embed. Worse, organizations often enforce training on people, which then fails to create any sustainable changes.[2] Thus, the investment in training often yields little to no return on investment. Can you, as an entrepreneur, afford to constantly throw money away on training without an accountability structure?

To master a comprehensive understanding of the challenges concerning traditional "employee training and development" programs, you should be aware of three distinct influences that play a major role in shaping that questionable reality. The first is epistemology—the study of knowledge. Epistemology includes studies on how people come to possess knowledge of events and how such knowledge is justified.[7] Within the context of entrepreneurs and business overall, what is "true" has a limited shelf life. For example, the primitive concept that the world was flat was "true" until explorers proved that theory wrong. The shelf life of that fact lasted a few hundred years. In today's fast-paced economy, the shelf life of a fact is significantly shorter. What had worked perfectly well in your business over the past year may not work so well this year. Most general beliefs do not hold for a long period of time.[4] When entrepreneurs hold on too tightly to what they knew worked, they can fail miserably, holding nothing but their pride. This is what I call epistemologically challenged people—those who think they know it all. Even for the smartest people, learning needs to be used as a tool to transform and create new knowledge on a regular basis.[8] Because what you know is constantly shifting, staying on top means a regular training program, rather than a single module approach.

Another distinct influence is the training program itself. Training is seen as a miracle cure for countless organizational problems. For example, since the Enron and Arthur Andersen scandals, ethics training is a growing fad in training and development. Countless organizations have mandated that their employees receive training on ethical conduct. Yet most of these programs fall short of creating an actual linkage into the daily practices within the organization, assuming that training itself is a solution. Specific scenarios in these programs create passive learning that is more entertaining than educational. Especially with external training entities, the training must incorporate a framework of connecting the knowledge with daily practices systemically. If the learner does not internalize the education, he or she will revert into old habits within a few days of the training.[4] For some organizations, that means an annual repeat of training. For others, the norm is to expect a monetary return. Cuts in training budgets tend to be the first when funds get tight.[5]

Training is a small part of a comprehensive learning strategy.[5] It does not heal organizational problems by itself. This brings us to the third distinct influence: knowledge management. Many technology firms today sell knowledge management applications that attempt to capture company knowledge and create learning organizations. They have ample features to maximize scalability and

---

Quick Tip: When you're looking at any training course/program, ask yourself the following questions.

- How new is the material covered in this course?
- What is the validated research (not some newspaper article, which is often biased; be sure the research is peer-reviewed at least by an accredited university) behind the content of the course?
- Does the course allow individual interpretation and application?
- How experienced is the individual delivering the course?

Although training courses/programs are in abundance, many fall short of providing the most up-to-date knowledge. It's one thing not to train your people; it's another, and often much worse thing if you trained your people with poor information that are actually just opinions.

ease of use. Some firms offer complete learning content, such as speeches from famous speakers on leadership and motivation.

One successful entrepreneur made the decision to purchase such a learning system. The system had a vast database of presentations by popular trainers and speakers. Each module came with its own set of presentation notes and questions to consider. As an external learning source, no linkage to the organization's daily practices existed. With such a heavy investment, he expected his people to jump on the system to learn. But after months of waiting, the system usage only showed that a few people had logged on. In hindsight, his staff had no motivation to take the extra time and effort to visit the site, much less learn from it. They also didn't have speakers in most of the desktop computers to listen to the presentations. This system went unnoticed for many months. Learning is much more than just a database you can access. Like any tool, knowledge management systems require human interaction. To make such a system functional, organizational processes need to encompass learning so that every individual has the desire to learn and the time to do it outside of their daily activities.

To move away from generic training practices and the respective connotations, the concept of organizational learning or a learning organization highlights the difference in organizational philosophies. Many companies are starting to realize that training is significantly more complex than a simple session alone. An integral part of any business is a holistic learning model that is woven through every aspect of the business.[1] Many well-established theorists speculate that in today's fast-changing environment, learning organizations are the only ones who will survive and achieve sustainable success.[1,3,4] No group or company is able to obtain and sustain a competitive advantage without a systemic process for organizational learning. Such a process requires a holistic view that integrates learning into everyday practices. Furthermore, rather than the traditional focus on specific content, skills such as learning to learn and adaptability become focal points of the learning process.[4] By enabling the natural instinct for all people to learn, entrepreneurs create the intrinsic needs that go well beyond the simplicity of simply earning paychecks.[5,6] Systemic learning must become a way of life; this chapter provides a foundation for this.

FOUNDATIONS OF A
LEARNING ORGANIZATION

The Harvard Business Review published an article that covered three crucial issues for a learning organization to thrive: meaning, management and measurement. Well ahead of its time, the article highlighted some crucial assumptions that contain epistemological challenges.[3] Expanding on these three areas, I call this the 3 M's of a learning organization. The 3 M's encompass a belief system that must exist within the organizational environment.

Meaning

The first of the 3 M's is *meaning*. As in contemporary literature on adult learning, meaning plays a vital part of human learning.[9] For people to learn, the ability to recall new information plays a crucial part. Meaning is the bridge that connects the information stored inside your mind with your ability to recall it. Did you know that the human brain has incredible capacity to store information? What is challenging is the *recall* of information. When development experts create meaningful content, learning is dramatically increased. At a basic level, meaningful learning connects an existing experience or memory with new information. When used to its fullest extent, knowledge experts attach powerful emotions and mental triggers that enable recall. The challenge here is that many people understand the theory but have limited practical experience with it.

Once I was sitting in the middle of a meeting of some 50 faculty members of one of the largest universities in the United States. The concept of engagement was a group discussion topic. One professor felt that creating meaningful learning is to connect the knowledge with relevant information. The discussion proceeded further into what is relevant. Some believed that to achieve relevance one had to tie the course knowledge in with current events. Others felt that connecting knowledge to specific case studies made it relevant. Regardless of the various tactics, the real question here is whether students really care about the current event or the case study. So much of today's business schools teach with a case study model that offers limited meaning for learners. Although it can be effective to get students to apply theories, the case study method falls short of creating true relevance for every learner. You might care about the company in the case if you knew someone working there; overall, most of the case studies are external to the learner and offer a degree of safety. Their utility in meaning creation is minimal.

To truly create meaning, each individual in the learning organization must have a stake in the outcome of the learning. The outcome of learning requires a personal impact. Meaning is unique to an individual, especially in a diverse population. Thus, learning organizations should assist in guiding individuals to meaning, rather than dictating meaning that tends to create sleep walkers.

Management

The concept of *management* is the second M of the epistemologically challenging issues. Traditional management theory tends to treat employees as disposable parts of a profit-making machine. A learning organization must change that mentality and move to a balanced focus on its people and the learning process, as well as the profits that result from the learning process. Blind management of tasks and goals will only reduce morale and secure organizational cancer.[10] Management and leadership have a middle ground in learning. Management is concerned with tasks, processes, and goals. Leadership is concerned with the people and the path for potentials to flourish. For entrepreneurs to succeed, management and leadership must occur at the same time. In other word, learning must be a carefully guided journey, whether you're leading or managing.

While I was at a UN global forum (Business as an Agent of World Benefit Forum: Management Knowledge Leading Positive Change) in Cleveland, Ohio, a fascinating series of events and a powerful discussion occurred on the subject of management/leadership. This occurred at the table where I was assigned to sit, along with seven other leaders from all parts of the world (Croatia, India, England, Mexico, and the United States). Most of these people were business leaders and well respected and published professors. Over lunch, after a group activity on establishing the vision of the world in 2020, the topic of who is a leader surfaced. Some felt that a leader is the person who takes charge of the group and leads the process. (This may also be a definition of a manager, since managers manages processes.) I interjected that the person choosing to follow is also a leader. The conscious choice to participate as a group member without a title is a leadership trait. In fact, the act of labeling someone a leader is hierarchical. Management principles require some form of hierarchy; leadership does not require such a hierarchy. Therefore, in group discussions, every individual involved is a leader and a follower at the same time.

I was in the process of writing this book at the time in addition to always having a curious mind, so I was very conscious of group dynamics and management/leadership principles at this conference. As I experimented with various methods of managing and leading groups, I found a solid balance between doing both at the same time to enhance the learning process. At a high level, appreciative inquiry was a methodology that drove the conference. Although this methodology provided the construct for the forum at a high level, group members determined processes in lower level discussions. One of the major challenges at the conference and in the discussions was the level of accomplishment and pride in the participants; almost all of the participants were well-educated business leaders in both academia and corporations.

Without going into too much detail, I'll just say that the last small group session illustrated the dynamics of management and leadership through a discovery and learning process. The session had a goal of "creating a state of the art curriculum for business education to reach a tipping point." Imagine a new company looking to create a product, as you read this story. A group of about 18 people sat in a circle with a large white board at the front and me next to it. Like the start of most meetings, much chatter filled the group as people were introducing themselves to each other.

I started with the following: "Let's get started everyone, since we have a limited amount of time. What does a 'tipping point' mean to you? Who defines it?" These leadership questions engaged the group to think further about the product. A few people responded with some degree of opposition. Another individual spoke and made another suggestion. "Can we all introduce ourselves before we get started?" This got people around the circle to state some surface information such as name, title, and affiliation. Such a suggestion aligns with management, as it attempts to focus on a process of introduction.

After everyone introduced themselves, someone in the group asked if there was a given facilitator or if the group had to nominate someone. One man, John, a business professor from Memphis, replied that there was no given facilitator in this process and nominated me to facilitate. A few others seconded the motion. I felt an incredible honor among such a group of leaders to facilitate along with some weight on my shoulders to produce the product.

Before moving forward, let's take a look at the two questions that were brought forth to the group. One asked for deeper thought and challenged people's minds. The other asked for basic information. Yet in the simplicity of two questions, the group chose the person with the deeper question to lead within the first 10 minutes of a meeting. Of course, there were other aspects of this situation that also influenced the choice (body language, authenticity, physical seating). The engagement of people to learn was the most influential impact.

After offering a few ideas on how to break down the product (manager role), I listened to the group's ideas (leader role). Putting the two together, I asked the group to form into three small groups of specific interest as a few others recommended (leader role) while keeping the timetable rigid (manager role). By allowing each individual to have a voice in the process, I led the group to own the process from a leadership perspective. By the end of the hour-long session, the group was ready to present the product to the conference. More important, we had a solid relationship with each other. As we returned to our tables, many commented that they enjoyed the process.

For a learning organization to function well, management and leadership co-exist to create learning. When walking into a meeting, leaders don't need to have a complete process designed. I had some ideas of how the session could be run, but I was not too attached to what I had in mind. I'm only one person

---

Quick Tip: Next time you're conducting a meeting, take on the following actions.

- Don't sit at the usual front of the room or head of the table.
- Walk in with a trust in the order that comes from chaos. Don't have a completely solidified process to managing the meeting. Allow the rest of the group to have input into the process, as well as the content. Let others have control.

If your leadership and management skills are sharp, both actions will lead you toward greater influence. This influence is not from authority or position but respect. Sometimes, being a successful entrepreneur is not about having all the ideas but knowing how to facilitate a process and making a product from nothing.

with a short lifetime of experiences; why not leverage the experiences of the group and allow each member to have input into the process? Allow the leadership component to weave through management desires and the need to control. By doing so, doors for respect and learning will open. As long as leaders learn in the process, the outcome will always astonish you. This is a basic fundamental principle of a learning organization—you should be willing to learn as the leader and the manager.

Measurement

The last of the 3 M's is *measurement*. Typically, financial figures dominate measurements in most organizations. Within a learning organization, measurements focus on the learning process and make a clear correlation between development investments and the return on individual and business performance.[5] Although the traditional financial measures still have value, they're only one dimension of the multiplicity of outcomes that small businesses encounter. You would not just measure physical dimensions of your body to determine its health. You would measure whole well-being through other aspects, such as your emotional state and stress levels. A holistic perspective of measurement enables the awareness of the entrepreneur. If learning is to occur at any level of the organization, measurements are the key to solidifying growth through learning. They can be as simple as a self-assessment of stress at the end of the day on a scale of one to five. It can also be complex, such as obtaining information from multiple perspectives such as customers, vendors, employees, and even family. The fascinating power of measurements creates a higher level of awareness. Such awareness creates a strong accountability structure that increases the likelihood of accomplishing a goal.[3]

KNOWLEDGE CREATION WITHIN A
LEARNING ORGANIZATION

To train or develop individuals within any organization, the knowledge creation spiral is a fundamental basic. This spiral is a continuous process of learning that transfers individual tacit knowledge into organizational knowledge. Furthermore, the process gives rise to endless innovations.[11] Can you imagine what it feels like to never worry about a competitor? Your knowledge creation spiral will always be creating innovations ahead of its time, and this gives any entrepreneur peace of mind.

To make this process as tangible as possible, I will use the example of one form of organizational knowledge—an orientation system, otherwise known as a job description. There are two general types of job descriptions: ones that don't exist with any substance due to lack of time and ones that have lots of detail from some time back when the business was initially created. As a result, when new employees start a job, the entrepreneur is often stuck conducting the training, instead of growing the business. With the knowledge creation spiral, the orientation system can be a living document that learns from people and teaches people how to grow. Can you envision a life where you no longer have to deal with employee training at all levels of the organization? Picture yourself going on vacation for months without having to worry about the business as it continues to thrive. What would that feel like?

Those images and feelings are prime motivators for creating such a system. The knowledge creation spiral has several distinct elements. The first is tacit knowledge, which later translates into explicit knowledge, the second element. Knowledge learning systems are the third element, and they transfer explicit knowledge throughout the rest of the organization for application. The final element is measurements, which solidify the impact of that knowledge application, creating new tacit knowledge (refer to Figure 6-2).

Tacit knowledge is personal knowledge inside each individual. This is often tough to formalize, because much knowledge rests as an unconscious competence. For example, many people know how to drive a car. If you asked them to write it down, they'd give you similar instructions. Certain people can use those instructions and rarely get into an accident or get a traffic ticket; others get into accidents regularly. Why is that?

One of the fun activities I've asked many leaders to perform is to write out directions of how to do something. Perform the exercise below and see how difficult it is to make your tacit knowledge explicit so that another person can understand.

Exploring Your Tacit Knowledge Exercise

You can conduct this exercise as a team building activity or with two other people.

1. Choose an activity you're comfortable with. Try something simple like putting on a jacket, tying your shoes, or putting on lipstick.
2. On a blank piece of paper, write down specific directions on how to perform the task. Make the assumption that your audience is an alien from another planet who has a command of the English language with identical body parts (i.e., knows which hand is right and which is left). List every step clearly, as explicitly as you can.
3. After writing these directions down, select a listener. The listener is to perform the actions with absolutely no assumptions about the intent of the direction. He or she is to follow the direction precisely.
4. Then ask someone else (reader) to read it aloud. Having another person read it aloud is a great method to reflect your tone and

thought process externally. If you try to read it, you'll change it as you go, thus defeating the point of the exercise.

5. As the reader dictates the directions, the listener performs them with no assumptions. If the listener gets stuck at any point, make a note of the assumption required to move forward and continue, bypassing the assumption.

When you have completed the exercise, see how far the listener got to completing the task. How many assumptions were made to complete the task?

In the countless times I've conducted this exercise with executives and entrepreneurs, very few people wrote directions that allowed the listener to complete the task without any assumptions. You can choose to perform the activity with something as simple as a daily task that everyone is familiar with, and then move on to tasks that are a bit more challenging, such as handling customer requests.

Tacit knowledge is also much more complex than just writing down tasks—that's only the management side. On the leadership side, various relationships and dependencies are crucial knowledge. Similar to the Testing Your Knowledge Transfer System Exercise in Chapter 6, alternative perspectives are needed to clearly identify how one's tasks impact other people. To initiate the transfer of tacit knowledge to explicit knowledge on a specific job function, every organizational member should perform the following steps.

1. Make a daily journal of tasks performed over the course of a week. Depending on the job, you might want to do this at the middle of the month or the end of the month, because many small businesses have end-of-the-month processes, such as accounting and inventory.
2. After a task list is built, complete the following for each task.

    a. Derive simple directions that clearly illustrate how the task is completed. Do your best to minimize assumptions in the directions.
    b. Seek out dependencies. What does the task require in terms of resources and people? What time lines are expected?
    c. Determine the multiple levels of impact. Who cares about the completion of this task? Who is impacted if the task is not completed properly?
    d. Go to each of the stakeholders listed and further define what is expected.

3. Create some basic measurements on how successful the task is using the following dimensions of measurement.

    a. Task effectiveness: for example, how many orders should one process within the hour? These are basic performance measurements.

    b. Self-impact: how should one feel on completing the task? What is the stress level? Is there a sense of accomplishment or fatigue?

    c. Relational impact: how do people feel receiving the completed tasks? Whether it's customers, peers, or family, are people content with the completion? Do they respect you for performing the task within a timely manner?

    d. Learning impact: what did I learn through the process? What can I add into the directions to make it more fun, more efficient, higher quality? What can I innovate?

4. Place the task list and its respective directions into a folder using a simple revision system (i.e., rev. 1.0 to start and increment as changes are made). This does not require a fancy database, although it is helpful to have one. For many small businesses, a simple text document is sufficient.

These steps just mark the beginning of knowledge transfer and creation. After completing these steps, the explicit knowledge requires transfer along with application. One basic method of knowledge transfer, application, and innovation is a simple job rotation. Although it may be tough because many entrepreneurs feel as if they are irreplaceable, every individual has something positive to add to any process. The question entrepreneurs should ask themselves is "what am I afraid of if someone else does this for a day based on what I wrote down?"

Job rotations are a perfect example of a form of knowledge transfer. This is a kind of experiential learning that builds a sense of community as well as respect for each other's roles. In a small business, it would look something like the following.

1. Choose one day a week or month, and ask someone else if they have a desire to learn what another person does. Make sure there is interest in learning about a different role. If motivation is not present, this exercise would be a waste of time. One method to find intrinsic motivation is to illustrate the connectivity of job functions between different people. For example, the connection between salespeople and accounts receivable would benefit from such discoveries of roles and dependencies; clearly illustrate the dependence on each other.

2. One that day, switch the people into "new" job roles. The person in the new role is now an apprentice. Empower that apprentice by providing explicit directions for each task. When a task appears, the apprentice can research the task and follow the directions.

3. This is where the learning process becomes challenging and exciting. Like the Exploring Your Tacit Knowledge Exercise, there'll be assumptions for each of the tasks. These assumptions create moments of confusion in ambiguity. Inside these moments, new knowledge is developed, and as long as workers are reasonable, they will refrain from running to the

source for help.[11] The apprentice will innovate new methods to connect the missing pieces within each of the assumptions. With a new and different mentality, the apprentice will likely create something new. Sometimes, this innovation may take a while; other times, the new thinking may be incredibly powerful.

4. The application of explicit knowledge provides a space for innovations to occur. Add the innovation into the explicit knowledge.

5. Once the task is complete, assess its impact using the measurements initially established. By recording the measurements, the organization can quantify the impact of the innovation and learn from that experience.

The execution of the job rotation took the concept of job definition and training through the knowledge creation spiral. It used multiple perspectives in the performance of tasks as well as the quantification of the task impact. This process allows organizations to be adaptable to most environmental situations. If a key member is sick and can't be at work, other members will be comfortable with taking on the responsibilities while also using that opportunity to grow the organizational knowledge. Such a process allows entrepreneurs to go on vacation without having to worry about the business. It also consistently fosters innovations that create internal efficiencies at all levels of the organization. The cost of such a system is minimal. The initial transfer of tacit knowledge to explicit knowledge may take a couple of hours each day for up to a week to establish. The technology is simple documents with a folder system for revisions. The job rotation may require some initial guidance at first but will run on its own with decreasing interruptions of tasks as the directions learn and grow.

There are occasions when organizations require outside assistance for new knowledge. A few key concepts to keep in mind when integrating outside expertise through consultants or academic courses are the following.

- Learning truly begins when the course or workshop is complete. Everyday organization practices need to envelop any major point learned.[5] If you send someone to take a class or if a consultant provides training on a specific subject, write down specific new knowledge gained immediately on completion. This is as simple as spending an extra five minutes to write down the top five lessons of the course. From those top lessons, write down specific actions to achieve in specific periods. For example, coming back from a communications workshop, one might learn about the importance of listening. An action that comes from that lesson is to ask more questions and speak less.

- Measurements must perpetuate actions to be complete. When you create a measurement, your awareness of the new action enables active engagement of your mind. Using the example of the communications workshop, one measurement might be the number of questions asked in a 10-minute conversation or the amount of talking versus listening in a conversation. Going a step further, one can also ask another person to rank on a scale of 1 to 5 if he or she believes that they were being heard.

- Create a learning agreement with someone who cares about your development.[5] As part of the left brain interpreter, our minds will create the most reasonable explanations for why an unspoken commitment to action failed follow through if there's no accountability. As long as there is someone else involved and watching, we're more likely to accomplish tasks simply because we don't want to let someone down. Try this and see what happens. If you have kids, tell them specifically what you intend to do and accomplish. See how much drive that gives you toward achievement.

One of the most important and challenging aspects to creating a learning organization is measurement. People don't like to fail. If there's a measurement, there is a chance of failure. Although some may embrace the challenge, others will run from it. This is where a successful entrepreneur creates new meaning behind the concept of measurement. No measurement is absolute, nor is any measurement, assessment, or test a prediction of future events. Measurements are only a marker in time, with relative relevance. Before conducting any learning event (training workshop or course), successful entrepreneurs stretch measurements across three different time periods—prelearning event, postlearning event, and at least two weeks after the learning event.[12] Because learning is a natural and ongoing process, measurements should occur at regular intervals. Establishing a holistic and timely measurement system informs the people in the organization what is important.

THE ROLE OF THE ENTREPRENEUR IN TRAINING AND DEVELOPMENT

Organizational learning is a context for success. The primary role of the entrepreneur is to establish the knowledge creation spiral. In addition, certain beliefs and behaviors lead people toward continued learning. These beliefs and behaviors also create an optimal organizational environment to foster individual growth that increases profitability.

The first and probably one of the most difficult behavior is the *willingness to unlearn* what you've mastered earlier.[4] Exhibiting behavior means that you lead by example. If an entrepreneur fails be to a learner who constantly reinvents him- or herself, no one else in the organization will authentically learn. As the study showed, business success is a mere reflection of the entrepreneur's internal growth.

Let's see how much you're willing to unlearn what you thought was a truth and behave accordingly for yourself. The myth and marketing of milk producers has the public believing that milk is good for healthy bones. Your mother may have even drilled that fact into your head when you were a child. In reality, there is no scientific proof that drinking milk guarantees strong bones. Some studies have even illustrated an increase in bone fractures in regular milk drinkers compared to nonmilk drinkers. Other studies have made a connection between milk consumption and prostate cancer.[13] (You can find much of this research for yourself online at www.pcrm.org.) Based on these facts, which I understand may be startling, will you unlearn old habits? No one is watching—only you will know the truth. This is just a simple test, but it touches on a core belief that most people hold. Will you change your behavior according to new information? Successful entrepreneurs do so on a regular basis.

Another key behavior associated with a learning organization is the *proper selection of your people*. According to well-published theorists, there are two types of people who work in organizations. As an entrepreneur, you should embrace people who are naturally curious and see life through the eyes of explorers. These people are open to interaction with different cultures and are willing to assimilate diverse concepts and perspectives.[4] Having these people on staff accelerates learning and success. The other types of people tend to have a dogmatic and pessimistic perspective on life. They interpret events using old beliefs that are out of date.[8] As long as you have people eager to learn within the organization, even failures become incredible lessons that fuel success.

In addition to selecting the proper people, entrepreneurs need to *embrace every employee*. Rather than using the traditional employee retention concept, consider employee embracement. When you retain or keep employees around, do you see excited workers? They may simply choose not to leave. Why not go beyond simple retention toward something with much more passion and fire? Embracement requires authentic emotional connection for both the employee and the entrepreneur. It speaks of passion for the work as well as the growth that comes with the job. To foster employee embracement, the entrepreneur is one of the key disseminators of information. Like sharing meals with one's family, informal discussions, small group workshops, and formal learning sessions share information freely. This sharing is symbolic of embracement practices. The impact is simple, yet powerful—employees feel a heightened sense of ownership through inclusion.

I was consulting at a technology firm once. They had a few employees who felt disconnected, and attitude was going down the drain. Because they were a service-based company, most of their people were out of the office, attending to customers. This practice minimized communications within the office. Some decisions failed to include those out of the office. The owners felt their key workforce slip away. The typical employee retention would seek rewards and incentives for them to stay with the company. Such extrinsic rewards are often temporary bandages that do not address the root issue of inclusion. We chose to implement an embracement process whereby weekly meetings on company events informed these people. Using a team-based approach (discussed in detail in the next chapter), we were able to understand how these employees felt and turned communication around within a few weeks. The meetings provided room for relationship development between all members of the organization. With this development, sensitivity toward each other's needs increased. This behavior change led to a complete attitude turnaround that yielded more than 30 percent revenue growth in three months, along with a few other minor strategy enhancements.

Empowerment is another vital behavior. The entrepreneur must authentically *empower his or her people*. Although many organizations use the concept of empowerment, most only give it lip service. At the core of empowerment is the fear of being alone. Think about it—if you truly empower people to take care of their lives, they will not need you anymore. That lack of need scares many people to maintain control and co-dependence. Ironically, when you truly empower people, they return by choice, instead of by need. The relationship is significantly deeper. Sometimes, empowerment is about letting people struggle to find their own way. Other times, it is about pointing people in the proper direction. Assuredly, empowerment is never about fixing the issue or maintaining control. The codependence chapter discussed that behavior in detail. Successful entrepreneurs know how to let go and allow people to fail and succeed.

The final behavior is *accountability* within the organizational environment. Learning is more effective if there is accountability. The entrepreneur is responsible for the environment of the organization. In your role as leader, accountability separates mediocrity from greatness. The accountability structure has no boundaries. Any member of the organization can share ideas and hold another person accountable for actions.[3] An accountability structure is fairly simple, but it takes a great deal of courage. Imagine an organization that replaced some of the generic "Hi, how are you?" statements with the following conversations:

- What have you learned lately?
- How have your actions change based on that lesson?
- What are you going to do differently? By when?

When you see that person later, ask the following: "Based on what you committed to last time, what was the impact of your actions?" These conversations require no real authority. They're simply meant as a mirror for other people to see their own lessons, actions, and impact. These conversations can happen by chance or by a systematic method in which accountability peers are established. This is not a two-person model like many coaching models. In the two-person model, if one person chooses to be NICE (Nothing Inside Cares Enough) and not hold the accountability on a tough issue, NICE begins to degrade the rest of the relationship. Instead, the accountability structure should maintain three or more people at all times.

Let's say you have four people in a group—Adam, Barry, Charles, and Darrel. The accountability structure would have Adam hold Barry accountable by Barry's own choice of commitments. Barry would hold Charles accountable; Charles would hold Darrel accountable; and finally, Darrel would hold Adam accountable. As time moves forward, a quarterly rotation of accountability peers builds understanding between every person and the challenges of others on a personal level. This not only creates strong connections between members of the organization but also fosters a supportive learning environment.

Through the conscious design of a learning organization, employee training and development becomes a systemic process of growth. As individuals in the organization grow, including the entrepreneur, the obvious reflection is increased profits. This chapter has outlined some of the basic principles required for a learning organization. If you desire the freedom to go on worry-free vacations while your business thrives, implement a new process on a monthly basis. As long as the business understands the basics of a learning organization and practices its principles, sustainable growth will occur.

REFERENCES

1. K. Kleponis, S. Christensen, and M. Hall (2005, November). Beyond a seat at the table. *T+D* 59(11), 60–63. This article defines enterprise learning as a holistic approach to enabling organizational learning. It also introduced a relatively new role—chief learning officer, who is responsible for organizational learning.

2. D. Goleman, R. Boyatzis, and A. McKee (2002). *Primal leadership: Realizing the power of emotional intelligence.* Boston: Harvard Business School Press. This text covered emotional intelligence and its significance to leadership. Goleman and colleagues offered much fascinating research concerning training programs and why they often don't work. The concept of a honeymoon effect is used to define the short-lived behavioral changes from training programs.

3. D. A. Garvin (1993, July/August). Building a learning organization. *Harvard Business Review* 71(4). Retrieved November 15, 2003, from EBSCO Research Database. This brilliant article defined some of the basic assumptions about management, meaning, and measurements with respect to learning. It offers some detailed strategies to assist learning, such as supportive learning environments and breaking down hierarchies.

4. S. V. Manikutty (2005, April–June). Manager as a trainer, a coach, and a mentor. *Journal for Decision Makers* 30(2), 57–64. This article challenges management concepts to also include coaching and mentoring. Manager must make the time to develop their people, rather than just manage day-to-day activities.

5. T. Kirkwood and A. Pangarkar (2004, August/September). Striking at the roots. *CMA Management* 78(5), 38–40. This article provides some of the top challenges of organizations in training their people. Some of the crucial ones are creating a supportive organization for learning and measure soft and hard results.

6. F. J. Landy and J. M. Conte (2004). *Work in the 21st century: An introduction to industrial and organizational psychology.* New York: McGraw-Hill. This is a great text on the foundations of organizational psychology. It connects various business leadership principles with wisdom from the psychology world. A specific theory taken from this text is the human relations theory in chapter 14, which adds the human element and the relationships between humans as a intricate part of organizational success.

7. P. K. Moser and A. Vander Nat (1995). *Human knowledge: Classical and contemporary approaches.* New York: Oxford University Press. This is very heavy reading on

the theory of knowledge. It provides a historical account of theories in epistemology from Plato to contemporary theorists. The overall theme is to illustrate the vulnerability of human logic in what we think we know. For humanity to move forward, we must derive a fluid definition of knowledge, rather than an absolute that proves someone else wrong.

8. C. Argyris (2002). Teaching smart people how to learn. *Reflections: The SOL Journal* 4(2), 4–16. Often, the smartest people are not very good at learning. This article provides some fascinating rationale for their lack of ability due to their success.

9. J. E. Ormrod (2006). *Educational psychology: Developing learners* (5th ed.). Upper Saddle River, NJ: Prentice Hall This book covers many theories of adult learning as well as measurements. Meaningful learning is one of the primary methods for knowledge construction. As people obtain new information, retention is increased as the new information is related with existing knowledge, creating a meaningful context that enables greater recall.

10. T. Sun (2005, November 25). Is there organizational cancer in your company? *Business First-Columbus, Bizjournals.* This is an article I wrote that defined organizational cancer as the lack of health from a humanistic perspective. Organizational cancers are what eat away at the company from inside. Many companies have structures and processes that create unfavorable work environments. Rather than blame people for their issues, organizations need to see the cancer and address it at the core of its structures, processes, and beliefs.

11. I. Nonaka and H. Takeuchi (1995). *The knowledge-creating company: How Japanese companies create the dynamics of innovation.* New York: Oxford University Press. This is one of my favorite books on the topic of a knowledge creation at all levels of the organization. Based on studies of successful Japanese companies, the book clearly defines the intricate aspects of a knowledge creation spiral. It outlines a process that translates tacit knowledge to explicit knowledge. A system of knowledge transfer moves explicit knowledge throughout the organization. Application of that knowledge created new tacit knowledge for the spiral to continue to grow organizational knowledge.

12. S. Geertshuis, M. Holmes, H. Geertshuis, D. Clancy, and A. Bristol (2002). Evaluation of workplace learning. *Journal of Workplace Learning* 14(1), 11–18. This article discussed effective evaluation processes for workplace learning. The authors believe that surveys to measure the effectiveness of workshops must be stretched over at least three different time periods—preworkshop, postworkshop, and at least two weeks after the workshop.

13. N. D. Barnard (2000). Preventive medicine and nutrition, Dairy and prostate cancer fact sheet. Physicians Committee for Responsible Medicine. Retrieved on October 19, 2006 from www.pcrm.org/health/prevmed/dairy_prostate.html. This is a validated source that does not take funds to bias any of its research. It provides great information on many common myths about foods that the marketing engines of producers have created. Countless agencies and universities have researched whether milk is good or bad for the human body. All who have not received money from the dairy industry have shown negative influences between milk and illnesses such as prostate cancer and bone fractures.

CHAPTER TWELVE

Behavior 8: Team–Based Decisions

How well have you incorporated the thoughts and ideas of your people in decisions? What processes have you established to ensure that everyone has a voice? What specific actions have you taken to listen to the diverse viewpoints from people of different backgrounds and interests?

Most entrepreneurs do not have a specific process for managing decisions. Although they are very capable of making timely decisions, the perception is that team-based decisions are time-consuming and inefficient. Based on this assumption, many successful entrepreneurs made decisions on their own with a negative impact to the team (as we found in the variable of action without full information). Our study also found that the lack of involvement in decisions is a reflection of a lack of process and time. Keeping people in the loop is vital to success. How does one maintain a level of efficiency while communicating what is important and meaningful to people within the organization? How can those impacted by decisions be part of the decision-making process? Especially with the current diverse nature of the workforce, how do successful entrepreneurs leverage the collective talents of their people?[1]

Studies have consistently shown that the collective intelligence of the group is more powerful than the smartest person in the group.[1] Intelligence is not a linear equation when more than one person is involved. When faced with a problem, decision making that involves the collective wisdom of the group will outperform those of a single individual or even the smartest entrepreneur.

Regardless of your intelligence level, you will have a certain bias toward specific choices and people. When making decisions, you'll also have unconscious rules of life that drive your decisions. For example, studies have found that people prefer other people who share backgrounds, beliefs/values, and goals. You may have a natural preference toward hiring or working with someone of similar values.[2] Or if you're looking for someone who has work ethics, your natural instinct may prefer Asian workers because they are well known for strong work ethics due their attitude toward collectivism over individualism.[3] Yet if you're looking for someone who has strong communication skills, you may prefer to have a man because the stereotypical expectation of men is to dominate communications. Studies have also found a global tendency to penalize women for attempting to take on the stereotypical male role of managers (in the United States, China, Japan, United Kingdom, etc.).[4] But other studies suggest that women would achieve greater successes as leaders due to the significant influence of emotional intelligence,[5] because their ability to identify emotions is stronger than that of men.[6]

All of these beliefs work in the background when making decisions about people. Some may have a tremendous influence on your decision; they may also cause a lack of in-depth analysis of a certain decision. Going back to your organization's need for strong work ethics, consider that not all Asian people have that quality. The same goes for Italians—not all speak with great animation. Much of your rules of life are formed based on your own experiences and how you've interpreted them. They're designed to save time when faced with similar future choices. As human beings have evolved out of the era when timely decisions meant life or death, fast decisions often fall on their faces due to the lack of applicability of your rules of life. These rules form assumptions that require additional analysis. Particularly in a varied environment, no two situations are alike, because the people involved are not alike. Sometimes sound decisions require the abandonment of your rules of life. In other words, to truly see the desired outcome occur, you need to challenge your assumptions. Some assumptions lie deep in an unconscious realm. The only way to reach them is to leverage the insights of others.

I remember a great concept at a seminar—"You don't know, what you don't know." Think about this for a second; you have conscious competencies like driving a car or starting a business. That is knowing what you know. There's also another part of you that knows that you have no idea of certain tasks. For example, you may have no clue how to fly a plane or how to conduct a symphony orchestra. Those are conscious incompetences. For the lack of competence, entrepreneurs can obtain services from those who do have a competence because they are aware of their own lack. What is dangerous to many people, especially entrepreneurs who have businesses resting on them, is what they don't know that they don't know (because this is a bit of a tongue twister, we'll called this WYDKTYDK—what you don't know that you don't know). Because there is no knowledge of such events, there is no way to plan for it. This is where the perspectives of other people become vital.

I conduced a training session on the concept of systems diagrams to understand organizational challenges facing a few organizations. Systems diagrams are based on system thinking. Within this theory, the interconnectedness of humanity fosters a web of relationships that influences one another. To truly understand the systems involved, one must lay out a diagram. The concept of a system contains great diversity. An individual is a system. Another system is an organization. A related system is customers, who contain individual systems.[7] The leadership group started out with a very simple example—the system of an individual (see Figure 12-1). Because each subsystem (intellectual, emotional, physical, spiritual) has many influences, each is connected to an entirely different system. Expanding on the physical system, one can envision the influences of food, shelter, and the environment as a starting point. As you look at Figure 12-1, you're probably thinking there are other influences that are not in the diagram. You are correct. There are many more factors that the original diagram did not have. You can add your wisdom to the diagram.

Once the concepts were understood by the leadership group, each group visited and analyzed an organization. After returning, they started to lay out a systems diagram for each organization and its challenges. Can you guess how many different systems were identified by the groups?

As I walked around the room at the seminar and observed the group dynamics, each group had many innovative insights, leveraging their collective wisdom. The systems diagrams didn't look anything as simple as Figure 12-1. Each of their diagrams had over 55 separate systems with many related subsystems.

Systems Diagram: An interconnected Human Being

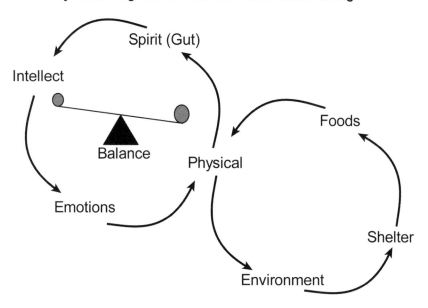

FIGURE 12-1.   Systems diagram of the individual self and a related system for physical needs. This diagram reveals the various intangible characteristics of a human being and lays out the physical influences from a systemic perspective. (You probably didn't know that you didn't know how to draw yourself as a system of multiple intelligences. This is a perfect example of a WYDKTYDK.)

They even broke the systems into multiple dimensions. Some systems were bodies of knowledge (such as a theory on education or business); others contained people and organizations. Can you imagine what your systems diagram would look like if you took a few minutes to draw out your web of connections for your organization (family or business)?

Capturing the Collective Wisdom Exercise

To value team decisions, let the brilliance of the collective wisdom surprise you. As discussed previously, I'm not interested in changing you. I'm only asking you to take the journey with me and discover some new thoughts and beliefs. This exercise reveals the power of the collective wisdom. (Note: Your understanding of systems thinking and diagrams is not relevant. As long as you and your team work from the same basis, a simple comparison of the number of systems identified reveals the collective wisdom).

1. Lay out the web of connections for your organization. Start with yourself and work from there. Label this diagram #1. See how many different connections your business may have.
2. After you've completed laying out your drawing, ask your team members to build another one from scratch from their perceptions of these connections. Feel free to facilitate only or allow someone else to do it with no bias towards the outcome. A couple of powerful questions to get the group started are "When you do a great job, who do you impact? When you don't get tasks complete on time, who do you hear from?" The team can design a web of connections from their perspective from these questions. Label this diagram #2. You may need to give them an explanation of systems thinking and the concept of a systems diagram. Don't show anyone your layout yet. You can choose to observe without input. Ideally, use the directions in the Group Empowerment Model below for using the whole "brain" of the organization.
3. Once the diagrams are complete, count the number of systems they've identified. Also, divide the number of systems by the number of people in the group (call that the system average). This represents a "systems per person" figure, assuming a linear relationship.
4. Add yourself into the group, and let the group build further on the diagram with your input. Label this diagram #3. When complete, count the number of systems you have and also the systems per person number by dividing the number of systems by the number of people with you included.

5. Take the number of systems in diagram #2 and add to it a respective systems per person number. This step assumes a linear relationship between number of systems and people involved. By adding the systems per person number, you're adding yourself theoretically to predict the number of systems created on diagram #3.
6. Is this number smaller than the number of systems in diagram #3?

Answer the following fascinating questions:

- Take a look at the number of systems your team identified in diagram #2.
- Did they come up with more systems than you did in diagram #1?
- Did they find some connections that you didn't think about at all?
- Is this a linear relationship?

The smartest people would rarely identify 15–20 systems of connectivity in a single attempt. Yet in a very short time of 20 minutes, the collective wisdom of the group using the process I'll outline shortly derived a very complete and complex image of the relationships between different systems. This work exemplifies the potential of functioning groups with well-designed processes to guide group dynamics.

REDEFINING THE TEAM
AND THEIR IMPORTANCE

Before moving forward to discussing team dynamics and decision processes, let's look at the concept of a team and its members. Traditionally, teams did not exist with the frequency that they do today. In the industrial era, much of the work completed required people to function alone, where a machine connected the work of people. Within this context, hierarchies of control dominated organizations.[8] Today, the concept of the team is significantly more dominant than before. Within a knowledge-based economy, mental function is greatly valued. To maximize knowledge creation and application, the growth of teams at all levels of organizations ensures a fluidity of knowledge that fosters the growth of sustainable success. Another major factor for team existence is the dramatic shifts in age differences in the workforce. Almost every country in the world is relying an aging workforce. Aside from the need to capture the knowledge and experiences of older generations, companies are facing age diversity visible at all levels.[2] Even if your organization is a local business, these factors play a significant role. And if your group is a multinational company, diversity takes on many more dimensions.

The incredible brilliance in embracing diversity is the power of the collective wisdom. When you have a team with diverse backgrounds, from education to culture, discoveries of hidden assumptions occur often. Another requirement for this to occur is the removal of hierarchies. Some of the entrepreneurs interviewed possessed a clear authoritative leadership style. Because they were the owners, their words had significant influence. This behavior was reflected in the management team as well. They were also unapproachable, operating with an iron fist. An authoritarian style of leadership has a negative impact on relationships in the long run. It does not promote team work, nor does it instill self-confidence in people. To minimize these behaviors, processes of equality must influence group decisions. Studies have shown that group heterogeneity enables creative solutions by the depth and width of approaches to organizational concerns.[2] As long as there is a process in place to capture that wisdom, teams within your organization will innovate with endless possibilities.

Another significant team is your customers. They are a vital part of your team in decision making. Successful entrepreneurs constantly involve their customers in many critical decisions. Some have gone as far as establishing advisory groups with their toughest customers. A common myth in business is that "the customer is always right." This creates tremendous stress on your business while it forces your people to swallow their pride. Consider the hierarchical relationship created by this mentality. Such a hierarchy would allow customers to act in any way they choose. I'm sure you have experienced or witnessed an event where a customer of a business takes advantage of this attitude to act like a spoiled child. You may even have some friends who may be ridiculous with their habits in forcing businesses to react to their every whim. From a business perspective, how profitable is that customer when you have to remake your product several times or change your service model just for that individual? Major corporations may be able to afford such entanglements with customer service departments (although only on the surface), but a small business can't afford to indulge this mentality. From an emotional perspective, there is no profit. Serving customers who demand everything for nothing offers little or no satisfaction. If anything, you're relieved when the deal is complete . . . except it's never really complete. The thought of that individual may stir horrific emotions.

Imagine when that customer leaves after getting what they want while you pay for it. They go back to their friends who are just like them and inform them of this. "Guess what, you'll never believe what I got away with! They gave me the deal of a lifetime. You should go check them out." Now more of these types of people will come to your business. How does that make you feel? What's the impact to your people as well, when they have to face these customers all the time?

The customer is not always right. If you allow such behaviors to perpetuate, your business will spend more time dealing with those type of customers than being productive and happy. Change the model of the customer relationships to that of a partnership in a team situation. There is no right or wrong in disagreements, only what could be done as the team works together to find an agreement that both sides authentically own.

In the face of disagreements or conflict, train your people to think in a team mindset. Use the following three steps to create cohesion between the customer and yourself.

Hierarchy to Partnership Transition System

1. Acknowledge the disagreement from an emotional perspective. All humans desire connectivity to other people. As social creatures, being heard and seen are necessities of humanity. You could make a simple statement that applies to most situations: "Wow, I can see what you see, and if I were in your place, I'd feel the same way. Our intent is not to have you feeling like this." After making this statement, pause for a moment to allow the comment to be absorbed. This basically tells the emotionally charged customer that you see them.

2. Partner with the customer for a solution. Rather than get busy in your mind with solutions that may or may not be sufficient, allow the customer to add his or her wisdom. Remembering that the collective wisdom is always greater than a single mind, ask the customer the following question: "How would you like to see this handled at this point?" By asking this, you're inviting the customer to take responsibility of their disagreement. You are transitioning the relationship from a hierarchy to a partnership where you both are on the same page, solving the same problem. This also shifts the mindset of the customer out of complaining mode and into an empowered mode that owns the solutions. From this point, move forward with the conversation to resolve the disagreement. You may have to ask more questions, depending on the complexity of the situation. In essence, your goal is to ask the customer to help solve the disagreement while you work together to execute within reason. If anything outside of your perceived reason appears, ask more questions and ask the customer to understand your position.

3. Once you address the disagreement, seek improvements from the customer. "I know the situation we had was not ideal. My intentions to serve did not meet your expectations. How would you like to see future situations like this handled?"

These steps facilitate a shift from an angry customer complaining to a calm partner participating in the solution. A crucial part of this process opens the door for ownership. Human relationships are delicate. Often, solutions in the first round do not solve the problem. Yet when the customer has ownership of the solution, additional rounds of working together enhance the relationship.

Imagine that—disagreements between customers and your business enhancing your relationship!

Since the initial development of this process, the concept of a customer has changed dramatically. Conventional wisdom looks at customers as a means of survival for any business. Customers are people who offer value in the form of monetary payment in return for products and services rendered. To be successful, you must have revenues and profit, which come from customers. To have customers, you must have capable people in your organization to serve them. Is it possible that the focus on the customer is a bit too far down the chain of relationships? What if you changed the mentality to the customer to the first line of relationships—your people? Without your people, you would not have customers that pay for your products and services. If you have disgruntled people, your customers would spread the word, ruin your reputation, and cause a slow demise of your business. One of the flaws in basic accounting principles is to cut costs when business is slow. Although it is a logical choice to provide the perceived immediate fix to low profitability or revenue, rarely does a company grow from cost cutting. The growth and resolution of revenue problems come from the people in the organizations. Any successful organization requires innovative and inspired people. They are the true customers of any business. As many studies have shown, when the employees of businesses are motivated, inspired, and working well together, creative innovations and success flow like ocean waves on the beach.

The customers of the business include both the employees who work with you and the people who make the purchases. They are all part of the team and require careful handling of delicate relationships. Active and conscious application of the hierarchy to partnership transition system creates the context for greater cohesion between people. This is where your success can thrive.

UNDERSTANDING GROUP DYNAMICS
AND DECISIONS

Having facilitated countless group meetings at all levels of organizations, I have seen many forms of group dynamics and decisions. The most interesting ones are those with lots of emotional history (some might call it baggage, although that is a judgment that we should avoid). One of the major problems faced by organizational leaders is groupthink. This practice moves everyone toward a single thought. Although it appears to exemplify cohesion within the team, the underlying issues lack understanding.[2] As mentioned before, a single idea that everyone conforms to lacks diversity of thought. Without depth and breadth of thought, problem identification and respective resolutions become limited. This occurs in many hierarchical structures, especially in large organizations where the perception of survival supersedes the need to voice one's unique ideas.

Within smaller organizations, the political clout or perceived values of the group play a key role in one's individual decisions. Groupthink occurs when individuals' desire to conform overrides their motivation to raise innovative ideas.[2] You have probably met many people who simple choose to not to make a stir. This is very dangerous for small businesses, because they don't have the large budgets to make such mistakes. For example, one of the entrepreneurs in the study runs a small firm. His style of leadership focused on complete control. Although team conversations existed with his staff, very few people were willing to speak up. All of the employees conformed their ideas to those of this owner. Can you imagine what it felt like to work in such a rigid and controlled environment? How long can you survive in an environment where individual identity does not exist?

This is a bit of a trick question, because some of you may be happy with this kind of environment. The answer is heavily influence by generational beliefs. For older Americans, especially those who are vets or early baby boomers, this is the expected environment and likely tolerated. On the contrary, if people of a younger age, later baby boomers, and especially those in Generation X and Y, this environment causes much dissonance and resentment.[9]

The emotional impact of groupthink is only one consideration. The lack of innovative ideas through a single mentality chokes organizations of any size. For example, remember the *Challenger* and *Columbia* space shuttle disasters? Studies have shown that groupthink played a role in both incidents. In the *Challenger* situation, basic logic and engineering understands that materials become brittle under cold temperatures. Some engineers raised the concern. Yet groupthink allowed the launch that resulted in the explosion. Those incidents choked the space shuttle program and shook the nation. As the owner of a small business, can you afford such catastrophic decisions?

Rather than protecting your organization from the negative consequences of a poor decision (which is fear-based motivation), let's look at the inspired outcomes of using an approach that minimizes groupthink. As a leader in any organization, understanding group dynamics and knowing how to empower individuals within a group is one of the most powerful methods to attract and retain your top talent. Furthermore, eliminating groupthink with a systematic process provides ample innovation for the organization and extraordinary empowerment for your people. This Group Empowerment Model (GEM) encompasses many different theories and ideas, such as transformational leadership, educational psychology, and Socratic methods.

The ultimate purpose of any meeting is not necessarily to cover the agenda and make decisions, although those are important. The context of meetings has the challenging goal of establishing self-leadership and positive relationships among people. The GEM process also creates a context with an accountability structure that ensures respective actions from people involved. It gives rise to well-rounded decisions.

Going back to the systemic diagrams that you had completed earlier in the Capturing the Collective Wisdom exercise, I now walk you through the GEM process. The process requires three stages of facilitation.

Premeeting Enrollment

1. *Feel the Group.* Before starting a meeting, request content from participants with a specific timeline. For some situations in which speed is crucial, you can ask people to return their topics within 36 hours before the meeting. For other, higher level meetings, 72 hours may be ideal. This gives you a feel of what's on the minds of your people. Too often, managers drive agendas that are important only to them or the organization. There is little to no time to discuss the people's concerns at the end of the meeting. This step also creates a level of ownership because the topics at the meeting are constructed by the team, not just the boss. Such a feeling of ownership opens the door for authentic involvement, which is a precursor to any successful outcome.

   In the case of the systems diagrams, ask each individual to think of the relationships he or she has with other people, groups, and organizations. After listing these entities, ask them to categorize them into fitting labels. Ask your people to deliver these labels at least three days before the meeting. The email would look like the following. Notice that the context of the memo values individual thought while providing a specific accountability with clear expectations. The questions are broad and ambiguous by design (throwing out the box concept—"think outside of the box"); this opens the door for innovation (there is no box that contains thought; no need to worry about thinking outside of the box).

   Hi team,
   Due to the current state of our business and its impact on you, I'd like to get your thoughts on the various effects you see influencing us. We're going to be using an exciting new method (called systems diagramming which I'll explain later) to look at our organization. Since you see and feel many different aspects of the organization in which I have limited knowledge, I'd greatly value your ideas and thoughts on who we impact and how to go about transforming our daily lives to be more fun and meaningful.

   Please take a moment to consider these questions and respond accordingly:

   1. Whom do you see influencing us or whom do we influence from your perspective, such as people, groups, or organizations? Customers and vendors are good starting points . . . please create a detailed list. Feel free to be creative and interpret this as you see fit. Then categorize them rationally and return them to my assistant.

   2. What do you see as the toughest challenges facing you on a personal level and on an organizational level? Feel free to be creative and interpret this as you see fit.

Please respond with your thoughts and ideas by Monday at 5 p.m. My assistant will collect your brilliance and place it on the agenda for our meeting. My assistant will return it to you by Wednesday at 9 a.m. with a confirmation for our team meeting on Thursday at 9 a.m.

See you soon, and have an inspiring day.

2. *Collect Wisdom.* When your assistant receives feedback, group the general concepts together. You, the entrepreneur, do not perform this task. One rationale is to maintain the objectivity of the collection, as your left brain interpreter will automatically bias the categorization based on your preferences. As an entrepreneur, take the role of a simple individual who is also responsible for the activity in step 1.

Your assistant (this can be anyone you choose—ideally, someone who knows little about the technical details of the business) combines the feedback within 24 hours and returns the agenda to the team by Tuesday at 4 p.m. Part of the early delivery is to illustrate the accountability of leadership. Going beyond sometimes means being early, rather than the traditional thought of working late to get something done.

There is a slight chance that nothing is returned. This may cause some room for concern and require additional analysis. One reason may be that no one got the request. Another more serious concern is that no one cares enough to respond, which indicates an organizational cancer that needs attention.

The Empowering Meeting

3. *Setting the Context.* Arrive at 8:45 a.m. on Thursday. While sitting in the meeting room, start with a blank piece of paper and lay out some ideas. This allows your mind to organize your thoughts without rushing into a meeting and switching hats. As people arrive, engage in deep conversations about their ideas. This will illustrate the value you see in their thoughts.

You may also want to challenge people not to have a cup of coffee before the meeting. As we all know, the caffeine in coffee has negative physical impacts, but it also influences mental states.[10] We're all familiar with the caffeine buzz when you drink too much coffee or soda. For your meeting to maintain a depth of thought, have some fruit and juices available. You'll be amazed at the conversations that result.

4. *Establishing the Rules.* The rules concerning the meeting are crucial to its success. When people are passionate about topics, especially ones that affect them personally, rules help establish guidelines of behavior so that no one can filibuster or dominate the meeting. Once the rules are clear, strategically choose to reiterate them for certain individuals in future meetings.

- When speaking on any subject, no one can speak for more than three minutes. Rationale: This pushes people to collect their thoughts, rather than "show up and throw up." In reality, most ideas can be presented in three minutes or less as long as the presenters are prepared.
- Establish ownership of thoughts by eliminating the word *you* in any statement. Rationale: You may have heard the concept of being tough on the problem and soft on the people. Using the word *you* in a statement often calls for some level of judgment, thus being tough on the people. Instead, use the word *I* in those situations. The only use of *you* is in the form of an open-ended question. For example, a common statement may sound like this: "You said that you would complete this project by Monday." Those are often fighting words. Translating into a tone of ownership, this statement becomes "I thought I heard that the project would be complete by Monday, is that correct?"

  I've simulated some of the toughest and most personal conversations using this rule. Removing the word *you* from statements softened the way topics like abortion, religion, or the war on terror, are perceived by other people. Rather than defending themselves, people are more inclined to authentically hear you. That is a beautiful place to be.
- Start any conversation with individual input on a piece of paper. For example, list the top five ideas you have on a problem. Rationale: In meetings, outspoken people often silence the introverts. For everyone to participate and stay engaged, getting people to write down their ideas not only helps them organize their thoughts but also gets everyone involved, regardless of the group size. Once they all have ideas, then you can ask each person to state their top ideas.
- Go around the room and ask for input from each person. Rationale: No matter what the topic, everyone has an opinion. Part of human nature is desiring attention from other people. The need for affiliation is a basic motivation. Providing room for every person to speak allows the depth and diversity of thought for the content crucial for success.[2]
- Identify a facilitator to enforce these rules of conduct. Rationale: Holding the context of these rules is a huge challenge. Though many organizations have rules, asking people to follow them, especially the CEO/president, is very tough. It requires someone who has strong confidence as well as an ability to be tough. Ideally, this individual should be someone who has minimal bias in the process. Sometimes it's best to bring in an outside facilitator; other times, a manager or assistant can take on that role.

You may find it difficult to implement all these rules at once. You may want to do one at a time, so that people can adopt slowly. If you believe that your people are up for a challenge, let them know that you trust them by using the specific phrase "I trust that you're all capable people who can adapt. Will you agree to a new way to conducting our meetings so that we all have a voice?" Asking for enrollment is much more powerful than dictating a process. This furthers the fact that you value your people's opinions.

5. *Establish the Goals.* Clearly state the goals of the meeting. In each meeting, there are two types of goals. One is for the content of the goal; the other is for the learning process and the development of relationships.

   In the case of the systems diagramming example, a leader would start with the following statement: "When I saw the number of emails concerning your ideas, I was very excited for this meeting. Thank you all for responding with such brilliance. John, you had an idea on XYZ. And Angela, your list included ABC. That's brilliant. I'm thrilled to be part of this meeting where we'll be putting all of your ideas onto paper and get a solid understanding of the influences surrounding us as well as a list of your top concerns."

   The example statement starts with addressing the emotional aspect of the team. Strategically select two or more individuals. John and Angela may be two individuals who are not as outspoken as others or may need a bit more attention to get involved. This statement confirms your ability to see the value in others while motivating them to actively contribute their creative ideas. The second part of the statement clearly lays out the goal.

6. *Empower Every Individual.* Open the dialogue for ideas by applying some of the rules established in step #4. Depending on the time allotted and people present, ensure that every person has the opportunity to speak. By asking everyone to put their ideas on paper first, you minimize the desire to be conforming. This also solicits many different perspectives for any topic of the meeting. Often, a carefully planned moment of silence gives people time to think clearly. The key is to engage every person at the level in which they are comfortable and sometimes, just outside of that level.

   Using the example of the systems diagramming, a question is initially asked to determine if anyone reviewed extra material concerning systems diagramming. If so, ask that person to share with the team what the theory is about. This empowers team members and motivates people to be proactive in research. If no one has done that, you can initiate the overview of the theory while making a note to determine what caused the lack of action for research.

   Once the theory is illustrated, each member of the team starts describing their elements of influence in under three minutes. As they present their ideas, the facilitator writes each system on the board. If a previous person mentioned the same system, make a check mark. The process of using visual drawing improves communication while also providing a much-needed acknowledgment of a person's ideas.

After each member has presented ideas, allow the team to build on each other's contributions and add to the drawing.

Once completed, use the same process to list the challenges they face. This list provides an overview of organizational challenges for future investigation.

7. *Efficient Team Decisions.* Efficiency is a crucial characteristic of a successful organization. Many of the successful entrepreneurs felt that team decisions would take too long, and loss of the collective wisdom would be a consequence. In the world of abundance, smart entrepreneurs have both efficiency and collective wisdom. When options are laid out from step #6, a voting process takes about two minutes to conduct. This multi-voting process is a bit more complicated than a simple majority vote.

   a. Each person gets 500 points to devote to any solution. The lowest breakdown is 100 points (if a person feels equally about five different solutions, they can put 100 points toward each solution).
   b. Clearly lay out each of the solutions on a wall. Ask each person to place their given points toward what they see as the most applicable solution on a piece of paper. (Asking each person to write it down is a form of commitment. In some cases, allowing people to vote immediately by walking up to the solution can sway the votes as the need for affiliation move their vote toward the majority.)
   c. On sticky notes, have each person write down his or her votes for each solution.
   d. Each individual walks up to the solution and posts their respective points on the wall.
   e. Total up the solutions and select the top choices.

8. *Create Accountability Structure.* Accountability is often one of the toughest aspects of being a leader. When someone you like fails to be accountable for something to which they have committed, calling them out on their lack of integrity is not easy. What many people fear is the potential battle or emotional fallout that results from the conversation. Thus, the accountability structure must be reflective so that individuals are not out to fight with excuses but own the task.

   At the end of each major topic in a meeting, close the topic with a list of accountabilities. These must be specific in nature on a deliverable timetable.

   For the example, an accountability that results after the meeting might look like this. "John, since you brought up the great idea of looking at the family unit as a system of influence, would you mind expanding on that through some research on the dependencies of family and how it impacts work life? Great, by when will you have that done? How will I see the research—a memo, an email, etc.?"

   The different questions engage the individual and allow him or her to establish the timeline and the deliverable details. By allowing the individual to establish the timeline, you value their opinions while providing the opportunity to take ownership of the task. When they own the task, the chances of completion are higher. If the task is not complete, you use their own words to reflect on their action. "You stated that you would complete this on Monday; what do you need next time so that you'll be able to follow through with your commitment?"

A reflective question to ask when commitments are not met and excuses are given is "Help me understand, what does your commitment have anything to do with your computer being down (the excuse)?"

There are also instances where you want the accountability to rest within the team members. Create a web of accountabilities by linking individual tasks with others. For example, John would have a report to Angela by Monday, and Angela may have a memo to Jason by Wednesday. Particularly if you have a large team, holding the accountability by yourself provides the perception of controlling. To empower the team, create self-corrective mechanisms so that everyone can be accountable to someone else. As the entrepreneur, you should create accountability to someone else in the organization. The person does not matter; allow yourself to be part of the game you've just created.

Postmeeting Reflections

9. *Capturing the Collective Wisdom.* Capture the discussions and accountabilities with a meeting summary. The summary needs to outline the major concepts as well as offer a detailed accountability of every deliverable. In some instances, name new ideas and processes after the people who created them. This is an incredibly powerful method of enrolling and rewarding people to take ownership of the business.

Also within the summary, schedule the next meeting where individuals present the impact of actions taken.

10. *Systemize Accountabilities.* For every task, place it immediately in your planner with at least a 24-hour reminder. Depending on the complexities of tasks, you may find that weekly reminders of tasks and acknowledgments of tasks completed create a higher level of awareness. The higher the awareness of integrity, the more success you will enjoy.

The GEM process does not have to always involve entrepreneurs. Ideally, the design creates a self-corrective process that is applicable to most meetings. The implementation of the process rests on the shoulders of the entrepreneur. By moving away from solving everyday problems, successful entrepreneurs who establish such a process remove themselves from having to be present at every challenge. The role of an entrepreneur is not to constantly put out fires. Once in place, any individual in the organization can take leadership for meeting

> Quick Tip: Physical representations of roles within meetings push people outside of their comfort zone. To make the meetings fun and exciting, get a few baseball hats with the different roles printed or embroidered on them. Some roles might include the facilitator, the pessimist, the optimist, the visionary, the timer, the recorder, and the star reporter. Especially when people have certain tendencies, asking them to put on the hat of the opposite role may resolve many of the challenges they pose.

initiation or facilitation. Empower the team to do that using the GEM process. Furthermore, an empowered team eliminates the possibility of co-dependence.

ENTREPRENEURS' MOST POWERFUL TOOL: SOCRATIC METHODS

Woven through the GEM process and organizational learning, Socratic methods are crucial skills of empowerment. Based on Plato's theory that knowledge is innate, the concept of Socratic methods is the art of asking questions with a fundamental belief that human beings are creative entities.[11] Socratic methods date back over 2,500 years. Although many theorists believe that communication is the key to getting stakeholder buy-in when facing change, Plato would contend that an internal communication through the application of Socratic methods by a leader creates true ownership of knowledge. For example, rather than creating strategies to communicate the vision, Socrates would ask multiple levels of questions to help the individual create that vision. With a basic belief that everyone is creative and has value to offer, this process empowers individuals while enhancing one's ability to learn. Although it is much harder work for the individual asking the questions, the process creates optimal learning as people discover knowledge for themselves.[12]

By using Socratic methods, leaders empower every individual in the organization. Within the accountability structure, Socratic methods create inspiration that enhances human behavior. Instead of the traditional fear-based and rigid rules and regulations of typical global corporations, each person is empowered to create the context that greatly increases accountability and ownership.

Summarizing Interpersonal Leadership

Organizational Function	Conventional Wisdom: Role of the Entrepreneur	Interpersonal Leadership (Humanistic View): Role of the Entrepreneur
CEO/president	• Set goals • Review performance • Control what needs to be done in specific situations	• Interaction is more personal; visions, goals, values are co-created by the team. • Allows the order in chaos to find itself, trusting in the people.

Employee selection/ retention	• Selection based on skill set	• Selection based on passion, because the individual development program is capable of training any skill set. • Seeks alignment of values between the individual and the organization.
Technical expert/ operations manager	• Tell and show people what to do • Perform operational duties	• Creates self-correcting processes that enable learning. • Transforms technical knowledge into organizational knowledge. • Focuses on organizational growth and establishment of processes that perpetuate growth.
Facilitation of learning	• Hire consultants • Personally conducts training	• Creates learning processes for individual development. • Fosters a learning environment along with learning goals to balance performance. • Maximizes individual expertise for knowledge transfer.
Decision making	• Makes all important decisions • Puts out fires constantly • Maintain center of attention	• Empowers team members with diverse decisions (apply the GEM process). • Maximizes efficiency of GEM. • Stays out of the center of attention.

REFERENCES

1. D. Goleman, R. Boyatzis, and A. McKee (2002). *Primal leadership: Realizing the power of emotional intelligence.* Boston: Harvard Business School Press. This book presents information concerning the wisdom/intelligence of the group as a collective. It provides information on studies that showed evidence to support the fact that significant intelligence improvements are exhibited in effective groups compared with individual intelligence. In terms of intelligence, the group is greater than the sum of its parts. When leaders can effectively manage the group dynamics, the collective intelligence will always be more than the smartest person in the group.

2. F. J. Landy and J. M. Conte (2004). *Work in the 21st century: An introduction to industrial and organizational psychology.* New York: McGraw-Hill. This is a text on organizational psychology. It contains countless studies on human behaviors. Many of the studies on group diversity offer insights into preferences of groups and the outcome of diverse groups. One study found that homogeneity appears to be a preference over diversity. Other studies found that heterogeneous groups are more effective in the long run, as long as groups resolved their differences and stayed intact.

3. E. K. Ngwainmbi (2004, Fall). Communication in the Chinese classroom. *Education* 125(1), 63–76. This article presented research concerning the communication preferences of Chinese students. It found that communication is impacted by both political principles and the Chinese attitude toward collectivism as opposed to individual values.

It also found that these students are inquisitive learners willing to acquire knowledge from nontraditional sources.

4. J. L. Juodvalkis, B. A. Grefe, M. Hogue, D. J. Svyantek, and W. DeLamarter (2003). The effects of job stereotype, applicant gender, and communication style on ratings in screening interviews. *International Journal of Organizational Analysis* 11(1), 67–85. This research article collected some great prior research on communication styles and gender expectations. The authors also conducted a study wherein the likelihood of being hired is assessed when males and females play their respective stereotypical communication styles (female—submissive communication style and males—dominant communications style).

5. W. Chen, R., Jacobs, and L. M. Spencer (1998). *Working with emotional intelligence.* New York: Bantam Books. This book found that emotional intelligence contributes up to 90 percent of an individual's performance. Based on these research studies, a high EQ is a sought-after characteristic in leaders of organizations.

6. D. A. Moran (2001, Fall). The emotional intelligence of managers: Assessing the construct validity of a nonverbal measure of "people skills." *Journal of Business and Psychology* 16(1), 21–33.

7. P. Checkland (1999). *Systems thinking, systems practice: A 30 year retrospective.* New York: John Wiley & Sons. This book is a bit on the technical side, but it provides an incredibly detailed perspective on systems thinking. It clearly lays out the process for analyzing organizational processes and concerns using systems diagrams that clearly illustrate the powerful forces at play between the numerous interactions that occur in the web of relationships. According to systems thinking, once you understand the interconnectivities of the system, you can solve many challenges at the root of problems.

8. R. Jacques (1996). *Manufacturing the employee: Management knowledge from the 19th to 21st centuries.* Thousand Oaks, CA: Sage Publications. This book provides a historical rationale for the concepts of management. The hierarchical nature of organizations is meant to place people into functional roles and control ideas. Because scarcity mentality dominates many organizations, ideas equal power. To control power and influence, people are placed into rigid contexts of job roles.

9. D. S. Chan (2005, July). Relationship between generation-responsive leadership behaviors and job satisfaction of generation X and Y professionals. ProQuest Dissertations. Chan's study of leaders from different generations reveals the need to be adaptable with specific behaviors. Not only are cultures important to building relationships, the different age groups also need different ways to lead them.

10. Physicians Committee for Responsible Medicine (2006). Retrieved on November 10, 2006, from www.pcrm.org. This Web site provides an enormous amount of research data that surprise many people, because the marketing message by producers often hides these facts. For instance, the caffeine in coffee has many negative side effects that people don't realize. For many people, caffeine slightly increases the loss of calcium. It also stays in our bloodstream longer than we think while increasing our metabolism. For some women, caffeine also makes PMS much worse than it has to be.

11. P. Boghossian (2006, March). Socratic pedagogy, critical thinking, and inmate education. *Journal of Correctional Education* 57(1), 42–64. Outlines the potential of Socratic methods as a tool for empowerment and education.

12. P. Areeda (1996, March). The Socratic method (Lecture at Puget Sound). *Harvard Law Review* 109(5), 911–23. This article illustrates the application of Socratic methods within a classroom setting.

PART IV

PLANNING AND SYSTEMS MANAGEMENT

This final section focuses on establishing processes and systems that help your organization thrive without you. One of the most challenging aspects of entrepreneurship is knowing how to make the business passive so that your freedom is not limited. As workplace stress and burnout continues to grow,[1] I've witnessed countless entrepreneurs with some degree of success lose interest after they've been working 60–80 hours per week with no real vacations. In one instance, one of the entrepreneurs had not gone on a vacation in nearly nine years. Utilizing the planning techniques and systems outlined here, many busy entrepreneurs learned to steal life back from their business.[2,3]

This section also begins to tie together many of the previous behaviors. As you develop an understanding in each of the chapters, you'll begin to realize that these behaviors are connected. Some of the external behaviors, although they appear to be easier to implement, require a foundation. For example, behaviors for constant learning and self-confidence are a prerequisite to planning and not being surprised. You may know someone, even yourself, who has been to a planning workshop in the past. How much sustainable impact did the workshop have on their lives? Within the foundations, the latter behaviors would likely be short-lived.

REFERENCES

1. C. Maslach and M. P. Leiter (1997). *The truth about burnout: How organizations cause personal stress and what to do about it*. San Francisco, CA: Jossey-Bass. This book highlights all the symptoms of workplace burnout and offers some methods to resolve these issues.

2. C. McCain (2003). True vacationing. *Business First-Columbus, Bizjournals*. This article featured some business owners who were able to go on real vacations, leaving the cell phone, pager, and email at work while mentally being apart from the business.

3. C. Bent Findly (2003). Holistic approach goes beyond the office. *Business First-Columbus, Bizjournals.* This article featured a client who learned that business isn't just about managing finances. This entrepreneur learned to understand the importance of balance in life.

CHAPTER THIRTEEN

Behavior 9: Being Surprised

Successful entrepreneurs are not often surprised. This behavior provides a sense of peace that links to the overall perception of success. On the surface, being surprised is simply a reaction to an event. Yet the makeup of being surprised is a bit more complex.

Being surprised is a state of emotional confusion. This confusion occurs between the actual events perceived by one's senses and the interpretation of those events. By understanding how to separate the interpretation from the events, successful entrepreneurs can use surprises as a reflection of their inner selves. Along with a focus on diligent planning, these entrepreneurs are able to embrace surprises.

SEPARATING INTERPRETATION
FROM EVENTS

An internal behavior to minimize surprises comes from the ability to separate one's interpretation of events from the event itself. When people see events as crises, the limiting reactions that occur lead to a mentality of fire-fighting. The lack of ability to make this separation causes this mental state.

In a leadership development course, the topic of being accountable for timeliness presented some fascinating discussions. The discussion on timeliness focused on being on time for course meetings. How to be on time and how to have integrity for one's own commitments presented a number of alternatives. The leadership group chose to allow self-management as a means to having integrity. As the program progressed (this was a nine-month program with sessions every other week), the number of late arrivals increased from one to two and then to four. Due to the increase in tardiness, a new discussion was sought to understand the rationale behind this phenomenon. The base of the rationale was a choice to be late, as other events perceived as important or crucial took priority over integrity.

Stop and reflect for a second on the last time you were late for something. Did you make a conscious choice to be late? What was the crisis that was more important than keeping your word?

As the group discussed the various crises, of which every late arrival had a rational explanation, it became obvious that the interpretation of the event dominated the rationale. As I listened to each of the stories, I saw a degree of co-dependence that placed the leader in an "I am needed" mentality. Shortly after a heated discussion, one of the late arrivals commented that if he had not scheduled his time so tightly, he would have never been there for this crisis to happen. Because he chose to leave at the last minute for the training session, the crisis caught him as he was stepping out of the door. What a brilliant deduction!

Let's go a bit further with that. When people come to you with a crisis, you help them resolve that issue. In that person's mind, you've just created a co-dependent relationship where you are the hero that saves the day. What if you weren't available to get the crisis? Do you think that individual is capable enough to find another way to resolve the problem? Sometimes, by *not* being there, you are truly empowering others. Think back to a time when one of your people tried to reach you with a challenge and failed to do so. Did that challenge eventually resolve itself without you? This is one of the ultimate accomplishments of successful entrepreneurs. They don't need to be the hero. If you feel like you need to be the hero, consider this thought—how arrogant are you to think that you have to be the one to fix that person's crisis?

I understand that this can be a bitter pill to swallow. But look at the consequences of not doing so. An average work week for entrepreneurs ranges from 60 to 80 hours; most of it is putting out fires—every spark and speck of smoke they can find. After a few years, they begin to lose sight of the reasons they started their businesses. Are you tired of working too hard? You do not have to. You have a choice!

The choice rests within your mind's filtering system. According to research, the human brain processes over 400 billion bits of information per second. Yet we're only aware of 2,000 or so, which include the environment, the body, and the passage of time.[2] In essence, we're not even aware of 0.01 percent of the information we receive. Think back to a time when you were in a busy room filled with people having multiple conversations. All of a sudden, your ears picked up your name from across the room. All of a sudden, your attention allowed you to listen to a specific conversation. Your mind has an incredible power to perceive what you place your attention on.

Your ability to filter what you want is an automatic response of pattern matching that enables your mind to make sense of all that information. When you're in fire-fighting mode or are stressed out, your mind will probably look for someone or something to blame. These negative emotions push you to respond with aggression and rigidity.[1] Regardless of how intelligent an individual is under normal circumstances, negative emotions limit responses because every situation becomes a crisis.

A few years back, I met an entrepreneur, Bobby, who had a multimillion-dollar business. Cash flow challenges placed Bobby in a tough place in the beginning of the year. He was under a great deal of stress. I was visiting him when a vendor stopped by to pick up a check for products delivered. Bobby informed the vendor that there was no check and asked if they could extend the invoice for 30 days. The vendor responded by refusing the request and putting Bobby's business on a cash only basis for the future. Under normal conditions, you know exactly how to handle such a situation. But under the negative emotions that Bobby was under, he saw that as an attack. All of a sudden, he went off the deep end and created a crisis. "Why are you doing this to me?" he screamed. "Do you want me not to pay my people or feed myself?" Immediately, Bobby became a victim who felt cheated and betrayed. After the vendor left, he informed me that he'd never work with this vendor again.

Such interpretations are devastating to small businesses. Shortly after the incident, more surprises hit Bobby. I learned that more incidents had occurred over similar issues with employees and other vendors. Each self-made crisis increased Bobby's stress level. As negative emotions increased, each crisis became more dramatic. Within the year, Bobby had to sell the business for a deeply discounted price.

To avoid such a downward spiral, successful entrepreneurs should understand the delicate nature of human emotions. They're able to think through surprises with a more delicate approach and separate interpretations from the events themselves. Here are the basic steps when you find your emotions stirring in the face of a situation. To make this meaningful, let's use an example that you've just discovered an employee talking on her cell phone while at work.

1. *Identify the feeling first.* This skill is one of the core basics of emotional intelligence. Unfortunately, we're raised to seek validation from others rather than acknowledge our own feelings and emotions.[3] It takes tremendous courage to face our own feelings, especially those that are negative. Stop yourself from reacting and ask yourself: "what am I feeling right now?" Regardless of what emotions come up, work to describe the emotion with multiple words. In some situations, you should state that emotion verbally. Let others know how you're feeling; allow the emotion to speak authentically and choose your descriptions to maintain ownership of those emotions. For example, you might say "I feel angry and hurt."

   When looking at the person on the cell phone, you might immediately judge that person to be unethical, because he or she is choosing to talk on the time that you're paying him or her. You may feel emotions of betrayal or anger. When describing the emotions you feel, you find yourself to be angry, irate, and hostile.

2. *Connect with the past.* As these describing words enter your mind, ask

yourself another question: "what happened in my past that caused similar emotions? What am I really responding to?" Often, your responses are programmed responses for protection. Because so much information hits our brain, responses are often automatic, especially when you're under stress. Once you see the past event, ask yourself to see the facts. What does this event have anything to do with the past event?

Having defined your emotions, thoughts of the past appeared when you last encountered a server at a restaurant who kept you waiting for several minutes while he talked on the phone with his girlfriend. You were in a rush to pay your bill and leave the restaurant for an important meeting. When you got to the meeting, your tardiness lost a huge deal that would have given your business a guaranteed revenue base over the next three years. Your anger at that server was intoxicating to the point that you would have hurt him if he was standing there. Thinking further, you find that the last situation has nothing to do with this one. You are in no hurry right now and have no idea why your employee is on the phone or how long she'll stay on.

3. *Separation*. While acknowledging the current emotion, begin the see the event by itself. When you have the ability to use both the talents of your heart in emotional intelligence and the wisdom of your head in intellect, you will successfully create a desired future. Based on the separation and a desired future, engage in a conversation that empowers you.

Now, you can clearly see the difference between your interpretation of an event and the actual event. You'll begin to shift a surprised mind reacting to a past event toward a calm mind that engages by choice. You'll choose from the following realities.

a. Interpretation and response: I can't believe she's on the cell phone during working hours. Doesn't she know she's being paid to work? Why is she stealing time from me and upsetting the customers? I'm going to tell her to get off the phone or else I'll find someone else to do the job. Better yet, all employees will turn in their cell phones when they enter work. No questions asked, just a new mandate.

b. Event and response: I feel angry, irate, and hostile, which has nothing to do with the employee on the phone. She's usually a great customer service person. There must be a reasonable explanation for this phone call. I'm going to ask her, "Is everything okay? Can I take over so that you can take this call?"

The two different realities create very opposite responses. The first is an emotional outburst/interpretation that causes a significant conflict. The second lets the employee know that you see the action and choose to be helpful by offering assistance. More important, what if the employee is on the phone with a doctor, discussing the health of her mother? How embarrassed would you be if you chose to see only your interpretation, if your employee ever tells you? Look at the opposite side—by choosing to respond to the event alone, you've increased trust.

Life is often a mirror of what we love and fear the most. For every pet peeve, there is an underlying fear that you may take on the trait yourself. Every hero or mentor in your life exhibits traits that you desire. Regardless of external realities, you're always empowered to look within yourself to understand the emotions that fire up your defenses and ambitions. Sometimes, a person in your life reminds you of your fears; other times, you will find someone to model yourself after. In both situations, your choice to interpret the event itself or to accept only an response to that event can create a paradise, a hell, or somewhere in between. Successful entrepreneurs choose wisely without being surprised.

ENTREPRENEURIAL PLANNING SECRETS

Another behavior that minimizes surprises is the process of careful and systematic planning. Successful entrepreneurs take time to plan, and their self-confidence helps them navigate the surprises as fascinating lessons. In traditional literature, both long-term and short-term perspectives on planning play a role in success.[4] The planning process also incorporates organizational communication. No plan will be successful unless the members of the organization truly embody its wisdom and insights. Communicating plans, visions, and core values help others set effective goals at individual levels that assist in creating a profitable business.[5] Clear communication skills are also consistent with transformational leadership.[6] Unfortunately, the lack of tactical information on communication significantly limits communication skills development. In my experience with teaching students across the world, most understand the importance of communication skills in leading an organization. Yet when asked to articulate what they intend to do to improve those skills, most fall short of any actionable ideas. Therefore, this section covers both the act of planning and its communication throughout the organization.

Planning and organizing are important to any business.[4] Specialists in corporate America teach planning and organizing knowledge. Large corporations may use many planning models such as Piercy and Morgan's model of strategic marketing planning.[7] They have the resources or funds to obtain experts in planning. Do entrepreneurs have such resources? You may not seen a model of good planning or communication until now. Research indicates that entrepreneurs rarely use or apply planning knowledge and formalized methodologies.[8,9] Due to the lack of formalized planning, reactive strategies negatively impact success.[10]

Two types of planning are crucial to success. Long-term planning includes strategic planning and visioning. Strategy is a high-level direction of the company. Although it presents some specific benchmarks and controls, strategy contains little detail. An example of a strategy is to be the lowest cost provider. The detailed actions are tactics. Short-term planning includes the design and execution of tactics. For entrepreneurs, long-term planning is an ideal starting point. The optimal time frame is more than five years out. In some case, 10 years is ideal because the further out in time, the greater the stretch of the vision.

One of the glass ceilings that weighs on many people's minds is the constant focus on "how to." During a focus group discussion on planning and visioning, a group of successful entrepreneurs had a tough time dreaming up an audacious vision for themselves. The majority ended up with the basics of a family and a passive business. A few found more ambitious visions such as changing the world and winning the Nobel prize for a technology innovation. This remarkable phenomenon had two distinguishing characteristics. Those who could dream of something great were immigrants, not born in the United States. Although we can get into many reasons on why this was the case, it's not something you can change in yourself. The other aspect that was interesting was the lack of focus on the how, while the others were all concerned with how they were going to get there. In further investigations, entrepreneurs with audacious visions realized the achievement well in the future (at least 5 to 10 years out). They were not concerned with limitations of today, nor were they concerned with the complexity of the strategies of how to obtain that vision. Based on the research, the following long-term planning process provides a path to your audacious vision. Utilizing the GEM process in the previous chapter, involving the people of the organization creates congruence and cohesion while minimizing the difficulties in communicating the plans.

Long-Term Planning Process

1. Start with a blank piece of paper and some magazines with lots of pictures.
2. Write at the top of the paper "10-year vision" and the question "who are we in 10 years?"
3. Push yourself to create at least 10 vision statements. Make sure they are impacts of actions, not actions or strategies themselves. For example, a common misstep is to say "to be the best in the country." Thinking further than being the best, what will being the best get you? What's the impact of being the best to the world? Who will you impact? Another common tactic in this process is to start with the mentality—if I have no fear of failure, where would I go and who would I be?

    In some cases, this process is visual. Particularly when communicating a thought, pictures can speak a thousand words. The internal dialogue with yourself in this process is to envision something great. The magazines represent some form of reality that you'd like to achieve. Especially for organizations that need an injection of motivation and creativity, I have used a vision collage to stretch the imagination. Remember the last time you made a collage? Probably sometime in elementary school was your last chance. Creating a visual image of your dreams is a powerful tool. For example, like most people, entrepreneurs would typically cut out their dream home or vacation. One specific trend that I've seen in dream collages is the picture of a clock or an hourglass representing freedom or control of time. Imagine the effort required to read a vision statement; compare that with the effort it takes to see a visual picture of that vision statement. The more often organizational members observe the visual vision, the more it motivates them.[11]

4. From the list, use a basic process of elimination to define the top vision(s). If you're conducting this as a group process, which is highly recommended, use the multivoting process to finalize the 10-year vision.

5. From the long-term vision, start moving closer to the present. Establish a 5- and a 3-year vision by looking at the steps required to achieve the 10-year vision. As you facilitate this process within a group or for yourself, maintain distance from the need to know exactly *how* to accomplish it. Depending on your industry, a three-year vision may begin to fold into a mission statement that provides a tangible goal.

6. Establish a mission statement based on the vision and values of the organization. You can choose to have a single statement or break it down into one-year and three-year statements, depending on the trends of your industry. Some of the fast-moving industries, such as the technology industry, may change too often to set a mission for three years out. The mission statement is usually one or two sentences with specifics on organizational functions and the target customer base. It may start with high-level strategies like "to enhance" or "to inspire and empower."

7. Once the high-level visions and missions are complete, allow the functional groups to design strategies, tactics, implementation plans, and measurements. One of the challenges for many entrepreneurs is to let go of some vital tasks. If you don't learn to delegate effectively, failure is likely.[12] Tasks such as strategic planning, tactical design, and tactical execution empower your people. Although many fears exist to justify the lack of delegation, consider the motivation of your closest customer. How much harder would you work on ensuring success if you're the one who came up with that idea? If you feel you need to be involved, play the role of a regular team member as discussed in the GEM process.

The long-term plans are complete but they are only a reflection of the current environment. Like any living document in fluid learning organization, annual reviews using similar processes ensure alignment of the organization to its people and the environment. Short-term planning naturally comes after the long-term planning is complete. On a strategic level, everyone's involvement in designing the strategies creates ownership. One of the primary competitive advantages to retaining your people rests with the level of involvement in higher level functions. The more involvement the organization realizes, the greater the ownership, which leads to greater effort. More important, it also allows entrepreneurs to work less.

With respect to short-term planning, the GEM process provides a context for optimal creation of ideas, tactics, and plans of execution. As you're walking through the process, create measurements that track every possible tactic. We'll discuss this later in Chapter 14.

Within the execution of various tactics, planning also involves organization of daily activities. The most efficient method of task execution and peace of mind is the purpose of a default schedule. I learned this from a coaching franchise called Action International. Further studies using default scheduling have noted incredible achievements based on clear focus of the mind. Although the default scheduling process takes a few months to plan out, it clearly identifies the amount of time required for each activity. Previous chapters established the foundation of tasks to values alignment; they also highlighted the importance of critical thinking before blind engagement (sleep walking). The default schedule is a tool that places all activities within a set plan.

Default Schedule Process

1. Determine the different roles you need to play in your organization. List them in order of importance with respective estimated time spent on them during the work week. This becomes your ideal time breakdown. If you've done the activities on task-values alignment in Chapter 10, you have a sufficient starting point of how you spend your time. For fun, compare the ideal time breakdown with those from the task-values alignment exercise.

2. Use a spreadsheet program and create a template like the one shown in Figure 13-1. Planning does not require expensive tools. A simple spreadsheet works fine.

3. Use the ideal time breakdown to block times out. To maximize your focus, mark key activities in at least one-hour time blocks. This dramatically increases your effectiveness in accomplishing tasks.

4. After you've planned out the entire week, this schedule becomes a guide for your work life. When you get requests from customers on concerns, you simply place them into an available time slot. This way, you'll always know exactly when times are available from week to week.

5. Share the default schedule with your entire organization. Ask workers to respect this schedule, as you will on their default schedules. Implementation of this concept at an organizational level reduces mistakes while significantly increasing productivity, because interruptions are minimized. The toughest part of this implementation is to hold your boundaries. When you need to focus on activities, turn off the phone and the email clients. Having an organized rotation for receiving customers and clients with the

Sample Default Schedule

Time	Monday	Tuesday	Wednesday	Thursday	Friday
8:00	Personal Reflection	Personal Reflection	Personal Reflection	Personal Reflection	Personal Reflection
8:30	Weekly Planning	Learning	Measurements	Learning	Measurements
9:00	Team Meeting	Learning	Measurements	Learning	Measurements
9:30	Team Meeting	Sales	Measurements	Sales	Measurements
10:00	Customer Relationsips	Sales	Customer Relationsips	Sales	Customer Relationsips
10:30	Customer Relationsips	Sales	Customer Relationsips	Sales	Customer Relationsips
11:00	Customer Relationsips	Customer Relationsips	Customer Relationsips	Customer Relationsips	Customer Relationsips
11:30	check email	check email	check email	check email	check email
12:00	Lunch	Lunch	Lunch	Lunch	Lunch
12:30	Lunch	Lunch	Lunch	Lunch	Lunch
1:00	Marketing	Marketing	Marketing	Marketing	Marketing
1:30	Marketing	Marketing	Marketing	Marketing	Marketing
2:00	Marketing	Marketing	Marketing	Marketing	Marketing
2:30	Org. Deve / Employee Dev.	Org. Deve / Employee Dev.	Org. Deve / Employee Dev.	Org. Deve / Employee Dev.	Org. Deve / Employee Dev.
3:00	Org. Deve / Employee Dev.	Org. Deve / Employee Dev.	Org. Deve / Employee Dev.	Org. Deve / Employee Dev.	Org. Deve / Employee Dev.
3:30	External Meetings	Systemiazation	External Meetings	Systemiazation	Systemiazation
4:00	External Meetings	Systemiazation	External Meetings	Systemiazation	Systemiazation
4:30	Systemiazation	Accounting	Systemiazation	Accounting	check email
5:00	Systemiazation	Accounting	Systemiazation	Accounting	Weekly Summary
5:30	check email	check email	check email	check email	Family
6:00	Task Review	Task Review	Task Review	Task Review	Family

FIGURE 13-1.   Sample of a default schedule for an entrepreneur during the growth years of a business. This default schedule lays out time blocks based on the priorities of the entrepreneur. Each time block focuses on a specific task without external distractions such as phone calls or emails.

rest of your team will provide a level of consistency as well as cross-training the staff.

The default schedule is an easy tool to design. After you've created it, adjustments are natural as you learn about your efficiencies throughout the day. For some people, learning times are ideal in the morning; for others, they prefer to learn in the evening. The toughest part of the default schedule is maintaining your personal boundaries. If your default schedule commits you to marketing activities such as searching for strategic alliances, do not engage in a different mentality such as answering phone calls. This schedule provides the maximum amount of focus.

One amusing method of enforcement that' has proven to be effective with many people is to have random boundary explorers. Ask a few people to push against your commitment to the default schedule. They can take occasional and random actions, like calling you when you're not supposed to be answering the phone. Others have chosen to walk into an individual's office with a random issue during a focus time. To win the game, all actions by boundary explorers are ignored or reorganized into the proper time slot. A successful entrepreneur will not answer the phone because the ringer is off. He or she will ask the boundary explorers in the office to look at the default schedule posted at the office door and return during the respective time slot.

Although these are simple concepts, it takes a great deal of courage to stand strong in your boundaries. I had one client who had a small office of five people, and the majority of the workforce served clients. The executive assistant, Marcy, was quite a capable woman. Her responsibilities were diverse and included handling customer issues, administrative duties for the two owners, scheduling service jobs, and accounts payable/receivable. Does this sound like some of your people, wearing many different hats? It's tough to manage all of it.

When I initially worked with the organization, evidence of stress between the various groups landed on Marcy's desk. Because she was the one who tied it all together, any mistake in one area could cause a ripple effect. As good as she was at her job, there was always a small amount of mistakes that led to conflict with the owners and challenges with customers. Like in normal workplaces, the blame went to Marcy because she was supposed to minimize errors at all costs. Yet no actual tools or strategies were given to her to accomplish such goals. Does this sound familiar? As you read this section, you should have the wisdom to provide and support your people with tactical methods of resolving problems.

Marcy, along with the rest of the organization, learned to use the default schedule. As a customer service individual, Marcy had a lot of resistance because she had to answer every phone call that came in. Yet these constant disruptions pushed her focus to a different area that led to mistakes. As a compromise, others in the office answered phone calls during certain times of the day. This provided Marcy room to focus and accomplish significantly more in that single-task time. The toughest challenge was to get the owners of the business to respect this default schedule. In the past, the owners were used to going to Marcy when they felt the need to ask a question. To stop this interruption, Marcy placed the default schedule on her desk with a plastic holder. Time blocks for no disruption were marked with red. For a few weeks, anytime someone went to Marcy's desk to ask for something during the blocked-out time, she chose not to respond and pointed to the default schedule. Soon, everyone in the office knew when not to interrupt her, including the owners. As a result, Marcy's productivity increased dramatically, errors in all aspects of her responsibilities decreased, and she was happy! Furthermore, the cross-training in answering customer calls by other staff members taught others lessons on the challenges of this task. Their alternative perspectives were able to produce innovations that enhanced communications throughout the organization.

This strategy of a default schedule planned respective responsibilities that enabled effective execution of tactics. In other situations, some innovative ways to establish one's boundaries used hats and lights. For instance, during single-task focus periods, some people wore hats that stated "Focused Wisdom at Work" or "Do Not Disturb The Brilliance." Some got more creative with little red lights on their doors or the walls of their cubical that indicated alone time. Regardless of what you choose to do, effective tactical execution comes from minimal interruptions throughout the organization. When individuals successfully lay out their default schedules, you will notice a dramatic increase in productivity and organizational knowledge. More important, each individual will find an inner peace about his or her work, leading to reduced stress and lower health care costs.

The final piece of the planning puzzle is the communication component. Because significant strands of literature talk about the key to effectively communicate emotions,[5] tasks,[12] goals, and visions,[6] the question to consider is, are all of this communication necessary? Is communication simply a bandage for not involving people in the first place? If you need to communicate anything to another person, that person has a stake in the information. What if you involved them in the beginning?

In some situations, the need to communicate indicates a systemic issue of the lack of involvement. When possible, in crucial areas such as business planning, strategy, marketing, and employee development/compensation, involve people with open-ended discussions. Make use of the collective wisdom of the team and watch the ownership of ideas, plans, strategies, and processes increase individual efforts across all levels of the organization. Of course, involving and empowering others requires self-confidence. Without the confidence in yourself, you'll be less likely to have confidence in your people. Your people, in turn, will have limited confidence in your abilities. Attempting to create such involvement under these conditions may not yield the desired results. This is why the analysis of self and self-leadership must be present before implementation of powerful concepts like this one. Human beings are a lot more complicated than machines that can just be reprogrammed.

In other situations where communication is required, knowledge and application of neurolinguistic programming (NLP) is a powerful persuasive tool.[13,14,15] Although the theory is much more complex than what can be covered here, a basic and powerful tenet of NLP is communication modalities. Human beings have three primary communication modalities: visual, auditory, and kinesthetic. Visual communication occurs in pictures, drawings, and reading. Learning by doing is kinesthetic communication. This form of communication does not always have to be doing the actual task. Writing down directions given is one form of kinesthetic communication. When people listen and write down what they hear, they're engaged in both auditory and kinesthetic communication. The most common form of communication is auditory, which is simply talking to one another, whether over the phone or in person.

Most business communication happens over conversations, but the majority of main communication modalities occur over the other two mediums, visual and kinesthetic. Auditory communication is the lowest of the three modalities (approximately 20 percent; visual and kinesthetic divides the remainder). Did you ever wonder why there are phrases like "in one ear, out the other?" For most people, auditory communication provides the least amount of retention. A study by Cornell University revealed that lecture or verbal communication of knowledge only yields a 5 percent rate of retention[16]. Those people whom you've judged to "not listen well" or be "poor listeners" may have stronger visual or kinesthetic communication modalities. Imagine that you're responsible for the communication and have the potential to change the outcome. Are you aware of your primary communication modality? Think back to your primary or secondary education—did you do well in some subjects and struggled in others? The conventional wisdom might blame your abilities; using several communication modalities, the teacher might have been influential in your performance. For example, if a teacher mostly lectured, visual and kinesthetic learners have to work harder to learn and retain the materials. (As a bonus for getting this far in the book, consider taking the time to determine your children's communication modality. Once they have an understanding, they can use it to reach excellence in any subject.)

From the business perspective, identify the communication modalities of those with whom you are communicating. Especially with plans, whether long- or short-term, the vast information involved in strategies, tactics, and dates is daunting. Using all three communication modalities will ensure that every individual retains maximum information. Using the GEM process for planning incorporates all three modalities, and thus inspires a significantly high ownership in the plans. The visual picture of long-term plans engages visual communication. Asking individuals to pass around the pictures and explain the vision of the organization engages kinesthetic as well as auditory and visual communication modalities.

The higher your consciousness in identifying and applying communication modalities in everyday relationships, the more success you'll achieve. The more you actively plan and communicate, the less you'll be surprised. In reality, the ultimate goal of an entrepreneur is to work less and get more—more inner peace, more free time, more enjoyment out of life. These tools play a key role in that attainment.

REFERENCES

1. C. Maslach and M. P. Leiter (1997). *The truth about burnout: How organizations cause personal stress and what to do about it.* San Francisco, CA: Jossey-Bass. This

book highlights all the symptoms of workplace burnout and some methods to resolve these issues.

2. *What the bleep do we know!?* (2004). Lord of the Wind Films (producer). Captured Light Industries. This is a great movie that points out the different realities that are available. The film provides testimony of many scientific minds to support the countless realities that we can choose.

3. R. K. Cooper and A. Sawaf (1998). *Executive EQ: Emotional intelligence in business.* Berkley, CA: Berkley Publishing Group. An excellent text on emotional intelligence. It provides many useful tools on how to understand your feelings. Emotional literacy is one of the four pillars of emotional intelligence.

4. K. H. Chadwick (1998). An empirical analysis of the relationships among entrepreneurial orientation, organizational culture and firm performance. ProQuest Digital Dissertations (UMI No. 9840688). This is a dissertation looking at the various dimensions of entrepreneurial orientation, which is a group of behaviors that entrepreneurs possess. Long-term and short-term planning had an impact on firm performance.

5. S. A. Kirkpatrich and E. A. Locke (1991, May). Leadership: Do traits matter? *Academy of Management Executive* 5(2), 48–60. This article highlights specific leadership traits that support organizational success. One specific characteristic that seems to be consistent with many other research studies is effective planning to achieve a vision, along with a drive for implementation. Other traits mentioned include drive, leadership motivation, honesty and integrity, self-confidence, cognitive ability, and knowledge of the business.

6. B. M. Bass (1985). *Leadership and performance beyond expectations.* New York: Free Press. A great book on transformational leadership and some of the basic leadership behaviors that attribute to organizational success. One of the key behaviors is clear communication of key information, such as organizational vision, plans, and mission.

7. N. Dennis and D. R. Macaulay (2003, September). Jazz and marketing planning. *Journal of Strategic Marketing* 11(3), 177–86. This article discussed the implications of rigid and structured planning processes such as Piercy and Morgan's (1994) marketing planning model. It highlights the greater levels of creativity and innovation that come from techniques of jazz improvisation. These techniques offer greater flexibility in planning.

8. R. C. Paige (1999). *Craft retail entrepreneurs' perceptions of success and factors effecting success.* ProQuest Digital Dissertations (UMI No. 9950110). This is a doctoral study of craft retailers. One of the fascinating findings is that entrepreneurs tend to lack a formalized planning process.

9. P. R. Stephens (2000). *Small business and high performance management practices.* ProQuest Digital Dissertations (UMI No. 3040560). This doctoral study looked at various practices that attributes to success. By using the Malcolm Baldrige National Quality Award for Performance Excellence as a measuring tool for entrepreneurs, one of the findings discovered the lack of formalized strategic planning among entrepreneurs.

10. M. Frese (2000). *Success and failure of microbusiness owners in Africa: A psychological approach.* Westport, CT: Quorum. This book illustrates some basic behaviors that leads to success and failure in microbusinesses. The research found that reactive planning, or the lack of formal planning, resulted in negative impacts that may lead to failure.

11. M. McPeek (2005, January 1). *New year resolution with Dr. Ted Sun.* NBC 4, Columbus, Ohio. Retrieved November 12, 2006, from http://www.videogateway.tv/index.php?link=p,details;stream_id,288.

12. R. C. Cuba and G. Milbourn (1982, October/December). Delegating for small business success. *American Journal of Small Business* 7(2), 33–41. This research article specified the impact of delegation to small business success. The authors also outline some basic reasons why entrepreneurs do not delegate. They include fear of losing control, unsure of employee abilities, reluctance to give up what they may enjoy, and lack of management skills.

13. R. Bandler and J. Grinder (1975). *The structure of magic: A book about language and therapy.* Palo Alto, CA: Science and Behavior. This book marks the start of neurolinguistic programming (NLP). It provides a powerful model for behavior and communication. It set the foundations for NLP in its many applications today from education to leadership. Many sales groups use many of its theories today.

14. P. N. Dixon, G. D. Parr, D. Yarbrough, and M. Rathael (1986, August). Neurolinguistic programming as a persuasive communication technique. *Journal of Social Psychology* 126(4), 545–51. This article discussed the power of persuasion that the application of NLP has on group dynamics.

15. S. Balvister and A. Vickers (2004). *Teaching yourself NLP*. Chicago: Contemporary Books. This is a great book on the key principles of NLP. It covered many concepts such as communication modalities and metaphors. To get the most out of this book, plan on taking a few years to read it. As each chapter has so much tactical information, you'll be amazed at the new concepts you can pick up and the impact they'll have on your life.

16. Cornell University, 2004. National Resources Conservation Service, USDA, "Instructional Systems Design (ISD)—Developing Performance Measurements." Retrieved from: http://www.nedc.nrcs.usda.gov/isd/isd8.html—this study found that lecturing only yields 5% retention of knowledge. While reading provides 10%, the combination of audio and visual increases retention to 20%. When action enters into the communication/learning process, retention moves up to over 75%.

CHAPTER FOURTEEN

Behavior 10: Measurements and Responsiveness

Successful entrepreneurs are aware of their environment. This awareness is much more than just a feeling. They often have scientific methods of determining quantifiable information. They monitor, interpret, and respond to both internal and external competitive, economic, and social events. These measurements are often not only outcome-based but learning-based as well. Once the measurements provide information, the entrepreneurs are adoptive and flexible in their response. This chapter covers some basic methods of measurements to obtain a further understanding of your organization and life. Once you have a deeper understanding of the issues, you're empowered to take action immediately. Better yet, empower the team (including customers, employees, vendors, partners, and family) to make self-corrective changes. A holistic measurement system includes multiple dimensions of financial, relational, and humanity. Such a system creates a self-correcting and auto-programming learning organization that thrives in success.[1]

EFFECTIVE MEASUREMENTS: CONTENT

One of the fascinating aspects of our system is that measurements are usually one-dimensional. Performance measures focused on financial numbers determine organizational success.[2] For example, according to business standards, Jack Welch is a respected leader. The typical performance measurements saw his success in the growth of General Electric. Looking beyond the performance, Welch had quite an interesting strategy. He believed in a "lean and mean" business strategy where cutting costs and maximizing efficiencies permeated every level of his organizations. Yet during his reign and in his retirement, Welch enjoyed enormous pleasures from GE, such as company jet, wine, clothes, and multiple residences.[3] Is only one dimension of performance measure enough to truly understand a person (not to mention entire organizations)?

Whether you're a fan of Jack Welch is up to you. Like many other leaders of our time, he obtained his status through a single perspective. Imagine managing a football team by only studying the statistics of the quarterback or only the offense. Would that ever win you the Super Bowl? Consider a popular sport like football. Countless measures look at the many dimensions of a player's emotional, physical, intellectual, nutritional, spiritual, social, and relational status. In this multibillion-dollar industry, a single perspective is far from sufficient. You, too, deserve to have such a multidimensional perspective. The challenge is learning how.

Once I was introduced to an entrepreneur, Ralph, who had a creative service. To start his business, Ralph had to take out some loans, like many entrepreneurs do. His accountant conducted performance measurements from the financial side. During a meeting, Ralph informed me that the accountant had projected a 25 percent increase in business revenues on a quarterly basis. Only seeing the numbers of the business, the accountant informed him that he needed to make sure he hit the numbers to meet his obligations. So, he asked me, "How do I make sure I get that 25 percent increase every quarter?" This was a shocking question. The condition of the business was nowhere near that growth potential, nor were there systems or capacities to enable it to happen. Ralph felt like he got his marching orders from the accountant and had to conform to this figure. Stressed out, Ralph had no idea on how to meet this number. The impact of the communication provided by the accountant was that of an emotional wreck. Ralph felt like he had to close his business, because he had no idea how to reach that 25 percent increase.

This situation illustrates the challenges of looking at a single dimension of a multidimensional business. What are the marketing strategies in place? What's the return on investment of marketing strategies? Where does Ralph's business stand in the industry? How do Ralph's customers feel about the creative service he offers? What alliances or partnerships are established? To fully understand the business, so many more questions needed answers before Ralph could draw a conclusion.

Although financial success is a founding principle of capitalism (the goal is gigantic profits made by individuals),[4] ask yourself this question from a purely logical perspective. Imagine yourself back in high school—would you focus on retirement? Better yet, remember the last time you had your hair cut? The barber used a mirror behind your head to show you in the mirror in front of you what your hair looks like after he is done. If you wanted to make some changes, would the barber attempt to change the image in the mirror behind your head by coloring or painting on that mirror?

This may sound absurd, but is it logical to place such emphasis of measure on something that is merely a reflection of many other contributing factors? When you're in high school, you might focus on getting into college. Once in college, you may focus on getting a job and then a better job. Retirement is many mores stages down the road. So why do organizations place so much emphasis on measuring profits and revenues when it greatly depends on the secondary customers who respond to the type of relationship with your people (see Figure 14-1)? The most crucial measurement one level immediately above the organizational leaders gets minimal attention in most organizations. Is there something wrong with this logic?

The first level of measurement starts with the entrepreneur. The previous chapters on self-leadership focused on the development of self. Once you've implemented a solid understanding of self from the multiple dimensions of intelligence, begin to seek the understanding of relationships and others. Various relational characteristics greatly influence organizational outcomes, such as the level of trust, the amount of empowerment, team cohesion,[3] and values alignment.[5] The next level of measurement is your first-level customers—your people, your employees. The concept of an employee often calls for minimal in-

A Systemic View of Business

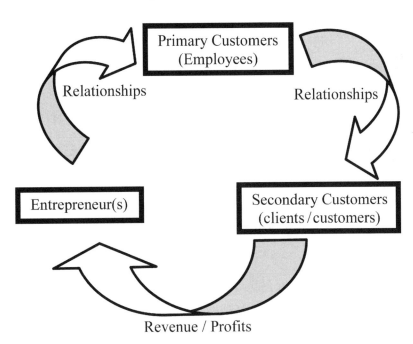

FIGURE 14-1.   A systemic view of business represents crucial dimensions of measurement in a business within relationships and customers. Although the profits/revenues are a few levels down the line, entrepreneurs who focus on relationships with their first- and second-level customers will result in ample revenue and profits. Without a focus on relationships, the existing revenues and profits will be extremely limited and short-lived.

novation and commitment. Ideologies such as "I just work here" doom the connotations of an employee. Instead, use the term *people* for a more neutral tone. The way you begin to think of people may also shift, because your job is not to just employ them but treat them as people.

The people measures include some of the self-leadership measures and a few others, such as a degree of innovation and job satisfaction.[3] The last of these characteristics—job satisfaction—is what most organizations use. Yet when you consider your level of satisfaction, how happy are you? Rather than measuring employee acceptance of you or your organization, seek optimal positive emotions. Measuring job bliss or happiness focus on positive emotions and speak clearly about the purpose of the organization. As you look at the various characteristics, ensure that an inspirational foundation is the basis of any measurement, rather than the conventional fear mentality that drives many measurements in today's organizations. For example, a typical measure is employee lateness or tardiness. Why not measure employee accountability and responsibility? Change employee retention to employee attraction or even employee referrals.

Intangible People Measures Exercise

This exercise is a sample of measures for your first-level customers — your people (Table 14-1). Feel free to expand on this and make your own version, but be sure to follow the contextual issues stated later this chapter.

These high-level statements measure job bliss, stress, and trust with the owner. You could give this measurement to your people on a weekly or even daily basis, depending on your relationship with them. Then input the data into a spreadsheet and plot the trends. You may be able to determine which day (in the week) or week (in the month) appears to be most stressful for your people. By determining a specific time, you can dig deeper to get at the root of what's causing the stress. Too often, organizations can only sense a rise in stress levels. Without

TABLE 14-1. A Quick View of Intangible Measures Concerning One's Responsibilities and Relationships. This is only a start; individual entrepreneurs can add to the list of what's important to them to these measures

Please Rate each Statement to the Best of Your Knowledge	Strongly Disagree		Neutral		Strongly Agree
I feel a sense of accomplishment every day.	1	2	3	4	5
My work is meaningful.	1	2	3	4	5
My present job is blissful.	1	2	3	4	5
I am challenged by my work.	1	2	3	4	5
I feel an acceptable level of stress at work.	1	2	3	4	5
I feel connected with the owner(s).	1	2	3	4	5

knowing what causes them or when it happens, increasing stress levels result in absenteeism, increased health care costs,[6] and unhappy second-level customers. If you learn to measure strategically, you can put a stop to the root cause well before it becomes a problem.

When looking at the relationships between your people and your second-level customers, a similar set of characteristics such as trust determines the relationship. The level of trust is a determinant of any transaction that occurs between your business and your customers. Measuring the amount of trust offers insights into the longevity of any business. For example, people are willing to pay more for a product from a trusted name, as opposed to common producer. Volvo has repeatedly generated a high degree of trust between its customers and its cars for safety. Based on that trust, people pay a premium for a Volvo. The majority of Ford and GM cars compete on price. As a small business, you can't afford to compete on price with larger businesses. Trust is a crucial competitive advantage that determines longevity.

Your customers provide the data for the final type of unconventional measure. Although they are similar to relational measures, there are fundamental tactics for measurement that increases trust. For example, many businesses use customer surveys to get feedback. Unfortunately, the surveys provide insufficient data to make systemic changes and only allow a one-way predicable communication. When using surveys, ask open questions that inspire customers to take ownership of the business. Open-ended questions should challenge customers to be part of the team. Here are a few sample questions to help you get started.

- What would you do to make this place more enjoyable?
- Imagine yourself as the owner of the business and, knowing about your experience with the business, how would you change it?
- What new value would add to your purchasing experience?
- Is there anything we should stop doing?

Because the amount of thought is much more significant than a few check boxes, the motivation for customers to answer these types of questions must be significant. Although the conventional thought is to give money or a gift with a drawing of some type, why give away your profits? Intrinsic motivators are significantly more powerful and sustainable. Imagine at the top of the customer questionnaire that said "thanks to John D., we now have a new JD process. This process enhanced the buying experience of every customer while decreasing the stress levels of our people. Thank you John D.!" This is a costless system where the reward for ideas is the customer name written in "stone" within the business. This measurement system provides further ownership for customers, similar to those who might own stock in a company. Furthermore, the likelihood of patronage to your business increases because we all want to bring our friends to see our names posted on the wall of the business, adding pride to the partnership between business and customers.

Other measures of the second-level customer use personal contact some time after the product is purchased or the service is provided. Most businesses only survey customers immediately after the transaction, so a personal touch some time later to inquire about the impact of the product/service provides a unique approach. Contextually, you're telling the second-level customers that you care about them and want to make sure everything is in working order.

EFFECTIVE MEASUREMENTS: CONTEXT

When you hear a poll conducted by a news station, do you believe its results? Many surveys in the business world lack validity from a scientific perspective. Doctoral students often take multiple courses in scientific research as an initiation to research. To obtain the best output from your measurements, the measures you create contain a specific set of considerations. Because you're looking to create the best measures for your business, these considerations are maintained regardless of your content. Here are four considerations.[7]

1. Keep the language simple and short. If people can't understand what you're asking, they won't answer or will provide the wrong answers. This also means avoid using abbreviations and slang.
2. Provide a single focus. Each question within the measurement should address only one topic. If you use words like *and*, this indicates multiple topics. Break these up into two separate questions. For example, a common question for your first-level customers might be "Am I treated with respect and enjoy my work?" This should be broken into two questions. "Am I treated with respect?" is the first question. "Do I enjoy my work?" would be the second question.
3. Make the questions specific. If you're going to use a scale (such as 1–7), be sure the questions are specific enough so that interpretations are consistent. For example, if you're asking a customer about his or her experience, ask about the specific experience of entering the building, being greeted, the purchase experience, and so on. I've seen many surveys that ask about the overall experience. Although that may be the norm, knowing how a customer enjoyed an overall experience does not give any tactical information. If the customer was unhappy, you still have no clue which part of the experience caused the unhappiness. But when you break the experience down into specific functionalities or personnel, you can make tactical changes immediately.
4. Be neutral with questions. This is where many people have challenges. Because they would like to obtain the best possible results, people often load the questions with biased terms that are leading. For example, "How do you like having the best service in town?" In this question, the term

like presents a bias. What's worse is the "best service" concept, which already tells the customer how to answer the question. An optimized question on service may be "Please rate the service you've received compared to what you expect." Ideally, you'll want to establish a baseline by asking if they have a certain expectation and if they found it positive. In one statement, you could state the following: "I like to be greeted within the first _____ seconds from entrance." Allow the customer to respond with 0–10, 11–20, 21–30, 31–40, and more than 41 seconds. This can establish an expectation so that you can make tactical adjustments.

As you can see, the various measurement considerations take into account the utility of the questions from a tactical perspective. Construct the questions so that the responses translate into responsive tactics. Because measurements provide crucial information, getting a graduate student from a nearby university to help can make the process easier. The entrepreneur provides the content on the various levels mentioned above. Pass that information to a student for them to assess the validation of the measures.

EMBRACE CONSTANT CHANGE

The reality of business is embracing change. Rather than react to change, design responses into the measurement system before events happen. This is how you can lead change and be ahead with minimal surprises. For example, greeting the customer sets the tone for relationship development. You can establish a number of greeting messages and measure the impact of each. Use the Group Empowerment Model (GEM) process to get your people's involvement in creating the greeting message. Start with four to five messages and rotate them over the period of a few months. One successful entrepreneur uses "Hi, welcome to XYZ, how can we make you smile today?" Another uses, "Good morning, how can we solve your challenges today?" You can easily use the team to derive many different tactics ahead of time and experiment with them on a regular basis.

Another key aspect of change for entrepreneurs to embrace is the ideas of others, especially those of the customers. Various open-ended questions established a framework for you to obtain customer ideas. As an entrepreneur, you don't have to be the one that comes up with all the ideas. Being responsive involves others in the problem resolution and empowers them to take it on. You always have two levels of customers that provide vital knowledge. First, your people in the organization have plenty of ideas. Have an open forum to hear them and empower them to make changes. Your second-level customers have ideas from a different perspective. Use open-ended questions and one-on-one discussions to obtain their insights. From either source, when you implement the ideas, name the new process or ask them to name it.

Imagine an organization with people's names all over the place. Each process has a story behind it; some are from your people in the organization who made a profound change; others are of second-level customers who suggested something. All of these improvements come from the people within your community. These people will often bring others to see their names in action. Some people may add their names to the honors list. Measurement systems empower organizations to be incredibly adaptive. As long as entrepreneurs create the context of responsiveness, organizations will thrive by leading change, regardless of size.

REFERENCES

1. P. Checkland (1999). *Systems thinking, systems practice: A 30-year retrospective.* New York: John Wiley & Sons. This book is a bit on the technical side but provides an incredibly detailed perspective on systems thinking. A crucial aspect of seeing organizations as systems is that they can become self-learning, self-correcting systems. As long as subsystems (people) within a system realize the interconnectedness of all members and their potential impact, perpetuation of success is possible.

2. G. H. Seijts and G. P. Latham (2005) Learning versus performance goals: When should each be used? *Academy of Management Executive* 19(1), 124–31. This research article refused the conventional wisdom of outcome-based goals. Because they creates competition and unnecessary fears on individuals, outcome-based goals are not appropriate in many organizational settings. The authors propose learning goals as an alternative, focusing on individual experimentation of new knowledge.

3. F. J. Landy and J. M. Conte (2004). *Work in the 21st century: An introduction to industrial and organizational psychology.* New York: McGraw-Hill. This is a great text on the foundations of organizational psychology. One of the studies illustrates lack of consistency between principles applied toward all aspects of Jack Welch's organization and those that applied to Welch himself.

4. M. Parker and G. Pearson (2005, August). Capitalism and its regulation: A dialogue on business and ethics. *Journal of Business Ethics* 60(1), 91–101. This is an article that captured a fascinating dialogue on what capitalism is and identifies the ethical challenges that exists in capitalism's basic principles.

5. T. Sun (2006, October). Leading sustainable change through self-discovery: A values accountability system defined. *United Nations Global Forum: "Business as an Agent of World Benefit: Management Knowledge Leading Positive Change."* Case Western Reserve University. This was a paper I wrote for a UN conference that focused on developing a values accountability system for organizations. Within the system, alignment of values between individuals and organizations create sustainable success and minimizes stress.

6. J. Schwartz (2004, September 4). Always on the job, employees pay with health, sick of work: The stress explosion. *New York Times.* This article had an enormous amount of data on stress within the United States. Stress contributed over $300 billion in health care costs and increased working hours.

7. W. L. Neuman (2003). *Social research methods: Qualitative and quantitative approaches.* New York: Pearson Education. This is a standard research text that presents the basics principles of scientific research. Survey construction requires 10 specific considerations, although they are a bit technical for entrepreneurs. I've broken them down into simpler concepts in this book.

CHAPTER FIFTEEN

Behavior 11: Action without Full Information

Remember the last time you made a decision and were filled with doubt? When was the last time you had trouble falling asleep as countless thoughts lingered through your mind?

Being decisive is a common myth. Although it might be efficient to choose a path, decisiveness can create emotional concerns that distract entrepreneurs. Successful entrepreneurs understand the negative emotional impacts of taking action without gathering *full* information. They make the time to understand the situation from a systemic perspective. My study revealed a fascinating equation for intangible success (the emotional aspect to success, such as happiness and sense of accomplishment). Out of all the variables, only self-confidence and the lack of uninformed actions made an impact to intangible success. Though self-confidence plays a larger role in the formula, taking uninformed actions has a negative influence of nearly 40 percent. The equation is as follows:

Intangible success = 3.604 + 0.261 (self-confidence) − 0.172 (uninformed actions)

The survey contained over 30 different variables. Yet the regression analysis only reveals two that were significant for intangible success. The fascinating aspect of this equation is that self-confidence is a state of being, whereas uninformed actions require thought and decisions. If you have a relatively high level of self-confidence, all you need to do to achieve intangible success is to create strategies and systems that ensure a depth of information about any situation before making a decision. This success includes happiness, gratification, satisfaction, and independence. It sounds fairly simple, but this behavior requires patience and a good understanding of epistemology (the theory of knowledge, how you come to have knowledge, how knowledge is justified) and systems thinking (the ability to see the interconnectedness of events and people).[1]

HOW DO YOU KNOW WHAT YOU KNOW?

Successful entrepreneurs have the ability to maintain an open mind and constantly search for new meaning. Understanding what you know and how you come to know it is a complex and cumbersome journey. Your years of experiences in what you believe and know define your personal epistemology. Because these experiences are different, multiple connotations of the same concept exist within unique individuals. Even among people of identical cultures, vast differences of thought exist. The pragmatic view of epistemology in conventional wisdom places these concepts into a chapter of psychology and semantics.[2] In recent decades, ethics violations reflect these differences in knowledge as one belief system attempts to judge another.

Although not all successful entrepreneurs understand the term *epistemology*, they have an innate understanding of what they know and are willing to debunk that knowledge base or belief system. How they come to possess such ability is usually by practical teachings from parents to schools. Some are lucky enough to be born with this ability. In earlier chapters, I've planted a seed of challenging your beliefs about the consumption of milk. Have you taken the time to research that subject? If not, what's holding you back? How much are you tied to what you know, and are you not willing to see other perspectives?

Let's look at something that may not be as intimate as a core belief. How do you feel about the color red? It might be your favorite color. You may see it as the color of romance if you're just starting a new relationship. From a biological perspective, red is one of the lowest frequencies of light visible by human eyes. Seeing the color red can also increase a person's breathing rate while pumping up the blood pressure. Red is the color of choice for many speakers in presentations because it represents power and prestige. Yet depending on the topic of the presentation, red may not be the best color if your speech is about relaxation and inner peace. In countries such as China, red represents joy, purity, prosperity, and happiness. In others, red was the color of communism, such as the former Soviet Union. During the cold war era, red was tainted with the fear of communist domination. Today, red is utilized often during Valentine's Day, representing love and romance. It also represents joy during Christmas. It has negative connotations, such as a red traffic light or a red flag signaling impending danger. Humans also avoid other basic uses of red, such as taking a red-eye flight. Another place you may want to avoid red is during game day in Michigan as The Ohio State University players enter the stadium. The color red (or scarlet) is associated with many college football teams. Wearing specific colors is a show of support for your team. Especially with heated rivals such as The Ohio State Buckeyes and the Michigan Wolverines, wearing red at Ann Arbor (home of the Wolverines) may yield certain dangers. For entrepreneurs, staying "out of the red" in terms of their bank accounts is a primary goal. There is a plethora of connotations for red that can be positive or negative. These connotations are harmless until the application of a specific connotation becomes a blind judgment of someone else's meaning. In other words, when people enforce their definition/connotation of a concept onto another, an ethical challenge appears that keeps them up at night.

For example, when I attended a United Nations conference and was fortunate enough to present some ideas, ample discussion on poverty and child labor existed. You may agree that the abolishment of child labor in the world may be a positive move for humanity; but have you stopped to consider alternatives? The popular opinion rests in eliminating child labor. Do you have the self-confidence and the depth of thought to go against that movement?

When the United States was going through an industrial revolution in the early 1900s, child labor was common. It played a role in assisting the county into becoming a world power. It also taught us incredible lessons about human and civil rights that created a nation of equality. This was a lesson we needed to learn to be where we are today.

Looking at another part of the world, a child who works in a factory is capable of bringing home income for the family. Otherwise, the child would likely be on the streets, influenced by other forces that may not be so positive. Through the work environment, the child learns about work ethics and understands the need to make a living. On an individual level, this child grows up learning from workplace experiences. On a national perspective, does every country have the right to find their path toward reaching the status of an industrialized nation? The popular opinion applied to other countries may strip that country of the lesson it needs in a journey toward its economic, social, and political success.

Check in with your heart rate or breath for a second—did it increase as you read an opposing viewpoint? If you're finding yourself fighting the alternative perspective, this example is a clear illustration of the norm—people tend to combat knowledge that opposes their own. The content just discussed may not be the entire picture, but in checking your tendency to fight, you have the opportunity to slow down.

What you know and believe in its justification is circumstantial. Especially in the case of technology advancements, nothing is absolute. The duality of right and wrong has countless ethical challenges and shades of gray. Duality enforces a blind judgment based on a single source of information. Multiplicity, on the other hand, begins to reveal alternative perspectives that draw from different experiences, cultures, and perspectives. The concept of acquiring complete information is much more complex than a single data source. It requires an understanding of personal epistemology that critically analyzes one's beliefs from multiple perspectives.

Intriguingly, you're not alone in this analysis. Humanity has grappled with these concepts since 300 B.C.E. The analysis of the source of knowledge started with Plato and Aristotle, who held beliefs that knowledge existed only in forms. Plato held the concept of innate knowledge from birth residing within the soul.[2] Other studies of historical figures has shown the power of this innate knowledge. Especially with one's purpose in life, innate knowledge of who you are and what you believe in will always be a powerful force.[3] On the other hand, Aristotle believed that knowledge was instantiated by sensory objects. What we see, feel, hear, taste, and smell determines what we know.[2] Yet this sensory-based knowledge is highly circumstantial because the same plate of distasteful food tastes fabulous if a person has not eaten in days.

During the early modern era, the epistemological focus shifted to rationalism in conjunction with the theories of sensation and reflection. Philosophers such as John Locke refuted the notion of innate ideas. He also brought a further division of knowledge with rationalism. Inductive and deductive reasoning entered the mix along with relations between knowledge and the physical object itself.[2] Contemporary philosophers gave way to pragmatism. Rather then quarreling about whether knowledge was innate or acquired by senses, they focused on the value of propositions.[2] If a certain piece of information provided an advantage, it then became a truth.

The most interesting historical analyses of knowledge came from Martin Heidegger. In his work, Heidegger saw knowledge as an interpretation of everyday experiences within one's being. Because the other theories of knowledge (such as rationalism) attempts to categorize concepts in terms of dualities, absolutes, and universal truths, they are counterproductive to the nature of human beings. Knowledge is existential (existentialism), not categorical.[4] This philosophy maintains multiple doorways for alternative beliefs and pushes one's mind beyond normal absorption of knowledge.

A life within existentialism is a life of endless possibilities. Imagine a free mind that does not fear differences or merely tolerates diversity. Instead, it embraces differences and uses them to benefit individual wisdom as well as collective knowledge. Connecting with previous chapters, major stakeholders within a small business include your family members, your second-level customers, your community, your vendors and suppliers, your people, and yourself. Getting full information about any situation includes a collection of wisdoms from your multiple intelligences.[5] Once you've gathered full internal information, acquire information from respective stakeholders. There are times when stakeholders are only one other group; other times, they may include multiple groups. As you've gathered by now, every stakeholder is part of the virtual team that forms when a situation arises. The partnership mentality allows a free flow of information that enables a multiplicity of perspectives.

What you know is always changing and shifting, whether you like it or not. Your brain's neurons and synapses constantly change. The process of learning may be strengthening, creating, or eliminating synapses. Your brain constantly adapts throughout your life.[6] The choice you have as a leader is to determine how you wish to adapt. Some choose to stick with what they know, because it brought them this far. The rest of the world will pass them by. Others choose to lead the changes and constantly reinvent themselves through absorption of new concepts, theories, and experiences. These entrepreneurs take action only after they obtain a comprehensive understanding from their internal wisdoms and the various stakeholders.

A SYSTEMIC THOUGHT PROCESS

In the face of decisions and various situations, learning to master a systematic thought process will empower the people around you and generate enormous wisdom and respect. This process first involves a self-check that includes one's triggers, rationale, emotional considerations, desired outcomes, and gut feelings. The second half of the process involves the team, because you're never working in a vacuum with no one else involved. While I was presenting at a UN global forum and completing this book, I found a small part of myself fearing the possibility of making a world change. Especially regarding my writing, a part of me feared the amount of world impact I would have on the readers. Although I've always known that it is my purpose to change the world, the child inside of me was afraid of being out there. One of my brilliant coaches, Alison Hazel-baker, taught me an incredible lesson that both acknowledged and embraced the fears of the child inside. She said, "The minute you're born, you're already changing the world, whether you want to or not." Imagine that your pure existence changes the world, whether you choose to or not. The minute you're born, your parents and family rejoice the event with happiness and chocolates or cigars. That celebration influences their friends and co-workers. Some of these people may find positive energies of life, others may experience anger because they're miserable and despise the scent of cigar smoke. Regardless of the type of influence, the actions of those people carry on to others around them. Especially with email and Web technologies, people pass these influences easily across the world with pictures and videos. All that happens when you're born, and you've done nothing but cry. Imagine the influence you've made to people around the world today.[7] No one lives a truly isolated existence. Part of the social and ethical responsibilities of that influence is to be a master at the systematic thought process. Otherwise, you will harm yourself and others, while potentially making a negative impact to the world.

The systematic thought process is ideal for all types of situations. Sometimes, the most simple decisions have many hidden impacts. Other times, the most difficult situations have simple solutions. This process will reveal the simplicity and hidden land mines. Although each step may appear to be difficult, change in perception and thought takes time. With a little bit of patience and a great deal of conscious effort, you'll master this process.

Systemic Thought Process

1. Choose to perceive and think in multiplicity. Your mind will categorize various events with similar situations of the past and take similar actions.

The challenge is the basic assumption that situations are the same. Your first responsibility is to check in with what you know.

a. Ask yourself, "What are my assumptions?" When looking at assumptions, they're not always obvious. There are three different kinds of assumptions: paradigmatic, prescriptive, and causal. Paradigmatic assumptions are the toughest to uncover. They structure the way our life is supposed to be. For example, working 60–80 hours a week as an entrepreneur is a way of life; it's what's expected. Prescriptive assumptions are ideas that place situations into an expected outcome. For example, if you're walking into a networking session, people will automatically see you and greet you. Causal assumptions are the easiest to uncover. They involve ideas on how the various aspects of the world work and the conditions that they can change.[6] For example, having a noncompete agreement with employees prevents company information from departing. As you may have guessed, successful entrepreneurs constantly challenge these assumptions. Sometimes, they completely debunk them. One method to breaking down the assumptions is with semantics.

   • Write the situation down as a simple problem statement
   • Separate each key word or phrase and investigate its assumptions

b. Look at emotional content. Leaders understand how they feel about certain situations. When they are able to articulate their emotions, they can see alternative perspectives.[8] Ask yourself three levels of questions:

   i. Present understanding: How do I feel about this situation?
   ii. Past recognition: Why do I feel like this? Was there a similar situation in the past that led me to feel this way? What was the lesson in that?
   iii. Future orientation: How would I like to feel about this situation? How can I act differently from before to reach that emotion? Keep in mind that emotions are often the true goals of your existence (i.e., being happy, being accomplished, being respected).

c. Consciously engage in seeing different perspectives. When you face any situation, your mind attempts to categorize it. It is a natural process, so don't worry about stopping it. Instead, accept it as a single perspective. Usually, this perspective will be from a fear-based mentality (i.e., what happens if my employees don't show up? Or if this project doesn't get finished?). Acknowledge the wisdom of seeing the worst. Then use the sense of duality to see the optimal. Push yourself to ask the positives—what happens when my people show up ahead of time? What's the impact when the project is completed perfectly ahead of schedule and within budget? Once you see the optimal possibility, expand the duality into multiplicity and ask yourself what other possibilities there are when my people show up ahead of time. What can I accomplish then? The key here is to have a multiplicity of perspectives.

d. Check in with your gut reaction. The instinct from the gut/spirit is quick and sharp. It possesses wisdom beyond comprehension. It is the intelligence of our soul.[3] We are all born with the ability to have a gut reaction to decisions and actions. You can engage in this wisdom by walking your mind through a decision. Think through it as if you've already taken the actions that follow a decision. Feel the reactions of your gut.

e. Consider the systemic impact of decisions/action: your decisions and actions will always influence the behaviors of other people. For leaders of an organization, understanding the systemic impact of decisions and actions separates mediocrity from excellence. The process of seeing the systemic impact creates the context of great leadership.

   i. Identify the groups under the influence of the situation. Capturing a systemic consideration includes both the internal groups (family, departments, teams, partners, your people) and external groups (vendors, second-level customers, suppliers, community).

   ii. For each of the influence groups identified, consider the above steps: (a) What are my assumptions about the group? (b) How do I feel about this group? (c) What perspectives might they offer that I don't see? (d) After going through the various alternatives and seeing its impact on this group, what's my gut reaction?

2. Involve the stakeholders. To decrease your stress, lower the hours worked, and minimize future issues, involving others makes a powerful strategy. Imagine having a bunch of capable people running around in your organization. Trust in your judgment in hiring them.

   a. Invite the stakeholders. In step 1, you identified the groups who will be impacted by the situation. Regardless of the simplicity or the difficulty nature of the situation, invite these groups to take part in its resolution.

   b. Utilize the GEM process. Sometimes, this process is done in a formal setting of a meeting; other times, let it be a standing-around meeting, where you ask for input as you walk through the hallway. After you get their input, share your thoughts and combine ideas. The more you involve others, the more you engage the collective wisdom.

   c. State the intentions. Before taking actions, summarize the process by clearly stating the intentions of the situation. This allows people to see the final outcome while encouraging each stakeholder to be creative in reaching it.

This process of thought combines the crucial components from self-leadership and interpersonal leadership to create a system of thought and process. It is up to you to take this information and make it your knowledge by implementing the process. When you place a conscious effort into this system, you'll be able to breeze through step 1 within a matter of minutes. This school of thought will earn you a great deal of respect, not to mention peace of mind. In the end, holistic decisiveness is a matter of practice that yields ample harvests for your organization. As you begin to explore the endless possibilities, openness to multiplicity of perspectives helps change your ways of thinking. Such a collection of perspectives enhances wisdom beyond your imagination.

REFERENCES

1. P. Checkland (1999). *Systems thinking, systems practice: A 30-year retrospective.* New York: John Wiley & Sons. This book is a bit on the technical side but provides an incredibly detailed perspective on systems thinking. It clearly lays out the process for analyzing organizational processes and concerns using systems diagrams. According to systems thinking, once you understand the interconnectivities of the system, you can solve many challenges at the root of a problem.

2. P. K. Moser and A. Vander Nat (1995). *Human knowledge: Classical and contemporary approaches* (2nd ed.). New York: Oxford University Press. This is a comprehensive text that covers the theory of knowledge from the days of Plato to present debates. It brings forth basic questions to challenge our knowledge and beliefs.

3. J. Hillman (1997). *The soul's code: In search of character and calling.* New York: Warner Books. This is a fascinating book on the source of you, written by a psychologist. The programming of one's soul determines one's life purpose. It uses world-renowned figures to illustrate the power of one's soul; the innate knowledge of purpose will always force its way to the surface of behaviors and professions.

4. D. F. Krell (Ed.) (1993). *Martin Heidegger basic writings: From being and time (1927) to the task of thinking (1964).* New York: HarperCollins. This is a very difficult read that has incredible wisdom. The basic tenets of Heidegger's thought are concerned with epistemology and human thought. Within his theories, Heidegger believes in existentialism, rather than rationalism, constructivism, or empiricism. Although many believe themselves to live within a context of categories, existentialism promotes the lack of absolutes. Each event deserves its own interpretation, free from quick judgments based on the past.

5. H. Gardner (1993). Multiple intelligences: The theory in practice. New York: Basic Books. this book was revolutionary in thought. It introduced the complexity of human intelligence with multiple dimensions that are interconnected and work in concert to help us achieve our goals. Gardner introduced seven different forms of intelligence.

6. J. E. Ormrod (2006). *Educational psychology: Developing learners* (5th ed.). Upper Saddle River, NJ: Prentice Hall. This text covers the basics of educational psychology. It has a small section that presents information on the cognitive development of the brain and how learning occurs using neurons and synapses.

7. F. Capra, (1996). *The web of life.* New York: Doubleday. This is a great short

read on the connectivity of humanity. It clearly provides examples of how each person is connected to the world in an endless web of relationships.

8. R. K. Cooper and A. Sawaf (1998). *Executive EQ: Emotional intelligence in business*. Berkley, CA: Berkley Publishing. This is an excellent text on emotional intelligence. One of the core pillars of emotional intelligence is an understanding of how you feel and how to articulate that emotion.

PART **V**

YOUR SUCCESS

How many strategies and behaviors from this book have you implemented so far? Although you may have sufficient rationale for not implementing some of them, the difference between successful entrepreneurs and those that fail is slight. Since the original study completed in 2004, additional data collection surveyed entrepreneurs who were in their first five years of operation. This group falls within the statistic of 80 percent failure due to their inability to implement crucial business and leadership skills.[1] Table 16-1 illustrates the findings as a comparison between those who has succeeded more than five years and those who are still within the 80 percent failure rate. With respect to knowing what behaviors are most important, there is a slight difference between the two groups. The difference is only 0.038.

The last column illustrates the ability to implement what is important. For those in the first five years of startup, their ability to execute is slightly less that what they believe is important (3.581 in execution and 3.775 in what they know to be important). The successful entrepreneurs also show a rift between what they know is important and what they choose to execute effectively. The difference highlights fact that cognitive development is often ahead of behavioral changes.[2] Furthermore, neurolinguistic programming also support this finding because behaviors appear at the surface what is visible. The knowledge and skills below the surface drives behaviors. To create a sustainable change in behavior, knowledge and skills must exist first.[3] You've acquired new information from this book, so how much of it are you going to implement?

The most fascinating finding in the follow-up study of startup entrepreneurs is the doubling effect of differences. Though the relative belief of which behaviors are more important differ slightly between the two groups, the execution of these respective behaviors more than double. One rational conclusion is that success and failure fall on slight differences in knowledge and behaviors. It also shows that every entrepreneur has the opportunity to be successful. In the face

TABLE 16-1. Comparison of Startup Entrepreneurs within Their First Five Years of Operation and Successful Entrepreneurs

Years in Business	Relative Importance of Behaviors (5 being the highest importance and 1 being the lowest importance)	Effectiveness in Executing Behaviors (5 being the most effective and 1 being the least effective)
1–5 years	3.775	3.581
More than 5 years	3.812	3.660
Difference	0.038	0.079

of decisions and actions, conscious choices that align what they know and what they act make the difference between success and failure.

REFERENCES

1. R. Monk (2000, July/August). Why small businesses fail. *CMA Management* 74(6), 12–13. This article highlighted the 80 percent failure rate of small business owners with their first five years of operation. It also provided some interesting rationale for these failures. The most significant is the inability to implement essential business and management practices.

2. J. E. Ormrod (2006). *Educational psychology: Developing learners* (5th ed.). Upper Saddle River, NJ: Prentice Hall. This book covers many theories of adult learning as well as measurements thereof. Cognitive psychology is one of the primary driving forces in understand human behaviors and creating learning environments. Expanding from the behaviorism that only focused on surface-level behaviors, cognitive psychology encompasses cognitive development within the mind, well before behaviors are visible.

3. S. Balvister and A. Vickers (2004). *Teaching yourself NLP*. Chicago: Contemporary Books. This is a great book on the key principles of neurolinguistic programming. The identity iceberg presents human cognition as a hierarchical model with behaviors and actions at the surface. Skills, beliefs/values, and identity are the driving forces below the surface.

CHAPTER SIXTEEN

Transforming Your Perception, Thought, and Behaviors

Contemporary literature on leadership primarily concerns itself with behaviors and styles.[3,4,5,6] Behaviors are a surface reaction to multiple internal influences.[1,2] As illustrated in the Humanistic Business Model in Chapter 14 (Figure 14-1), entrepreneurs need to focus on the first level of influence (your people and respective relationships) rather than the primary focus on profit, which enters the process of business many levels later. The same applies to leadership—focusing primarily on behaviors yields minimal value to entrepreneurs. The true focus of leadership development for successful entrepreneurs is perception and thought. Behaviors are only a result of perceptions and thought.

As this book draws to a close, I've realized that the journey of articulating my research results has led me to a different understanding of leadership than what I started with. The many concepts within the self-leadership section (Part II) focused on perceptions and thought. Starting with the perception of self, understanding and acknowledging your potential is the first step toward success in any organization. Constant learning seeks to reinvent your perception of self. With every step forward in confidence and the lack of co-dependence, you'll begin to see yourself as a great leader, capable of leading any organization. The perception of others and events external to you is the second step in the journey. Regardless of what happens externally, you have a choice on how to perceive others and events.

Recently, I had a close friend, Nicole, who was going through a tough time. In an email at 2:31 A.M., part of her message stated the following: "You've always told me that if I need to talk to you, to call you and, if I'm meant to talk, you'll answer. Well, I guess tonight was a night where I had to think it through for myself."

As I read this email the next morning, my heart had a huge smile in seeing the impact I've had on her choice of perceptions. A typical reaction to such a need would have been to blame the other person for not being there. I'm sure you've had people that called and left interesting messages concerning why you didn't answer the phone when they needed you. Of course, that perception shifts the blame to you. The choices you make in perceptions drive the reality in which you live. For some people, reality is dogmatic and gloomy. The entire world is against them. For others, reality is full of brilliant lessons that help them grow. By choosing to see the opportunity of being alone and reflect within herself, Nicole chose the reality that blessed her with powerful lessons. In her time of reflection, she realized some important revelations. A latter part of her email reads: "I just feel like everybody is letting me down. Sadly enough, though, I think a lot of that is a projection of my own self-doubt on everyone else."

The first sentence is one of blame; the second part clearly empowers her as a leader. This moves us to the third step of your journey—thought. How you think about what happens is a result of your perceptions. As Nicole choose to empower herself in reflection, her thoughts provided the internal means to overcome her challenges in life. You too have that option at any time.

The way you choose to think about yourself, others, and events has a profound effect on the behaviors you adopt. Entrepreneurs' ability to consciously

An Internalized Leadership Model

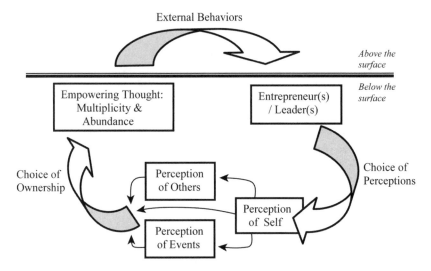

FIGURE 16-1.   This Internalized Leadership Model depicts the importance of a focus on self, rather than the typical external view of leadership approaches. To achieve sustainable success, the perception of self must be one of balance and congruence. From that balance and congruence, perceptions of others and events grow to be systemic in nature. Thus, transformational thought creates empowerment within the mentality of multiplicity and abundance.

choose perceptions and thought determines their level of success (see Figure 16-1). As you learn to heal the rift between perceptions, thought, and behaviors, always look for the lesson inside each event. Even in the worst outcomes, the best lessons exist. Consider that failure does not exist in the area of entrepreneurship. Failure is not a single dimension of financial solvency or business operations. Failure only occurs if you choose to discontinue the journey. The minute you make the choice to travel on the journey of entrepreneurship, you've already achieved success called independence (the pinnacle of American history). As long as you stay on this journey, great lessons that help you grow in perceptions, thought, and behaviors will always bless you. The path of your future is in your hands. Choose to live in abundance, rather than scarcity. Perceive a multiplicity of possibilities over duality. Discover an inspirational perspective instead of the common fear-based choices. Constantly grow with a deliberate effort; the knowledge of this book is here to support you.

REFERENCES

1. J. E. Ormrod (2006). *Educational psychology: Developing learners* (5th ed.). Upper Saddle River, NJ: Prentice Hall. This book covers many theories of adult learning as well as measurements thereof. Cognitive psychology is one of the primary driving forces in understand human behaviors and creating learning environments. Expanding from the behaviorism that only focused on surface-level behaviors, cognitive psychology encompasses cognitive development within the mind, well before behaviors are visible.

2. S. Balvister and A. Vickers (2004). *Teaching yourself NLP*. Chicago: Contemporary Books. This is a great book on the key principles of neurolinguistic programming. The identity iceberg presents human cognition as a hierarchical model with behaviors and actions at the surface. Skills, beliefs/values, and identity are the driving forces that is below the surface.

3. B. M. Bass (1985). *Leadership and performance beyond expectations.* New York: Free Press. A great book on transformational leadership and some of the basic behaviors that attribute to organizational success. One of the key behaviors is clear communication of important information, such as organizational vision, plans, and mission.

4. B. M. Bass, (1990). *Bass & Stogdill's Handbook of Leadership* (3rd ed.). New York: Free Press. This is a great resource for obtaining a high-level overview of leadership theories from the beginning of humankind to today's global economy. Although it is a bit on the technical side with ample historical references, it covers most dominant leadership theories and styles.

5. L. C. Spears and M. Lawrence (2002). *Focus on leadership: Servant leadership for the twenty-first century.* New York: John Wiley & Sons. This book is a collection of articles with a primary focus on servant leadership.

6. S. P. Robbins (2005). *Essentials of organizational behavior* (8th ed.). Upper Saddle River, NJ: Pearson Education. This is a common text for organizational behavior. Leadership is one of its many chapters. Robbins states that the leadership research is mostly concerned with styles.

APPENDIX A

Successful Entrepreneur Knowledge Competence Questionnaire

This is a simplified version of the survey instrument that initiated the research project. A combination of focus group studies and literature research of previous studies provided the foundation for this instrument. Feel free to take this survey yourself to get a better understanding of where you stand personally compared with successful entrepreneurs (compare with averages in Appendix B).

The following questions are designed to gain an understanding of your thoughts on specific bodies of knowledge and the level of competence you possess.

The "to what extent scale" is designed to seek your level of knowledge and/ or behavior frequency on the statement. The following key applies to the To What Extent Scale:

A: Never

B: Rarely

C: Sometimes

D: Often

E: Always

Planning and Organizing		*To What Extent Scale*			
1. I take time to plan the path of my business.	A	B	C	D	E
2. My employees can clearly articulate the goals and values of my company.	A	B	C	D	E
3. I value long-term potential over short-term thinking.	A	B	C	D	E
4. On average, I tend to work a lot more hours in the business compared to other employees.	A	B	C	D	E
5. I have a written business plan.	A	B	C	D	E
6. I act as a role model to communicate my values to subordinates.	A	B	C	D	E

Planning and Organizing		*To What Extent Scale*				
7. I react to events as they occur rather than make detailed plans.	A	B	C	D	E
8. I am caught by surprise by events occurring outside the company.	A	B	C	D	E
9. When planning, I use information from stakeholders such as customers, suppliers, and employees.	A	B	C	D	E
10. I make constant changes to my business plan according to environmental factors.					

Self-Leadership					
11. I exhibit a high degree of technical proficiency in my field.	A	B	C	D	E
12. I have the courage to make commitments that would be considered risky by others.	A	B	C	D	E
13. I am quick to take action without spending a lot of time to find out all the information about the situation.	A	B	C	D	E
14. My business cannot survive without me, since I am responsible for producing products and services.	A	B	C	D	E
15. I project a high degree of self-confidence.	A	B	C	D	E
16. I solicit critical suggestions to improve my performance.	A	B	C	D	E

Interpersonal Leadership					
17. I make most of the decisions in the business.	A	B	C	D	E
18. I encourage decisions to be made at the lowest level of accurate information.	A	B	C	D	E
19. I encourage cooperation and collaboration across functional areas of my business.	A	B	C	D	E
20. I encourage my employees to experiment with new ideas and concepts to create innovative approaches.	A	B	C	D	E
21. My employees know they should avoid failure in my business at all costs.	A	B	C	D	E
22. I provide training and development to my employees.	A	B	C	D	E
23. I successfully select people.	A	B	C	D	E
24. Decisions in the business are based on information from my staff.	A	B	C	D	E

Systems Management					
25. I measure the results of important goal-achieving actions and their impact.	A	B	C	D	E
26. I actively seek knowledge about my customers and the marketplace.	A	B	C	D	E
27. I am aware of the products/services and pricing structure of my competitors.	A	B	C	D	E
28. I know the return on investment of my advertising campaigns.	A	B	C	D	E
29. I know what my gross margins are.	A	B	C	D	E
30. To keep updated with technology and information, I participate in learning activities through seminars, workshops, trade shows, and talking with suppliers.	A	B	C	D	E
31. I understand how financial statements depict my business.	A	B	C	D	E

Systems Management	To What Extent Scale				
32. I monitor, interpret, and respond to external competitive, economic, and social events.	A	B	C	D	E
33. I critically analyze past performance and future opportunities and take actions to enhance performance.	A	B	C	D	E
34. I am actively involved in market analysis.	A	B	C	D	E
35. I actively engage in surveying my customers.	A	B	C	D	E

The following key applies to the rest of the questions.

The "satisfaction of performance scale" is designed to seek your level of knowledge of the statement. The following key applies to the this scale.

A: Very dissatisfied

B: Somewhat dissatisfied

C: Neither satisfied nor dissatisfied

D: Somewhat satisfied

E: Very satisfied

Success Measures	Satisfaction of Performance Scale				
36. Sales growth	A	B	C	D	E
37. Net profit	A	B	C	D	E
38. Yearly increase of your personal net worth	A	B	C	D	E
39. I have achieved my own personal happiness and fulfillment.	A	B	C	D	E
40. I enjoy complete independence and control over my life.	A	B	C	D	E
41. I feel satisfied with owning my own business.	A	B	C	D	E
42. I receive personal gratification working in my field.	A	B	C	D	E
43. I consider myself to be successful in my life and the pursuit of my goals.	A	B	C	D	E

APPENDIX B

Simple Data Analysis

The following data provide the average results of successful entrepreneurs. These data enable you to gauge your own responses from the survey in Appendix A. You may notice that some areas are strong and others are weak when compared to successful entrepreneurs. This is a simple overview of the data analysis. As you will see in Appendix C, many other statistical analysis tools derived the results of the study. If you scored lower than average in any of these areas, cross-reference the behavior with the top 11 most influential behaviors discussed in this book. Otherwise, the return on your investment in developing a specific behavior may present insignificant impact to your business.

Planning and Organizing	Abbreviated Behavior Names	Average Response of Successful Entrepreneurs
1. I take time to plan the path of my business.	Business planning—time	3.823
2. My employees can clearly articulate the goals and values of my company.	Communication: goals	3.885
3. I value long-term potential over short-term thinking.	Long-term thinking	4.145
4. On average, I tend to work a lot more hours in the business compared to other employees.	Long hours	3.806
5. I have a written business plan.	Business planning—written	3.279
6. I act as a role model to communicate my values to subordinates.	Role model	4.393
7. I react to events as they occur rather than make detailed plans.	Reactive	3.246
8. I am caught by surprise by events occurring outside the company.	Being surprised	2.500

Planning and Organizing	*Abbreviated Behavior Names*	*Average Response of Successful Entrepreneurs*
9. When planning, I use information from stake-holders such as customers, suppliers, and employees.	Well-informed	4.129
10. I make constant changes to my business plan according to environmental factors.	Business planning—adoptive	3.541

Self-Leadership		
11. I exhibit a high degree of technical proficiency in my field.	Technical proficiency	4.262
12. I have the courage to make commitments that would be considered risky by others.	Risk taking	4.065
13. I am quick to take action without spending a lot of time to find out all the information about the situation.	Action without full information	2.721
14. My business cannot survive without me, since I am responsible for producing products and services.	Co-dependence	3.419
15. I project a high degree of self-confidence.	Self-confidence	4.339
16. I solicit critical suggestions to improve my performance.	Feedback solicitation	3.952

Interpersonal Leadership		
17. I make most of the decisions in the business.	Independent decisiveness	4.098
18. I encourage decisions to be made at the lowest level of accurate information.	Delegation	3.500
19. I encourage cooperation and collaboration across functional areas of my business.	Teamwork	4.419
20. I encourage my employees to experiment with new ideas and concepts to create innovative approaches.	Team innovation	4.242
21. My employees know they should avoid failure in my business at all costs.	Employee fear of failure	2.532
22. I provide training and development to my employees.	Employee training and development	3.869
23. I successfully select people.	Hiring ability	3.677
24. Decisions in the business are based on information from my staff.	Team-based decisions	3.550

Systems Management		
25. I measure the results of important goal achieving actions and their impact.	Measurements	3.639
26. I actively seek knowledge about my customers and the market place.	Customer awareness	4.210
27. I am aware of the products/services and pricing structure of my competitors.	Competitor awareness	3.968
28. I know the return on investment of my advertising campaigns.	Measurements—marketing ROI	2.967

Systems Management	Abbreviated Behavior Names	Average Response of Successful Entrepreneurs
29. I know what my gross margins are.	Measurements	4.032
30. To keep updated with technology and information, I participate in learning activities through seminars, workshops, tradeshows, and talking with suppliers.	Constant learning	3.952
31. I understand how financial statements depict my business.	Financial understanding	4.197
32. I monitor, interpret, and respond to external competitive, economic, and social events.	Measurements—responsiveness	3.855
33. I critically analyze past performance and future opportunities and take actions to enhance performance.	Measurement—Action Orientation	3.987
34. I am actively involved in market analysis.	Measurements	3.323
35. I actively engage in surveying my customers.	Measurements	3.500

Measures of Success	Average Response of Successful Entrepreneurs
36. Sales growth	3.419
37. Net profit	3.468
38. Yearly increase of your personal net worth	3.355
39. I have achieved my own personal happiness and fulfillment.	3.903
40. I enjoy complete independence and control over my life.	4.131
41. I feel satisfied with owning my own business.	4.419
42. I receive personal gratification working in my field.	4.597
43. I consider myself to be successful in my life and the pursuit of my goals.	4.258

APPENDIX C

Research Details

RESEARCH METHODOLOGY

The methodology used in this study was quantitative. To establish a wide range of basic areas of knowledge for small business success, a correlational, descriptive, quantitative analysis examined a sample of successful entrepreneurs who had been in business for longer than five years. A quantitative analysis, having a relatively short duration of study and low tolerance for ambiguity, provided the most meaningful data.[1] There were three primary sources for the survey design: the *Craft Retailer Entrepreneurs' Perception of Success* survey;[2] the *Entrepreneurial Orientation, Organizational Culture and Firm Performance Research Instrument*;[3] and the *Chief Executive Officer Leadership Questionnaire*.[4] In addition, literature review and subject matter expert interviews further strengthened the design. The key perspectives from current research and interviews were synthesized into the survey design to provide further support.

The research design included data gathering from entrepreneurs from a business list broker. In addition, a portion of the participating entrepreneurs was generated from personal, business, and professional organizational relationships. The respondents participated through a Web-based survey. The respondents' degree of general knowledge possessed was correlated to the personal and business successes.

A survey approach was selected to "include cross-sectional and longitudinal studies using questionnaires . . . for data collection with the intent of generalizing from a sample population."[1] In addition to existing literature, validation of the survey was conducted through the use of subject matter experts and a pilot study consisting of 10 participants within the sample population. The survey was conducted through email invitations that bring the subject onto a survey Web site. The email database consisted of entrepreneurs in the Franklin County,

Ohio, area. Statistical analysis was used to correlate general knowledge competence to entrepreneurial success.

RESEARCH RESULTS

The presentation of data thus far has been grouped by various analysis types.
The tables and figures provided a quick overview of successful behaviors attributed to entrepreneurial success as supported by each statistical method of analysis. In this section, each specific variable is defined in more detail. The performance level was the indicator for the behavior of a participant. It was measured
according to the following frequency values: 1: Never, 2: Rarely, 3: Sometimes,
4: Often, and 5: Always. The importance indicator dealt with the perceived
significance of a variable by successful entrepreneurs. The following response
key applied: 1: Very Unimportant, 2: Unimportant, 3: Neither Unimportant nor
Important, 4: Important, and 5: Very Important. The analysis is illustrated in
relative order of overall significance to entrepreneurial success. The tables reveal the multifaceted view that is provided by using different statistical methods
to analyze the data. It also demonstrates that the data can generate seemingly
contradictory information, which generates the need for an overall contextual
analysis.

Variable Name	Regression Equation Coefficient	Impact on Success	Type of Success Impacted	Pearson Correlation Coefficient with Respect to Success
Measurements—responsiveness	0.515	Positive	Traditional	0.561 (Traditional) 0.314 (Overall)
Measurements—responsiveness	0.427	Positive	Overall	0.561 (Traditional) 0.314 (Overall)
Technical proficiency	0.466	Positive	Traditional	0.477 (Traditional) 0.271 (Intangible) 0.258 (Overall)
Constant learning	0.213	Positive	Overall	0.282 (Traditional) 0.240 (Intangible) 0.245 (Overall)
Self-confidence	0.265	Positive	Intangible	0.467 (Traditional) 0.266 (Intangible) 0.267 (Overall)
Employee training and development	0.201	Negative	Traditional	0.218 (Traditional) 0.210 (Intangible) 0.210 (Overall)
Team-based decisions	0.363	Negative	Overall	−0.211 (Overall)
Co-dependence	0.357	Negative	Traditional	0.255 (Traditional)
Risk taking	0.354	Negative	Overall	0.245 (Traditional)
Being surprised	0.244	Negative	Overall	0.358 (Traditional) 0.271 (Overall)
Action without full information	0.172	Negative	Intangible	−0.245 (Traditional) −0.238 (Intangible)

Variable Name	Regression Equation Coefficient	Impact on Success	Type of Success Impacted	Pearson Correlation Coefficient with Respect to Success
Reactive	N/A	N/A	N/A	−0.408 (Traditional) −0.333 (Intangible) −0.293 (Overall)

The results from the analysis of the Successful Entrepreneur Knowledge Competence Questionnaire data support the hypothesis that entrepreneurs possess specific bodies of knowledge that have a statistically significant positive impact on entrepreneurial success. They are measurements—responsiveness, team-based decisions, constant learning, risk taking, being surprised, self-confidence, action without full information, co-dependence, technical proficiency, employee training and development, and reactive. The analytical, graphical, and contextual data support these survival tactics as vital to entrepreneurial success.

REFERENCES

1. J. W. Creswell (1994). *Research design: Qualitative, quantitative and mixed methods approaches.* Thousand Oaks, CA: Sage Publications. This is a standard research methods text book.

2. R. C. Paige (1999). *Craft retail entrepreneurs' perceptions of success and factors effecting success.* ProQuest Digital Dissertations (UMI No. 9950110). To create the optimal instrument for this study, validated instruments from similar studies provided a solid foundation. Paige's work was one of the sources for the instrument used in this study.

3. K. H. Chadwick (1998). *An empirical analysis of the relationships among entrepreneurial orientation, organizational culture and firm performance.* ProQuest Digital Dissertations (UMI No. 9840688). Chadwick's research was one of the sources for the instrument used in this study.

4. F. Toney (1995). *A research study to determine traits, actions, and backgrounds of leaders that result in goal achievement.* ProQuest Digital Dissertations (UMI No. 9608646). Dr. Frank Toney served as my mentor during my dissertation. Toney's work was one of the sources for the instrument used in this study.

Recommended Resources

This list of recommended materials includes a variety of fields of study, from business to psychology. Exploring these resources will further your fundamental understanding of leadership and entrepreneurship. Furthermore, as you apply the concepts, your beliefs will begin to reinvent you as a leader.

Abbeduto, L. (2006). *Taking sides: Clashing views in educational psychology* (4th ed.). Dubuque, IA: McGraw-Hill.

Ambrose, L. (1998). *A mentor's companion*. Chicago, IL: Perrone-Ambrose.

Argyris, C. (2002). Teaching smart people how to learn. *Reflections: The SOL Journal* 4(2), 4–16. Retrieved January 14, 2004, from EBSCO Research Database.

Baker, D., Greenberg, C., & Hemingway, C. (2006). *What happy companies know: How the new science of happiness can change your company for the better*. New York: Prentice Hall.

Balvister, S., & Vickers, A. (2004). *Teach yourself NLP*. Chicago: Contemporary Books.

Bass, B. M. (1990). *Bass & Stogdill's Handbook of Leadership* (3rd ed.) New York: Free Press.

Capra, F. (1996). *The web of life*. New York: Doubleday.

Checkland, P. *Systems thinking, systems practice: A 30-year retrospective*. New York: John Wiley & Sons, 1999.

Cohen, R. J., & Swerdlik, M. E. (2004). Psychological testing and assessment: An introduction to tests and measurement (6th ed.). Mountain View, CA: Mayfield.

Cooper, R. K., & Sawaf, A. (1998). *Executive EQ: Emotional intelligence in business*. Berkley, CA: Berkley Publishing Group.

Creswell, J. W. (2003). *Research design: Qualitative, quantitative and mixed methods approaches* (2nd ed.). Thousand Oaks, CA: Sage Publications.

Gardner, H. (1993). *Multiple Intelligences: The theory in practice*. New York: Basic Books.

Gazzaniga, M. S. (1998). *The mind's past*. Berkeley: University of California Press.

Goleman, D., Boyatzis, R., & McKee, A. (2002). *Primal leadership: Realizing the power of emotional intelligence.* Boston: Harvard Business School Press.

Harvard Business Review on Knowledge Management (1998). Boston: Harvard Business School Press.

Hillman, J. (1997). *The soul's code: In search of character and calling.* New York: Warner Books.

Hosmer, L. R. (2003). *The ethics of management* (4th ed.). Boston: McGraw-Hill.

Huang, C. A., & Lynch, J. (1995). *Mentoring.* San Francisco: Harper Collins.

Kirkpatrick, D. L. (1976). "Evaluation of training," in Craig, R. L. (ed.), *Training and development handbook* (2nd ed.). New York: McGraw-Hill, pp. 1–27.

Kirkpatrick, D. L. (1998). *Evaluating training programs: The four levels.* San Francisco: Berrett-Koehler.

Landy, F. J., & Conte, J. M. (2004). *Work in the 21st century: An introduction to industrial and organizational psychology.* New York: McGraw-Hill.

Morgan, G. (1998). *Images of organizations: The executive edition, abridged.* San Francisco: Berrett-Koehler.

Moser, P. K., & Vander Nat, A. (1995). *Human knowledge: Classical and contemporary approaches.* New York: Oxford University Press.

National Commission on Excellence in Education (NCEE). (1983). *A nation at risk: The imperative for educational reform.* Washington, DC: U.S. Department of Education.

Nonaka, I., & Takeuchi, H. (1995). *The knowledge-creating company: How Chinese companies create the dynamics of innovation.* New York: Oxford University Press.

Ormrod, J. (2006). *Educational psychology: Developing learners* (5th ed.). New Jersey: Pearson.

O'Toole, J. (1996). *Leading change: The argument for values based leadership.* New York: Random House.

Robbins, S. P. (2005). *Essentials of organizational behavior* (8th ed.). Upper Saddle River, NJ: Prentice Hall.

Schein, E. H. (1997). *Organizational culture and leadership* (2nd ed.). San Francisco: Jossey-Bass.

Seijts, G. H., & Latham, G. P. (2005). Learning versus performance goals: When should each be used? *Academy of Management* 19(1), 124–31.

Shea, G. (2001). *Mentoring: How to develop successful mentor behaviors* (3rd ed.). Menlo Park, CA: Crisp Publications.

Smith, M. K. (2002). Malcolm Knowles, informal adult education, self-direction and andragogy. *The Encyclopedia of Informal Education,* retrieved August 21, 2006 from www.infed.org/thinkers/et-knowl.htm.

Sun, T. (2004, May). *Knowledge required to achieve entrepreneurial success.* ProQuest Dissertations.

Sun, T. (2005, July). Meaningful learning: An effective methodology that yields tremendous leaders today. *Conference Proceedings on Global Conference on Business and Economics.* Oxford, England.

Sun, T. (2006, October). Leading sustainable change through self-discovery: A values accountability system defined. *United Nations Global Forum: "Business as an*

Agent of World Benefit: Management Knowledge Leading Positive Change." Case Western Reserve University.

Whitworth, L., Kimsey-House, H., & Sandhal, P. (1998) *Co-active coaching: New skills for coaching people toward success in work and life*. Palo Alto: Davies-Black Publishing.

Williams, L. C. (1993). *The congruence of people and organizations: Healing dysfunction from the inside out*. Westport, CT: Quorum Books.

Index

About the Author

TED SUN

A dream maker is a master at developing people and organizations. As early as high school, Ted Sun coached other runners on the track team and achieved great success. In college, he refined his leadership skills to coach a dance team toward their first ever national finals qualification. As an executive development expert, he's taught many leaders the basic principles that reshaped life as they knew it. Today, Dr. Sun is the owner of multiple businesses as well as a well-respected educator and researcher around the world. His work and expertise has been featured or recognized by ABC, NBC, *Entrepreneur Magazine*, *Inc Magazine*, *Harvard Management Update*, *Columbus CEO*, *Diversity Inc*, HR.com, *LA Times*, *Chicago Tribune*, *Business First*, and many more. In addition to being one of the top 100 coaches worldwide according to Action International, Dr. Sun was featured on ABC commenting on the presidential debate of 2004 and on NBC for the 2005 New Year's show. Furthermore, his recent research has repeatedly received the attention of a world audience, such as when the *International Journal on Business and Economics* invited him to present his studies and expertise at the Global Conference on Business and Economics in 2005. In 2006, a major publishing company (Praeger) honored Dr. Sun with a book deal to publish his research in a new book, *Survival Tactics*. Furthermore, Dr. Sun was selected as the Faculty of the Year at the University of Phoenix Columbus Campus, achieved a perfect student rating in course evaluations at The Ohio State University, and received the honor of presenting to a UN Global Forum. Currently, Dr. Sun has appointments at six different universities where he teaches on leadership and organizational learning systems. He also leads the leadership development with many executives and organizations, such as Leadership Worthington. As you get to know Dr. Sun, you'll experience the passion that he has for helping people live their dreams.

BACKGROUND

Dr. Sun was born in Shanghai, China, and moved to the United States when he was 10 years old. At a very young age, Ted had to learn to survive and mastered the art of street smarts while living in New York as an immigrant with nothing. After three years of tough city life, he moved to Columbus, Ohio, at the age 13 and has been there ever since.

Ted's desire to help people succeed hit him like a ton of bricks in high school. As a district track champion, he trained a group of younger runners. An indescribable excitement hit him when these runners won their first race. It was a life-changing moment to go from being successful himself to playing a critical role in helping others succeed. In that moment, Ted found a greater passion and bliss in developing other people.

Ted has carved a path of success in each and every role he has played. He coached many organizations to national success, such as The Ohio State University's first ever national finals appearance in dance team competition. He was also one of three Outstanding Seniors of the Year for Mechanical Engineer at Ohio State. While studying for his MBA, he served as the class representative to provide feedback with university officials on course/program development. He was awarded the Service Legend award after only one year of service in a national telecommunications company. Today, as a business coach, Ted recently qualified as one of the top 100 business coaches in the world.

EDUCATION

Not fully understanding the feeling that came from helping others achieve success, Ted had initial interest in engineering. At The Ohio State University (OSU), he successfully pursued a BS in mechanical engineering with honors. Shortly after graduating, he began to consciously realize the incredible feeling of helping people succeed. Thus, Dr. Sun completed an MBA from OSU in hopes of creating a bigger impact by reaching more people in management. He also holds a doctorate degree in management on organizational leadership from the University of Phoenix. Currently, he is pursuing a second doctorate in organizational psychology at Capella University.

Dr. Sun is part of the faculty at OSU, the University of Phoenix, Argosy University, South University and Southern New Hampshire University. Using his expertise in working with various organizations at all levels, he teaches graduate-level classes (online and in person) such as Organizational Behavior, Management Ethics, Leadership, and Computer Information Science to students across the world. Even in an online environment, Dr. Sun has changed many lives in the United States as well as other countries, such as Saudi Arabia, the Bahamas, Greece, and Bosnia-Herzegovina.

COACHING

While at OSU, Dr. Sun began his career in coaching. As the trainer for the Ohio State dance team (The Buckeye Dance Force), Dr. Sun played a key role in their first national finals appearance. He also had a successful track club at OSU that won every track meet as a team. With each opportunity, he coached people to regional and national successes. He learned to love the feeling of the team's success.

Dr. Sun started ballroom dancing in 1995 and has achieved a number of championship titles on a national and international level. His passion is to dance, and allowing music to carry him away into the magic of a new language is only second to his love of helping people succeed at their dreams. This is the source of much of his incredible creativity. Recently, Dr. Sun's research on leadership (body language) and trust has led him toward the development of communication skills workshop utilizing ballroom dancing as the medium.

Working with various management teams across the country, Dr. Sun also played a vital part to the network management implementations for Verizon Wireless. He not only led a team of specialists to implement systems, he also coached many leaders and their teams through the tough transitions of a merger. Within the first year of his employment, Dr. Sun was one of the youngest people to receive the most prestigious awards in the company, a Service Legend. Today, he continues to enable leaders to achieve their dreams.

As the founder and principal partner, Dr. Sun is leading Executive Balance and Knowledge Builders toward a new horizon of success. His clients have doubled profits, established financial stability, been featured as success stories, found new focus and balance, and discovered their own path to leadership.

Even in the toughest of economies, Dr. Sun's clients are growing, hiring, and expanding to new and bigger locations. His path of success has enabled his clients to live in their field of dreams. *Business First of Columbus* even compared Dr. Sun as a coach with the great legend of Woody Hayes (a legendary coach in of college football).

PROFESSIONALLY

Today, Dr. Sun owns Creative Innovations Enterprises, a holding company with three different entities. He is also the founder of Executive Balance and Knowledge Builders. Leadership Worthington has also recognized his expertise by engaging his expertise to head up the city's premier leadership Development Program. His role as the Chief Dream Maker is to help change the world and enable others to achieve their dreams.

Dr. Sun's successes with his clients have been highlighted by a number of features in *Business First* and *Columbus CEO*. His expertise is well recognized by both ABC and NBC news, and they have featured his commentary on various subjects such as the blackout of 2003 and the presidential debates of 2004. Many universities engage Dr. Sun's services to design or lead both undergraduate and graduate courses. His latest work with Southern New Hampshire University on the design of a new Leadership and Ethics course is the first to integrate student experiences from a holistic level. The design also incorporates many technological advances and artificial intelligence to further enhance the cognitive development and emotional intelligence of students. Dr. Sun is also nationally respected for his expertise from the *Los Angeles Times* and *Chicago Tribune* to *Entrepreneur* and *Inc.* magazines, and even the *Harvard Management Update*.

VISION

Dr. Sun enjoys his life very much due to the fact that he is living his dream of helping people. With each new piece of knowledge he gains from research and teaching, he finds that most of it has tremendous power in creating learning organizations where people are happy with the improvements in their life. As he continues to live the reality of a life with endless possibilities, his success is defined in the number of hearts he can touch in helping others reach their goals.

The personal vision of Dr. Sun and his organization as of March 2004: *To lead humanity toward systemic evolution from within.*